THE MAKING OF
AMERICA

THE MAKING OF
AMERICA

The History of the United States

from 1492 to the Present

★

Historian Robert D. Johnston, Ph.D.

with a foreword by First Lady Laura Bush

NATIONAL GEOGRAPHIC

WASHINGTON, D.C.

Published by the National Geographic Society
1145 17th Street, NW
Washington, D.C. 20036-4688

National Geographic Society
John M. Fahey, Jr., *President and Chief Executive Officer*
Gilbert M. Grosvenor, *Chairman of the Board*
Nina D. Hoffman, *Executive Vice President, President of Books
and School Publishing*

Staff for this book
Nancy Laties Feresten, *Vice President, Editor-in-Chief of Children's Books*
Suzanne Patrick Fonda, *Project Editor*
Bea Jackson, *Art Director, Children's Books*
Janet Dustin and Sadie Quarrier, *Illustrations Editors*
Thea Glidden, *Designer*
Cinda Rose, *Contributing Designer*
Carl Mehler, *Director of Maps*
Martin S. Walz, *Map Research and Production*
Judy Gitenstein *Contributing Editor*
Alex Novak, *Managing Editor*
Jennifer Emmett, *Editor*
Jo H. Tunstall, *Assistant Editor*
Adam Schaeffer, *Image Collection*
Arzin Amin and Natasha Scripture, *Illustrations Assistants*
Jocelyn Lindsay, *Fact Checker*
Judy Klein, *Copy Editor*
Connie D. Binder, *Indexer*
Rachel Graham, *Marketing Manager, Children's Books*
Heidi Vincent, *Director of Direct Response Sales and Marketing*
R. Gary Colbert, *Production Director*
Lewis R. Bassford, *Production Manager*

Manufacturing and Quality Control
Phillip L. Schlosser, *Managing Director*
Vincent P. Ryan, *Manager*

Cover: Two symbols of America's freedom: The Statue of Liberty and the historic Stars and Stripes that flew at Fort McHenry during the War of 1812.

Half title page: The Liberty Bell, which bears the inscription "Proclaim Liberty throughout all the land unto all the inhabitants thereof," was made in England in the mid-1700s. It is on display near Independence Hall, in Philadelphia.

Full title page: "Union," painted by Constantino Brumidi in 1869, contains all the symbols of the Great Seal of the United States: the bald eagle clutching arrows and an olive branch and the Union shield with its 13 stripes for the Colonies that declared independence from Britain.

Flag note: The flags that appear on the opening page of Chapter One represent (left to right) the three major European colonizers of North America: Spain, France, and Great Britain. The flags at the beginning of Chapter Two are (left to right) the Union Jack of Great Britain; the Continental Colors, which was created in 1775 and served as the first official flag of the United States; and the Stars and Stripes, which replaced the Continental Colors as the official flag of the United States in 1777. The flags that appear on the opening page of the six other chapters indicate the flag or flags in use at the beginning and end of the time period that is the focus of the chapter.

Library of Congress Cataloging-in-Publication Data

Johnston, Robert D.
The making of America : a history of the United States from 1492 to
the present / by Robert D. Johnston ; foreword by Laura Bush.
p. cm.
Includes bibliographical references and index.
ISBN 0-7922-6944-6
1. United States—History—Juvenile literature. I. Title.
E178.3 J735 2002
973—dc21
2002004825

One of the world's largest nonprofit scientific and educational organizations, the National Geographic Society was founded in 1888 "for the increase and diffusion of geographic knowledge." Fulfilling this mission, the Society educates and inspires millions every day through its magazines, books, television programs, videos, maps and atlases, research grants, the National Geographic Bee, teacher workshops, and innovative classroom materials. The Society is supported through membership dues, charitable gifts, and income from the sale of its educational products. This support is vital to National Geographic's mission to increase global understanding and promote conservation of our planet through exploration, research, and education.
For more information, please call
1-800-NGS-LINE (647-5463) or write to the following address:

NATIONAL GEOGRAPHIC SOCIETY
1145 17th Street N.W. ★ Washington, D.C. 20036-4688 ★ U.S.A.

Visit the Society's Web site: www.nationalgeographic.com

Printed in the United States of America

To Sandy Perry Sequoya Johnston, my brilliant budding historian
who makes sure that all days are GLORY DAYS
—RDJ

★

ACKNOWLEDGMENTS

I WISH TO ACKNOWLEDGE THE HELP OF A NUMBER OF PEOPLE associated with the
National Geographic Society for their extremely thoughtful help with *The Making of America*. First
and foremost, my editor Suzanne Patrick Fonda went above and beyond the call of duty to conceive
and shape the book, as well as to see it into its final form. Judy Gitenstein showed great wisdom and
sensitivity in making sure that the language in the book was simultaneously accessible and intellectually engaging for a young audience. Lydia Lewis, educational consultant and a teacher at the National
Cathedral School, gave the book's outline and the manuscript close attention to make sure that it
covered a wide variety of necessary issues. Jocelyn Lindsay was the best fact checker I've ever dealt
with, going beyond extremely careful attention to the accuracy of the information presented in the
book to helping out with the style of the writing as well. Bea Jackson and Thea Glidden designed the
book in the usual masterful NGS way. Sadie Quarrier and Janet Dustin gathered the book's numerous
images, while Carl Mehler, director of maps, and his crew—especially Martin Walz—created the carefully researched maps. Nancy Feresten kept the project on track and helped us clarify our purposes
and prose. Michael Mullins filled in critical transatlantic research gaps, and Aaron Sachs, a Ph.D.
student in Yale University's American Studies program, proved once again that he is one of the best
readers (and writers) in the world as he looked over the entire manuscript. And a very special thanks
to First Lady Laura Bush and her aide Charlie Fern.

I composed most of this book while spending the year on sabbatical in Jerusalem. It has been a
most difficult year, but an amazing one as well. Above all, being in Israel reminds me how much all
of us—no matter how much history we know—still need to learn more. The people who have most
helped me understand this most complex of places in the world were my family. My wife Anne is a
Jewish educator with an incredible talent for reaching out to children of all ages. Her thoughtfulness
has significantly contributed to the improvement of the book. My six-year-old son, Isaac, who this
year attended a joint Jewish-Arab kindergarten, helped convince me even more that education can
play an important, even joyful, role in creating a better world. But most of all, my 13-year-old son,
Sandy, was the book's most demanding reader. Sandy knows so much about history that I am continu-
ally awed. When taking a break from reading Herodotus, or *The Groovy Greeks,* or naval histories of
the American Civil War, or a biography of Suleyman the Magnificent, Sandy consented to read
The Making of America. He had innumerable and terrific suggestions, prevented me from making a
number of errors, and spoke forcefully for the viewpoint of what children would want from a work
of history. I immediately knew to whom I should dedicate this book.

ROBERT D. JOHNSTON

TABLE OF CONTENTS

First Lady Laura Bush

YOU AND I SHARE A VERY SPECIAL PRIVILEGE: We live in the United States of America—a country founded on the principles of freedom. Throughout our nation's history, brave men and women have been willing to risk their lives to defend the principles upon which our country is based. They believed, as we do today, that every person has the right to life, liberty, and the pursuit of happiness.

We are a diverse nation, made up of many people from many lands. Yet we are united in our love of freedom. The world watches the United States—in times of war and peace, of great depression and economic growth. We must show the world a country at its best by living our lives in a way that reflects America's freedom-loving values. How do we do this? By using our own history as a guide.

The Making of America helps us understand America's principles and values and how they have adapted to our way of life through the years. The book tells us stories about the times we made wise decisions and about the times when we made mistakes. It also tells us stories about the brave heroes as well as the misguided cowards of our past.

To learn history is to learn what it takes to be a good leader and a citizen of the United States of America. If you understand the lessons of the past—what Americans did right *and* wrong—you will know what's right when it's time for you to make decisions about our nation's future.

As America's future leaders, you will have many opportunities to show the world what it means to be citizens of this remarkable country—to live in this wonderful place we call home.

You have the responsibility to keep our society growing and changing for the better. And you have the responsibility to make sure that the United States of America always will be "the land of the free and the home of the brave."

Laura Bush

Laura Bush

CHAPTER ONE

A NEW WORLD FROM MANY OLD WORLDS

★ Beginnings to 1763 ★

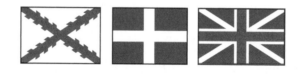

"A New World...more densely peopled and abounding in animals than our Europe or Asia or Africa."

AMERIGO VESPUCCI

Pre-1492	**1492**	**1513**	**1607**
These ancient handprints on a wall in Arizona's Canyon de Chelly National Monument were made by ancestors of the Puebloans, tribes who have flourished in America since centuries before Europeans arrived.	*The arrival of Christopher Columbus in the West Indies marked the beginning of the European conquest of North America and forever changed the lives of the native peoples already living on the land.*	*The search for the Fountain of Youth, a fabled spring that promised longer life for those who drank its waters, led Ponce de León to Florida, which he claimed for Spain. Within about 50 years the Spanish established St. Augustine.*	*The first permanent English colony in North America was established at Jamestown, in Virginia, where John Smith, one of the leaders of the colony, was saved from death by the Indian princess Pocahontas.*

IF YOU LOOK AROUND the United States today, it is easy to see the many cultures and peoples who have come together from all over the world to produce our rich and diverse way of life. Some came seeking the great opportunities that this nation has to offer; others were brought against their will. Each group has brought with them distinctive customs, religions, languages, food, and clothing.

The culture of the United States has been shaped largely by European culture—its laws, religions, and intellectual life. Yet this is far from the whole story. The peoples of all continents have played crucial roles in the making of America. And they have done so from the very beginning.

1620

In 1620, the Mayflower *arrived in Massachusetts. Aboard were both Separatists, seeking religious liberty that was not available in England, and adventurers looking for economic opportunity.*

1638

People from Sweden and Finland settled in Delaware. They cleared the land of trees to plant their crops and used the timber to build the first log cabins in America. Each European group built its own distinctive type of house.

1647

Massachusetts established the first public school system in America in 1647. Children of many different ages gathered together in a single room. Eventually all of the states established public schools.

1673

Transportation improved with the opening in 1673 of the Boston Post Road, connecting Boston, New York, and Philadelphia. But as late as the mid-1700s, a coach could take a full day to travel 30 miles over muddy roads.

America's beginnings involved a fascinating set of interactions among many groups: Indians, who had been on the continent for many centuries; the Spanish, who moved mainly north from Mexico after conquering much of Latin America; the French, who settled along the St. Lawrence and Mississippi River Valleys; and the English, who moved west after reaching the Atlantic Coast. Slaves arrived later from Africa after surviving a long and torturous ocean voyage.

As Americans, we often think we are unique in our diversity. We are not. Many countries have had remarkable combinations of peoples and cultures. One of the most striking characteristics of Americans, however, is the pride we take in how we came together as a people. To understand the roots of our diversity, we must journey back to the time just before the first Europeans reached our shores.

THERE ARE MANY DIFFERENT names for the original inhabitants of the North American continent. Historically, indigenous Americans have preferred to be called by their own tribal names, such as Diné and Lakota, rather than those given them by outsiders, such as Navajo or Sioux. There are many such tribes, collectively known as Native Americans or Indians. On the eve of contact with European explorers, there were many more.

Each tribe had its own culture, including a separate language. Indians on the Great Plains used sharp spears to hunt bison for their food, shelter, and clothing. They often killed the animals by forcing them to stampede over a cliff.

The Pueblo peoples of the Southwest were farmers who took their name from the apartment-like structures they lived in. Some 300 years before the Europeans arrived, the ancestors of these Indians built a remarkable multistoried complex consisting of more than 600 rooms. Today you can see some of the ruins of Pueblo Bonito at Chaco Canyon in northern New Mexico. Farther east, along the Atlantic Coast, the Abenaki and the Pequot were farmers, hunters, and fishermen.

There was a great diversity of social life and culture among the many Indian peoples. But there were some common patterns that distinguished Indian life from European life. For example, women held considerable political power in a number of tribes—much more than women did

Native Americans in the southwestern part of what is now the United States built magnificent structures in the desert (left). This site can be visited at Mesa Verde National Park in Colorado. The arrival of Europeans (above) and the colonization that followed brought unimagined devastation to the Indians through disease and war. Yet Native Americans found ways to survive and have contributed greatly to American culture.

in European communities. Europeans found it strange that in the Indian world, women, not men, worked in the fields to harvest the corn, tomatoes, squash, and other foods unique to the Americas. Indian men fought wars, hunted, and in woodland areas did the extensive burning necessary to clear forests and fields so crops could be planted.

Land was held by all members of the tribe collectively. Different tribes did claim certain areas as their own territory, but Indians did not have a system by which individuals held ownership over a particular piece of earth. This led to a greater sense of equality within Native American communities than within European society.

Indian religions were quite different from Christianity, the religion that dominated Europe. Indians believed that the world was populated with many spirits, not just one supreme being. Nature and the supernatural world—the world we can't see—were connected. Humans shared kinship with plants, animals, and trees.

From 1492 on, Europeans and their many descendants destroyed most of this world. The first evidence of European contact with the Americas comes from more than a thousand years ago, when Vikings from Scandinavia came to L'Anse aux Meadows in what is now Newfoundland, Canada. But this early exploration did not lead to permanent settlement. It was Christopher Columbus who set in motion the most dramatic and devastating assaults on Native American life and culture.

Columbus, a sailor from Genoa, Italy, was hired by Queen Isabella and King Ferdinand of Spain to discover a faster route to Asia's riches. Columbus, and the conquistadors who came later, were often greedy and brutal. Columbus wrote: "The best thing in the world is gold." On one of his trips to the New World, he advised Isabella and Ferdinand: "Should your majesties command it, all the inhabitants could be made slaves."

Many historians argue that Columbus, along with many settlers over the three centuries that followed his arrival, committed genocide—the systematic attempt to destroy an entire people for reasons of race, ethnicity, culture, or religion—against the native peoples of the Americas. There is strong evidence to support this viewpoint. When the Europeans arrived, the population of North, Central, and South America was about 60 to 70 million people. Between 5 million and 15 million of them were spread throughout the land that

John White, an English colonist and artist, drew respectful views of Native American life on the East Coast of North America. In his drawing of the village of Pomeiooc near Roanoke Island (above), White showed the strong defense around the outside of the village. In another drawing (left), an Indian mother carries "a gourd full of some kind of pleasant liquor" while her daughter holds a doll dressed in European clothing.

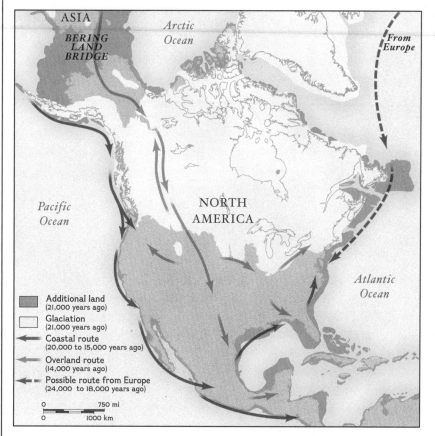

ASIA
BERING
LAND
BRIDGE

Arctic
Ocean

From
Europe

Pacific
Ocean

NORTH
AMERICA

Atlantic
Ocean

Additional land
(21,000 years ago)

Glaciation
(21,000 years ago)

Coastal route
(20,000 to 15,000 years ago)

Overland route
(14,000 years ago)

Possible route from Europe
(24,000 to 18,000 years ago)

0   750 mi
0   1000 km

Bering Land Bridge

THIS MAP shows how a land bridge connected the continents of Asia and North America when the most recent ice age lowered sea levels. Scientists once theorized that the ancestors of today's Native Americans reached North America by walking across this land bridge then made their way southward by following passages in the ice as they searched for food. New evidence shows that some may have arrived by boat, following ancient coastlines.

The Clovis point (below) was used by hunters more than 12,000 years ago and shows their great toolmaking skill.

is now Canada and the United States. Over the next four centuries, that figure fell by more than 90 percent before it began to rise again. Millions of Indians died in what many scholars, and most Native Americans, consider the greatest human disaster in all history.

The Spaniard Bartolomé de Las Casas boldly accused his own country's priests and soldiers of cruelty and destruction. Las Casas, who believed "the entire human race is one," was a lonely voice speaking out against the brutality of the conquest of Indian America.

This illustration shows Christopher Columbus landing on an island in the Bahamas. He named the island San Salvador (it is now called Watling Island) and took possession of the land "in the name of Our Lord Jesus Christ, for the crown of Castile." Believing he had reached the East Indies, he called the native people who greeted him Indians, a name that is still used for the indigenous people of the Americas.

However, not all of the Native Americans who died were killed in war or were massacred by Europeans. Instead, smallpox, measles, and other diseases brought by the Europeans killed a large number of Indians. Their bodies had no immunity to these foreign diseases because they had never been exposed to them.

Native American Cultures

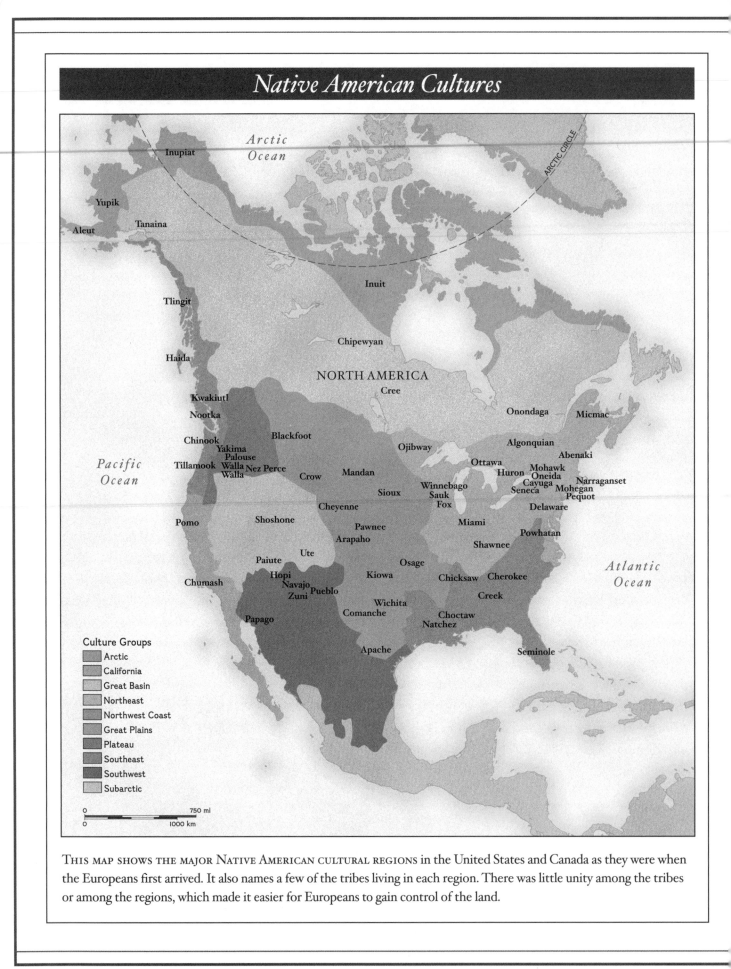

Arctic
Ocean

Inupiat

ARCTIC CIRCLE

Yupik

Aleut
Tanaina

Tlingit

Inuit

Chipewyan

Haida

NORTH AMERICA
Cree

Onondaga
Micmac

Kwakiutl
Nootka

Blackfoot

Algonquian
Abenaki

Chinook
Yakima
Palouse
Ojibway
Ottawa
Huron
Mohawk
Oneida

Pacific
Ocean

Tillamook
Walla
Walla
Nez Perce

Crow
Mandan

Winnebago
Sauk
Fox

Cayuga
Seneca
Narraganset
Mohegan
Pequot

Sioux

Cheyenne

Miami

Delaware

Pomo

Shoshone

Pawnee
Arapaho

Powhatan
Shawnee

Atlantic
Ocean

Paiute
Ute

Osage

Chumash

Hopi
Navajo
Zuni
Pueblo

Kiowa

Chickasaw
Cherokee

Creek

Wichita

Papago

Comanche

Choctaw
Natchez

Apache

Seminole

Culture Groups
- Arctic
- California
- Great Basin
- Northeast
- Northwest Coast
- Great Plains
- Plateau
- Southeast
- Southwest
- Subarctic

0 ___ 750 mi
0 ___ 1000 km

THIS MAP SHOWS THE MAJOR NATIVE AMERICAN CULTURAL REGIONS in the United States and Canada as they were when the Europeans first arrived. It also names a few of the tribes living in each region. There was little unity among the tribes or among the regions, which made it easier for Europeans to gain control of the land.

European countries sent explorers, soldiers, missionaries, and traders to North America. Holland, France, Sweden, and Russia all attempted to colonize parts of the continent, but the biggest competition was between Spain and England. Spain achieved an early advantage when explorers landed in Florida in 1513 and established St. Augustine, the first permanent colony in North America, in 1565. As late as the 1840s, Spain, and after Spain, Mexico, controlled vast portions of the land that is now the southwestern United States. When the British Navy defeated the Spanish Armada in 1588, putting an end to Spain's naval supremacy in the Atlantic, England became the single most important force north of Mexico.

Permanent English colonization began in 1607 with the settlement of Jamestown. Named for King James I of England, Jamestown served as the foundation for one of the most successful and significant English colonies: Virginia.

Jamestown did not thrive at first. Almost all the original settlers died of disease or starvation within the first few years of settlement. Many starved because they were not willing to plant a crop of corn. Why?

England was a very unequal society. Members of the upper classes viewed physical labor as being far beneath their dignity. And common English folk who had endured the long, difficult trip to America expected to get rich quickly without hard work. So they died, having failed to adapt to life in a new world.

Death came from another direction, too. The powerful Algonquian confederacy of Powhatan and his half-brother Opechancanough, fearful that the English wanted to take their land, periodically launched fierce attacks on the colony.

> "It is probable that this land contains as many riches as that from which Solomon is said to have obtained the gold for the temple."
>
> HERNÁN CORTÉZ, SPANISH EXPLORER OF MEXICO

This artist's drawing of Flowerdew Hundred shows what a plantation along the James River looked like in the 1620s, soon after Jamestown was founded. Representations of the buildings and the location of fences are based on archaeological findings. This plantation boasted the first windmill built in British America (far left).

Pocahontas

★ *Indian Princess and Cultural Ambassador* ★

POCAHONTAS is frequently thought of as our country's first symbol of peace and friendship. By helping to free Indian prisoners held by the English colonists and saving the lives of some of the Englishmen her fellow Native Americans wanted to kill, she became a cultural ambassador.

Little is known about the real Pocahontas. She did exist—historians know that for sure. But even her true name is uncertain. Her birth name may have been Matoaka or it may have been Amonute. We know that later in her life, after her conversion to Christianity, people called her Rebecca.

Historians know of Pocahontas's most famous adventure from only one source. John Smith, one of the governing leaders of the Virginia Colony, told how Pocahontas rescued him just as her father, Powhatan, was about to have him killed. Pocahontas would have been about 12 years old at the time. Historians do not know if this story is true, but they do know that in 1613 the English, with the help of an Indian, succeeded in kidnapping Pocahontas.

While a captive, Pocahontas met the English colonist John Rolfe. The two fell in love and decided to marry. First, though, Rolfe had to ask his superiors for permission. They agreed on the condition that Pocahontas would convert to Christianity. Rolfe also sought Powhatan's approval—which the chief granted, hoping the marriage would improve relations with the colonists. Indeed, their marriage brought a temporary peace between the Indians and the Virginia colonists.

Pocahontas and Rolfe had a son, Thomas, who grew up among the English and later became a wealthy tobacco farmer.

In 1616 the family left for England, primarily to attract investors for the colony of Jamestown but also to show off Pocahontas and her son to British society. Church leaders, and even the king and queen, celebrated her arrival. King James jokingly asked her if she, as a princess, had made a mistake in marrying a commoner!

The next year, as Pocahontas prepared to return to Jamestown, she became ill—most likely with smallpox—and died. She was probably only 21 years old. Powhatan, heartbroken at the news of his daughter's death, gave up his position as chief and died a year later.

Today, Americans honor Pocahontas in countless ways. The country has given her name to ships, towns, and counties. Her story has even been told in movies. Although many details of her life remain unknown, she was clearly a remarkable individual.

TOBACCO, which King James described as "loathsome to the eye, hateful to the nose, harmful to the brain, and dangerous to the lungs," became the salvation of Jamestown and indeed of all Virginia. The mild-tasting variety that John Rolfe discovered became an overnight sensation in Europe.

At first, most of the workers who labored in the tobacco fields were indentured servants. These were poor Europeans who agreed to work for a master for a given time—usually seven years—in exchange for a trip to the New World. This was rarely a good deal for the servant. Many died of disease before they became free. One song from Virginia tells how difficult life was for them:

> Now in Virginia I lay like a hog.
> Our pillow at night is a brick or a log.
> We dress and undress like some other sea dog.
> How hard is my fate in Virginia.

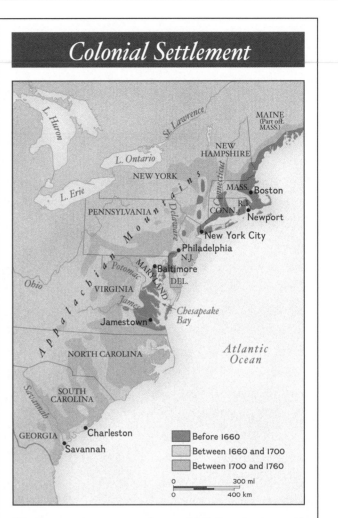

Colonial Settlement

Before 1660

Between 1660 and 1700

Between 1700 and 1760

0   300 mi
0   400 km

EUROPEAN SETTLEMENT began in the region around Chesapeake Bay and in the Northeast, then spread south and west into the Appalachian Mountains.

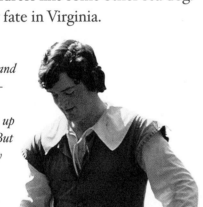

The crop that both saved and cursed Virginia was tobacco. Plantation owners became rich trying to keep up with European demand. But the labor required to grow tobacco ultimately led to massive slavery.

Those indentured servants in Virginia who did win their freedom generally moved to rural areas away from the ocean. In this backcountry, poor men who finally had a chance to own land quickly proved to be thorns in the side of the increasingly rich and powerful Virginia ruling class, which consisted primarily of tobacco planters. In 1675 and 1676, under the leadership of Nathaniel Bacon, a band of poor, white backcountry Virginians murdered a number of Indians who were blocking the way of their westward settlement. Bacon and his followers then moved on Jamestown, hoping to seize power from the wealthy planters. When the governor of Virginia tried to stop the raiding and killing, Bacon and his followers burned Virginia's capital to the ground.

Bacon's Rebellion soon collapsed, but it taught Virginia's leaders an important lesson: Relying on white indentured servants for their labor was dangerous. They turned instead to the slave trade of Africa.

The first slaves had come to Virginia in 1619, but as late as 1680 slaves made up only 7 percent of the population of the Chesapeake Bay region. Many blacks in 17th-century Virginia were free farmers, having won their freedom after serving as indentured servants. Some even owned slaves and used them to work their farms.

The need of white plantation owners to replace indentured servants with a more permanent labor force created a demand for African slaves from the late 1600s until Congress outlawed the American slave trade in 1808. It was slave labor that made Virginia wealthy, and slaveholding Virginians would play an important role in the American Revolution and in the drafting of both the Declaration of Independence and the Constitution. Slavery provided the economic foundation necessary for American freedom. This is one of the most bitter ironies in all our history.

Slavery had existed as a human institution throughout the world for thousands of years before the American slave trade began. Many African societies had long practiced slavery, especially for criminals and war prisoners. Slavery within Africa was usually relatively humane. Slaves were considered part of the general community, and their food and clothing were much the same as everyone else's. Often they could marry, and their children were free at birth. Slaves could receive an education.

But Africans also sold their slaves to slave traders. The development of New World plantation agriculture caused more than ten million Africans to be brought against their will to the Americas during the 18th century, with the majority going to South America and islands in the Caribbean. Europeans organized this mass kidnapping, though the actual kidnappers were almost always Africans. "I must own to the shame of my own countrymen that I was first kidnapped and betrayed by those of my own complexion," noted a slave named Ottobah Cugoano.

It is almost impossible to imagine the shock and the horror that enslavement brought. Children were ripped from their mothers and fathers, never to see them again. Forced marches from the African interior to the coast could take up to two exhausting, hunger-filled months. Once at the coast, ship crews performed humiliating physical examinations and branded slaves on their buttocks with searing irons.

Then the terrifying trip across the Atlantic, known as the Middle Passage, began. Chained to each other, Africans were "rammed like herring in

"With the loathesomeness of the stench and crying,...I became so sick and low...I now wished for the last friend, Death, to relieve me.

OLAUDAH EQUIANO, describing the Middle Passage

From the late 1600s until 1808 the demand for slave labor to work southern plantations involved Americans in the most brutal and horrifying forced mass migration in our history. The painting above shows the cruelties endured on the months-long voyage from Africa and the resistance of many slaves to their treatment. The symbol below was adopted by an antislavery movement in the late 1700s.

a barrel" underneath a ship's deck. They had barely enough room to move about or even to breathe comfortably—and no separate place to go to the bathroom. Disease ran rampant. Approximately two million Africans died before the ships reached the Americas. Slaves revolted and resisted—some committed suicide—but in the end the power of the slave traders was overwhelming. At least one in seven slaves did not survive the Middle Passage.

Slavery was part of the fabric of American society in the North and South well into the first decades of the 1800s. On the eve of the American Revolution, slaves made up roughly 10 percent of the populations of New York and New Jersey. Although many New Englanders built huge fortunes from the slave trade, a full 90 percent of all slaves in colonial America lived in the South. In South Carolina, slaves outnumbered whites.

Slavery was always brutal and often deadly. Through it all, enslaved people worked hard to preserve as much of their own culture as they could. Marriage was not legally allowed. Masters could break apart slave families to sell members to other slaveholders. In spite of this, slaves created families, nurtured and cared for their children, and when possible formed long-term relationships. They continued to recall their heritage by giving children African names. Though they came from many cultures in Africa and spoke different languages, slaves in America developed their own new languages, such as Gullah, so that they could understand each other.

To fortify themselves spiritually, slaves turned to Christianity—the religion of the master. Slaveowners recognized that Christianity was in many ways a religion of equality and liberation. It

This watercolor from the 1790s is titled "The Old Plantation." It provides a rare glimpse of slaves relaxing and enjoying themselves in the slave quarters. The depiction of dancing to a drum and banjo shows how important music was to the nurturing of the spirit and to maintaining a sense of dignity. Despite their masters' tyranny, slaves were still able to create their own culture in America.

was a dangerous weapon in the hands of slaves. "Ten times worse a Christian than in his state of paganism," commented one planter.

Slaves imported many African elements into their religion, especially in rituals related to birth and death. The rhythmical swaying and music that Africans brought to their religious gatherings greatly influenced white people. Slaves created spirituals, religious songs that spoke of trials and troubles as well as of their deepest hopes for God's deliverance. Slaves introduced banjos to the South and words like "goober," African for peanut, and even the word "OK." Southern culture, including the culture of the slaves themselves, was becoming a distinctive mix of African and European elements as early as the 18th century.

Although Northerners also held slaves, the culture, economy, and society of the North became increasingly distinct from those of the South throughout the 18th century. Yet not all the

North was the same. The Middle Colonies—New York, New Jersey, and Pennsylvania—were different from New England in important ways. New York was becoming an important global financial and shipping center unlike any other place in the colonies. And Pennsylvania, founded by William Penn in 1681, became a special kind of haven for a variety of peoples.

In contrast to Pennsylvania, New England's society was made up mostly of people with related ancestry and beliefs. The first two settlements in Massachusetts set the tone for the later development of the region. In 1620, about a hundred people, many of them devout Christians, sailed from England aboard the *Mayflower,* landing at a site they named Plymouth. Some of these Pilgrims, as later generations called them, were Separatists, or people who thought that the religious establishment in England was so corrupt that they should remove themselves completely from it.

William Penn

★ *Founder of a Haven for Quakers and Others* ★

WILLIAM PENN was a member of the Society of Friends, or Quakers, in his native England. Quakers were a small religious sect that emphasized the need for peace and harmony. Most were pacifists who refused to fight in wars. Quakers believed that each human being had an "inward light" that allowed him or her to connect with God. They considered men and women to be equal before God.

The authorities in England—and in New England—persecuted, and sometimes even killed, Quakers just as they did other dissenters. William Penn himself was thrown in prison several times for publicly announcing his Quaker views. Anxious to be free of religious harassment, Penn and some other Quakers established a colony in West Jersey (now part of New Jersey) in 1674 that aimed to "put the power in the people." Then, to repay a debt to Penn's father, King Charles II provided Penn with a very large tract of land to the west of the Delaware River. Penn planned to use his new territory, which he named Pennsylvania, to establish a "holy experiment"—a religious haven for Quakers.

Penn's experiment was a great success. Quakers influenced the social and political life of Philadelphia, the colony's capital, for decades. In his Frame of Government, Penn guaranteed religious tolerance, political freedoms, and the right of citizens to elect their own representatives. These values were later incorporated into the U.S. Constitution.

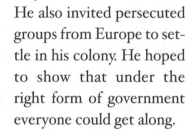

Penn was ahead of his time in many ways. He dealt fairly with Indians, making sure that settlers did not forcibly take over Indian land. He also invited persecuted groups from Europe to settle in his colony. He hoped to show that under the right form of government everyone could get along.

After William Penn died in 1718, much of the colony's holiness wore off. Relations with Indians took a turn for the worse as Protestant settlers grabbed Indian land. Economic inequality increased as Quakers kept many of the best jobs in the colony for themselves. Still, the colony's Quaker culture continued to prove critical to the development of human freedom. Much of the earliest anti-slavery thinking and political agitation against England came from Quakers. In this and many other ways, William Penn's experiment had long-lasting and beneficial consequences for all Americans who value a society made up of people from various cultural backgrounds.

The Mayflower brought 102 passengers, many seeking religious freedom in America. But their journey was difficult. Quarters (1 in the painting above) offered little chance for privacy. Only when the weather was calm could the crew cook meals in the galley (2). A typical meal was cold salted meat or fish and a biscuit. Much of the food (3) spoiled before the end of the two-month journey. Still, the crew, led by Captain Christopher Jones (4), showed great skill. In this painting, an officer on the quarterdeck (5) relays the captain's instructions to a helmsman (6). Meanwhile, three sailors turn a capstan to hoist the sails (7), and another raises the anchor (8). The men aboard the Mayflower signed a compact (below) promising to write and obey "just and equal laws." This was an important step toward democracy.

IN 1630, THE PURITANS arrived in New England. They settled in Massachusetts, north of the colony at Plymouth. The Puritans wished to purify England's religion rather than keep themselves away from religious institutions they did not support. Like the Separatists, Puritans were faithful Protestants and strong dissenters against the established order in England. They believed that Catholics were ungodly and that the Church of England, with its powerful priests and its love of luxury, was almost another Catholic Church.

Their protests, though, did not make them any more tolerant when they themselves were in charge. The Puritans were more than willing to

Colonial Trade

THE COLONIAL ECONOMY depended on international trade. American ships carried products such as lumber, tobacco, rice, and dried fish to Britain. In turn, the mother country sent textiles and manufactured goods back to America. Equally important was the "triangular" trade among the Colonies, Africa, and the West Indies. Colonial merchants shipped rum to Africa, where it was used to pay for a human cargo of slaves. After enduring the horrifying Middle Passage to the West Indies, slaves worked on sugar plantations. From there, sugar and molasses, which came from sugarcane, was shipped to New England to make more rum.

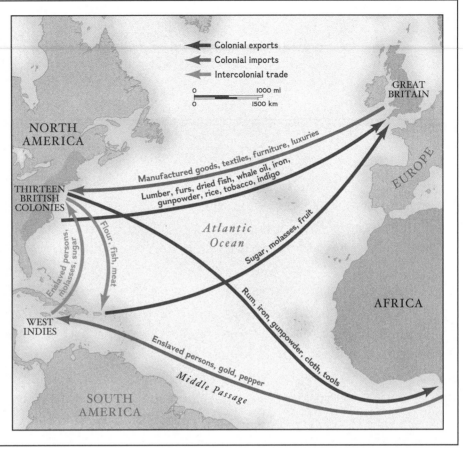

crush any signs of dissent within their own ranks. In 1635 they banished Roger Williams, who believed in religious tolerance and questioned the right of the Puritans to take Indian land. (Williams went on to found his own colony, Rhode Island.) Soon afterward the authorities expelled Anne Hutchinson, a woman who had attracted many followers by claiming that the Puritan leaders were not godly enough and that she could communicate directly with God.

Puritans executed Quakers in their midst. And they burned and stoned people—mostly women—whom they accused of being witches. Even if the accused managed to prove that they were innocent of practicing the devil's magic, their reputations were destroyed.

The Puritans also believed that the native inhabitants of New England were pagans who needed to be converted. One of the official goals of the Massachusetts Bay Colony was "to win and incite the natives to the knowledge and obedience of the only true God and Saviour of mankind and the Christian faith." Their sense of religious superiority made them feel justified in using any means necessary to accomplish this goal.

Puritans believed dunking an accused witch in water (above) would reveal whether she had the spirit of the devil.

The Great Debate

PURITANS MAY HAVE BEEN INTOLERANT and repressive, but they had surprisingly generous and even idealistic goals that have echoed throughout American history. Some of the most important of these ideals were expressed in 1630 by Puritan Governor John Winthrop aboard the *Arbella* as he and his fellow passengers were headed to Massachusetts. In an eloquent sermon titled "A Model of Christian Charity," Winthrop asked his fellow Puritans to reach deep into their Christian faith and use it to make themselves and their new community different. The rich must take care of the poor, and the strong the weak, Winthrop urged. Community mattered more than the individual: "We must delight in each other, make others' conditions our own, rejoice together, mourn together, labor and suffer together." And the Puritans must not fail in their efforts, Winthrop warned, because the world was watching them as if they were a "city upon a hill."

The Puritans took Winthrop's ideas quite seriously. Most of them lived in rural communities where farmers labored together, women sewed together, and children learned a common moral code together. And, of course, the Puritans went to church together. The Puritans often referred to their communities and their government as a "commonwealth." The word "commonwealth" meant that the Puritans knew that they would prosper only if they lived their lives in "common."

No Puritans in the 17th century directly disagreed with the ideals that Winthrop expressed. Still, not everyone actually lived by them. Rich merchants sometimes charged higher prices than seemed fair to the rest of the community. Neighbors fought over who owned a particular piece of land, and farmers quarreled when someone else's livestock trampled their crops. In other words, the Puritans were not perfect.

Yet, in the nearly 400 years since Winthrop expressed his vision of a distinctive community, many Americans continue to be inspired by the idea that they have a special responsibility among the nations of the world. They see America as far more than a subject of close observation. They believe that America is different, unique, and even *better* than other nations. In this view, Americans are more democratic, freer, wealthier, and more moral than other people. Some politicians have gone so far as to say that America is God's chosen nation. Even those who see our country's faults as well as its virtues find it difficult to escape the sense of mission that Winthrop expressed so long ago. Americans are so good, it seems, we must change the world!

President Ronald Reagan, who believed strongly in America's special mission, often quoted Winthrop. In 1980 Reagan remarked: "I have always believed that this land was placed here

> "For we must consider that we shall be a city upon a hill. The eyes of all people are upon us."
>
> JOHN WINTHROP

Here Governor John Winthrop (1588-1649) comes ashore in Salem, Massachusetts. Winthrop served as governor of Massachusetts Bay Colony for 12 years. Under his leadership, Puritanism developed both high religious ideals and intolerant religious practices.

between the two great oceans by some divine plan. It was placed here to be found by a special kind of people—people who had a special love for freedom and who had the courage to uproot themselves and leave hearth and homeland and come to what in the beginning was the most undeveloped wilderness possible.... We can meet our destiny and that destiny can build a land here that will be for all mankind a shining city on a hill."

Some Americans believe that such talk is simply wrong, even dangerous, because Americans have been just as greedy and materialistic as other people. These critics argue that the dollar has always been the great god in American history. They say this thinking makes Americans feel they have the right to change the world even if it requires coercing or even killing others. The notion that Americans have a special mission, they argue, has too often led to brutality rather than to generosity, to the drive to control other countries rather than to help them.

Who is right in this great debate? Both sides, it seems. The United States does have a unique history that has produced some of the most humane values the world has ever known, above all democracy—government by all the people—and equality. But Americans are much more like other people than we sometimes want to believe. And the distinctive values Americans do have can lead to arrogance as well as to charity.

If Americans can be both proud and humble about our distinctive history, then we can rightly hope that our country can be the right kind of city on a hill.

English settlers lived in constant fear of attacks by Native Americans. The conflicts between the two peoples were often murderous. In this painting Mary Rowlandson, a settler in Lancaster, Massachusetts, flees her burning house, clutching her children, only to be taken prisoner by the Indians. After spending 11 weeks in captivity, she was ransomed and freed.

OCCASIONALLY THE PURITANS' APPROACH to the Indians was peaceful. But any time they thought the Indians were out of line, or when Puritan farmers needed more land, their sense of religious superiority took over. They tried to get rid of the native population, women and children included. In retaliation, Indians often conducted raids on Puritan villages, burning buildings, scalping residents, and carrying off prisoners. (It is interesting to note that some Puritans who were taken prisoner by the Indians found Indian life so attractive that they chose to stay with their captors and become part of the Native American culture.)

The climax of these encounters came in what the colonists called King Philip's War of 1675 and 1676. The Wampanoag leader Metacom (King Philip to New Englanders) decided to form a multi-tribe Indian alliance to fight off the intrusion of the Puritans. The Indians attacked with stunning success at the beginning of the war,

destroying 12 villages and coming within 20 miles of Boston and Providence.

In the spring of 1676, the tide turned against the Wampanoag when the powerful Mohawks joined the Puritans and took the field against them. Eventually Metacom was killed. The Puritan authorities carried his head around from town to town on a pike, then displayed it for 20 years after the war ended. They sold his wife and son into slavery in the West Indies. Four thousand Indians and two thousand New Englanders lay dead. Considering the size of the population at the time, this was one of the bloodiest wars in all of American history.

The Puritans had problems within their society, too. They believed that their children were less religious than the older members of the community. As one member of the second generation put it when his minister became upset that he had not been in church: "My father came here for religion, but I came for fish." Puritan ministers tried to involve the younger generation in the church, often without success. "The spirit of God appeared to be awfully withdrawn," one Connecticut citizen noted wistfully.

A century after the founding of the Puritan colonies, New England and the Middle Colonies were engulfed in what became known as the Great Awakening. It began in the mid-1730s and lasted through the 1740s. Ministers such as Jonathan Edwards reached out to people, using an emotional preaching style to bring them back to God.

Towns and cities were multiplying at a faster pace than churches, so people had to travel farther to attend a church. Their need to be a part of a church community was met by traveling ministers called "itinerants," or wanderers. They preached wherever they could find an audience—in meetinghouses, in city streets, on village greens, and even at campsites in forest clearings. These traveling revivalists spread the Great Awakening throughout the colonies.

Among the most popular of these wandering evangelists was George Whitefield. Like the other itinerant ministers, he challenged the established clergy. He urged all Christians—women and men, black and white, children and adults—to feel and speak about the holy spirit without any threat from political or religious authorities. Although not specifically political, these revivals contributed to the democratic spirit of America.

But at the end of the Great Awakening not all signs pointed toward democracy. Americans soon felt that the British empire was more a source of tyranny than of protection. Slavery was becoming a much stronger institution in both the northern and southern colonies. And the economic and political progress made by Europeans in the New World had come at the expense of Native Americans. So, by the 1750s, it was unclear that America would indeed be a land of freedom.

Then the American Revolution tilted the scales decisively in the direction of democracy.

George Whitefield (left) was among the most popular religious figures in America during the Great Awakening. His powerful sermons sometimes attracted as many as 30,000 people. Whitefield was so emotional as he described the horrors of Hell that his listeners often sobbed and trembled.

CHAPTER TWO

A
REVOLUTIONARY
AGE

★ *1763-1789* ★

"Liberty, when it begins to take root,

is a plant of rapid growth."

GEORGE WASHINGTON

1763

The Seven Years' War ended. Americans cheered the British victory over France until they learned that the king had forbidden the colonists to settle in the newly won lands.

1765

Parliament passed the Stamp Act. Colonists resented being forced to pay a tax on newspapers, playing cards, and other everyday items to finance the housing of British troops on American soil.

1770

On March 5, nervous British troops fired into a threatening crowd, killing five. The Sons of Liberty used the so-called Boston Massacre to encourage rebellion.

1773

On December 16, Patriots dressed as Indians protested a tax on tea by tossing several hundred chests of tea from British ships into Boston Harbor. According to tradition, this chest washed ashore.

THE NEXT CHAPTER OF AMERICAN HISTORY tells the story of a small group of mismatched British colonies and how they became a new, unified country. From the perspective of the 21st century, thinking back to the time of the American Revolution and its outcome, ask yourself: What if you were part of the group that started the new nation? How would you organize the government? What kinds of laws would be needed? What people would you allow in? How much freedom would you grant people? Would everyone have the same rights?

Americans of the 13 Colonies had the grand and difficult opportunity to wrestle with these questions during the late 1700s. The choices that they made affect us to this very day.

1775

The American Revolution began on April 19, when Minutemen, like the one commemorated by this statue, fought British troops at Lexington and Concord.

1776

New Yorkers celebrated the news of the Declaration of Independence by toppling a statue of King George III. Munitions makers melted down its lead to make bullets for the Revolution.

1778

After spending a bitter winter at Valley Forge, Washington's troops learned that France and Spain would help fight the British— support that eventually helped win the war in 1781.

1789

On April 30, George Washington took the oath of office as the first President of the United States. The ceremony was held at Federal Hall in New York City.

As late as 1763, most inhabitants of the 13 Colonies were content to be ruled by the British king. They had not dreamed that anything like independence might be possible. But within 12 years, Americans would be fighting a deadly war against Great Britain, the most powerful empire in the world. And they would win.

Our Founding Fathers, such as George Washington and Thomas Jefferson, contributed enormously to the fight for our liberty. At the same time, some of their values were very different from ours today. Many of them were slaveholders. Of those who did not have slaves, many held the belief common at the time that only white men who owned property had the right to govern.

Should we be critical of the Revolutionaries for not doing more for the cause of freedom, for justice, and equal rights? Or should we admire them as brave and brilliant men who contributed so much to the country that they created for us?

Historians encourage us to do both. Some scholars argue that it is unwise to judge the past by current values and standards because we cannot fully understand the thoughts and lives of people who lived centuries ago. Those who came before us had tough issues to face, just as we do now.

At the same time, most historians believe that in a democracy we must continue to ask critical questions about the past, even about people as important to our very existence as our Founding Fathers. We can do this and still honor those who made difficult decisions, paid the price, and paved the way to a better future for us all.

LET US FIRST GO BACK 12 YEARS before the American Revolution, to 1763. Most people in 1763 considered their first loyalty to be to their colony, whether it was Virginia, Georgia, or New York. Their second loyalty was to their country, Great Britain. Things were, however, beginning to change.

Those same colonial subjects had just fought on behalf of their king to drive France from the main-land of North America in the French and Indian War. They were proud of what they had done to help Britain, the place where many of them had been born.

Still, that war—a small part of the European Seven Years' War—had troubled many Americans, and it drew them together. The British soldiers they fought alongside were often rude and violent. These soldiers were professionals who looked

---

American colonists showed their opposition to British tyranny by raising liberty poles (left). Although Boston was the location of the most vigorous resistance to the British, it was the bustling port city of Philadelphia (above) that was chosen as the meeting place for delegates from each of the Colonies when the time came to figure out how to free America from British control.

Treaty of Paris 1763

THIS MAP SHOWS how Britain and Spain carved up the bulk of North America after the British defeated the French in the Seven Years' War. France lost all territory on the mainland of the continent. Its only profitable remaining North American colony was on the island of Hispaniola in the Caribbean Sea. The British government, realizing it needed to maintain good relations with the Indians, established the Proclamation Line of 1763. This boundary roughly followed along the Appalachian Mountains and separated Indian lands from the 13 Colonies. British troops had orders to stop American settlement west of this line. This greatly angered the Americans, who insulted the red-jacketed British soldiers by calling them "Lobsters." The cartoon below shows the colonists' contempt for having to pay taxes to support these troops.

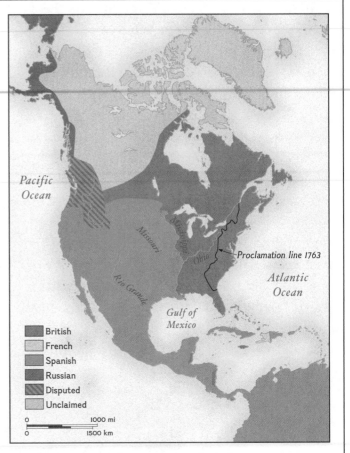

Pacific Ocean

Missouri

Rio Grande

Mississippi

Ohio

Proclamation line 1763

Atlantic Ocean

Gulf of Mexico

- British
- French
- Spanish
- Russian
- Disputed
- Unclaimed

0   1000 mi
0   1500 km

down their noses at the Americans, who were untrained volunteers. The British called the Americans "riffraff," and the New Englanders in particular "Yankees." (This was not meant as a compliment.)

Mostly, though, it was the way in which the British handled the period after the war that eventually drove the Americans to rebel. The French and Indian War ended in a clear victory for the British over the French, who had controlled much of what is now Canada. But the British still needed a lot of money to keep their empire in North America going. The French and Spanish populations were never happy with British rule, and Indians frequently rebelled. Americans themselves constantly sought new

land. Mostly to keep peace with the Indians, the British refused to let the colonists move west of the Appalachians, and this caused much friction between frontier settlers and the authorities. The British government decided to station 10,000 soldiers in North America to keep order.

Who would pay for these soldiers? And who would pay the huge debt from the war? People in England were already protesting increased taxes. George Grenville, the British prime minister, asked Parliament—the British legislature— to pass a measure known as the Revenue Act, or Sugar Act, in order to shift more of the tax burden onto the Americans.

The Revenue Act doubled the taxes colonists

British soldiers relax by playing checkers and swapping stories at a camp on Manhattan Island (above). Below, Bostonians tar and feather a tax collector. Such illustrations of resistance to tyranny greatly aided the cause of the increasingly rebellious Americans.

had to pay on imported molasses. The act increased the number of goods that the colonists could export to England only. The act hit colonial merchants especially hard because it reduced their trade with other countries.

Even more shocking was Grenville's next measure, the 1765 Stamp Act. Americans were required to pay an extra tax on every newspaper they printed, and every calendar, pair of dice, or deck of playing cards they bought.

The Stamp Act caused a true crisis. Americans already felt an economic pinch because of the taxes. Now they began to look upon the British government as the enemy of liberty. Americans argued that because they were not allowed to send their own representatives to the British Parliament, Parliament should not tax them. This is the origin of the famous cry "no taxation without representation."

In response the British reminded the colonists that most people in England were not represented in Parliament either, but they still had to pay taxes. Taxes in the colonies, they pointed out, were much lower than in Britain.

Still, Americans began a round of strong protests. Patrick Henry, a young lawyer with a reputation

Patrick Henry speaks out against British tyranny at a Virginia courthouse (above). News of his words as well as other speeches and events were printed in newspapers and spread throughout the Colonies. Eventually, political resistance changed to violent revolution. Henry's words "Give me liberty or give me death!" became a rallying cry in America's war for independence.

for being a liberty-loving radical, pushed resolutions through the Virginia Legislature denouncing the Stamp Act. Henry came close to committing treason—encouraging the overthrow of the government—when he argued that King George III should be worried about losing his head, as had happened to King Charles I during the English Revolution of the 1640s.

The slaveholding elite in Virginia, because of its wealth and unchallenged authority, was able to keep the demonstrations against the Stamp Act orderly. In Boston, though, protests became violent. Many of the leaders of the community— businessmen and lawyers—lost control of the people. Inspired by Patrick Henry's fiery words, a group of Bostonians hanged an effigy—a straw

dummy—of stamp official Andrew Oliver from an elm tree. When Lieutenant Governor Thomas Hutchinson, who had been appointed by the Crown, ordered its removal, a hostile crowd led by a shoemaker named Ebenezer MacIntosh took Oliver's effigy and paraded it through the streets. MacIntosh's followers proceeded to destroy the new building designed to collect the hated taxes. The rampage continued and led to the destruction of the lieutenant governor's house the following week. The governor of Massachusetts, Francis Bernard, denounced this "war of plunder" and accused the rebels of trying to take away the proper "distinction between rich and poor."

The so-called mob succeeded in getting Parliament to back down. The next year British legislators, although declaring that they had the right to tax and make laws for the Colonies, repealed the Stamp Act. This was an exceptional victory, especially for lower-class Bostonians, who until then had not been considered a legitimate part of the political community.

Officially, peace prevailed during much of the decade leading up to the Revolution. But things were never quiet for long. In 1768 the British placed additional taxes on paper, lead, and other products imported from Britain. This set off another round of protests in Boston. An angry crowd forced customs officials to flee to a British warship in Boston Harbor, where they had to stay for months. That was the last straw for the government in London. It responded by ordering more than a thousand troops into Boston to regain control from the rebels and restore order.

Outraged colonists in Massachusetts and other colonies refused to buy British goods. Women were the key to the success of this boycott. They began to spin thread and weave their own cloth instead of using British fabrics, and they figured out how to cook tasty meals without using imported spices. "The industry and frugality of American ladies," wrote one Boston editor, "are contributing to bring about the political salvation of a whole continent." Meanwhile, newspapers published the names of Americans who refused to cooperate with the boycott, and this often led to violence against them.

The boycott was so successful that the latest round of taxes was repealed in 1770. There was one exception: The tax on tea was kept as a way to "mark the supremacy of Parliament." Parliament's action was too late to prevent what came to be known as the Boston Massacre.

On March 5, 1770, a group of working-class Bostonians hurled insults and snowballs at British troops. The frightened soldiers fired, killing five and wounding four more. The first man killed was Crispus Attucks, son of an Indian mother and an African-American father. Thomas Hutchinson, now the governor of Massachusetts, pulled the troops out of Boston and ordered the arrest of the soldiers who had fired. This served to calm things down, but the damage had been done. In the next few years, more than 80 towns in Massachusetts,

Women played an important role in resisting British tyranny. During the crisis leading up to the Revolution, women used spinning wheels to spin their own thread and looms to weave their own material so the Colonies could boycott fabric imported from Britain. They instilled political ideas in their children, and some served as spies. When war broke out, a few even disguised themselves as men in order to serve as soldiers. Others began to speak out for greater political rights for women.

On March 5, 1770, British soldiers fired into a crowd of taunting Bostonians. When the shooting ended, five Americans were dead or lay dying. Post riders, like the one shown below, quickly spread word of the Boston Massacre, fueling anti-British feelings.

led by a group called the Sons of Liberty, created Committees of Correspondence to resist British tyranny. In many cases, they organized what were clearly new governments.

When Parliament passed the Tea Act in 1773, resistance was prompt and effective. The Tea Act gave the East India Company a monopoly on tea imported into the Colonies. Parliament's idea was to help a floundering British-owned company by providing Americans with cheap tea.

The colonists saw the Tea Act as another way for the British to interfere with their affairs. In Philadelphia, a group called the Committee for Tarring and Feathering asked those who tried to import tea if they would like "ten gallons of liquid tar decanted on your pate [head]—with the feathers of a dozen wild geese laid over that to enliven your appearance?"

In Boston, at least 5,000 Patriots met at Old South Church on December 16 to protest the new policy. That night, a few dozen men dressed as Indians went to the wharf, proceeded to the tea ships, and threw 45 tons of tea into Boston Harbor.

That was the final straw for the British. Parliament passed the Coercive Acts (known in America as the Intolerable Acts) to restore order to Boston. The British shut down trade in and out of the city. The port would be closed until all the spilled tea had been paid for. British soldiers and officials who had been arrested for earlier clashes with local people were freed. The power of the Massachusetts legislative assembly was

Paul Revere's now famous ride to warn colonists in Lexington and Concord of British troop movements ended in his arrest three miles beyond Lexington. His fellow Patriots, William Dawes and Samuel Prescott, escaped capture and warned Minutemen in Concord.

dramatically reduced. Almost all town meetings—the heart of local government—were banned. The commander in chief for British forces, Thomas Gage, was appointed Massachusetts governor.

When the rest of the Colonies heard what had happened in Boston, they rallied to support their New England brethren. In September 1774, a group of 55 delegates from all the Colonies (except Georgia) assembled as the First Continental Congress to debate how best to respond. National unity slowly began to develop. As Patrick Henry proclaimed, "The distinctions between Virginians, Pennsylvanians, New Yorkers, and New Englanders are no more. I am not a Virginian, but an American."

Most colonists began to foresee the inevitable. War came in April 1775 when the British government, tired of continued resistance and troubled by the strength of the Continental Congress, ordered General Gage to arrest Samuel Adams, John Hancock, and other Patriots. Gage then sent 700 redcoats from Boston to Concord with orders to seize weapons colonists had stockpiled there in case of British aggression.

Because of the warnings of Paul Revere and others, Minutemen—villagers who volunteered to be ready to fight at a minute's notice—met the troops at Lexington. The dawn skirmish resulted in eight American deaths. The British marched on to Concord, where they met a fierce response. They retreated, the targets of gunfire all the way back to Boston. In all, 273 British and 95 Americans lost their lives on this first day of the American war for independence.

What exactly would these rebellious Americans be fighting for? At first, the goal of most Americans was loyalty to the Crown, but with more control over their own affairs. One of the most important acts of the Second Continental Congress was to send the king a list of grievances called the Olive Branch Petition. George III responded by sending 20,000 additional troops to put an end to what he called an "open and avowed rebellion." The rebels were now committing treason, an act punishable by death.

In January 1776, Thomas Paine came out with his pamphlet "Common Sense." Americans responded enthusiastically to his passionate challenge to the idea that kings should rule. Paine called George III a "royal brute" and made it clear that people everywhere should rule themselves in a direct way, rather than being ruled by a monarch.

Paine's pamphlet is the foundation document for genuine democracy: Rule by all the people. Paine wrote "Common Sense" in a simple style that could be understood by all. He drew from the Bible, which people then knew well, and captured the hearts and minds of ordinary Americans— farmers, craftsmen, laborers.

"Common Sense" sold more than 100,000 copies in the six months leading up to the Declaration of Independence. Copies were passed around and often read aloud to those who could not read. For Paine, and for many of his fellow citizens, America was the only hope for humanity.

An unexpected volley from British light infantry ends the lives of eight Minutemen at Lexington on April 19, 1775 (above). Later that day, Major John Pitcairn lost this pair of pistols (top) when his horse threw him as he and his troops retreated from Concord.

Thomas Paine

★ *Inspiring a New Nation* ★

IN WORDS THAT BECAME a rallying cry for Patriots, Paine wrote: "O! ye that love mankind! Ye that dare oppose not only the tyranny but the tyrant, stand forth! Every spot of the Old World is overrun with oppression. Freedom hath been hunted round the globe....O! receive the fugitive and prepare in time an asylum for mankind."

When people think of America's Founding Fathers, they usually recall George Washington, Thomas Jefferson, or Benjamin Franklin. These were all rich and powerful men. In contrast, Tom Paine was the Founding Father closest to the common people.

Paine's life had not gone well in England, so, like many others, he looked to America for a better one. He arrived in 1774 and threw himself into the rabble-rousing world of Philadelphia's artisans and small-business owners. He worked as an editor and later became a volunteer in the Continental Army. He was with George Washington at one of the Revolution's darkest hours, in December 1776 before victory at Trenton, New Jersey. Most American troops had signed up to fight only until the end of that year. Congress had no money to pay them, and they did not want to stay any longer. Washington used Paine's words to rally his men: "These are the times that try

men's souls. The summer soldier and the sunshine patriot will, in this crisis, shrink from the service of their country; but he that stands it now, deserves the love and thanks of man and woman. Tyranny, like Hell, is not easily conquered; yet we have this consolation with us, that the harder the conflict, the more glorious the triumph." The troops were inspired to stay and fight on, and Paine became much more than a writer. He was now a true freedom fighter.

But after the war, Paine was soon forgotten. In 1787 he returned to England but was thrown out of the country for writing in defense of the French Revolution. Then he nearly lost his life in France when he criticized the violent turn of events that revolution had taken. The most hard-line revolutionaries had begun to chop off the heads of their enemies.

Paine came back to America in 1802. He settled on a farm in New Rochelle, a town near New York City. Until his death in 1809 at the age of 72, he was treated as a villain in the Federalist newspapers. Most of our country's founders died knowing that they had won the admiration—even the love—of a grateful country. But Tom Paine, the man who first electrified the new nation and did so much to give voice to our democratic spirit, had only six mourners at his funeral.

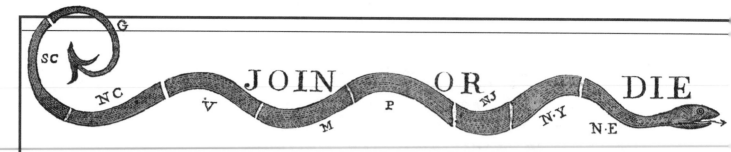

If Paine was the one who provided the emotional push to break away from Britain, the Declaration of Independence was what made it actually happen. Much of the declaration is a catalogue of complaints, documenting what Thomas Jefferson described as the "repeated injuries and usurpations" against American liberties by George III. Yet what we remember most—and what history should remember—are the immortal words "We hold these truths to be self-evident, that all men are created equal, that they are endowed by their Creator with certain unalienable Rights, that among these are Life, Liberty, and the Pursuit of Happiness." This statement, and the rest of the declaration's words of hope, have resonated throughout world history, letting people everywhere know that they were created equal, with basic human rights, and that governments deserve the loyalty of their citizens only so long as they meet their needs.

The signers of the declaration were subject to death for their disloyalty to the Crown. Their courage still inspires us. Yet, for all their courage, the revolutionaries had their shortcomings. They were intent on promoting liberty, yet they excluded half of the population by declaring all *men* equal. Abigail Adams spoke eloquently about this in one of the most famous letters in American history.

The snake was a popular symbol in colonial America. In Paul Revere's engraving (top) the Colonies, arranged in geographic order from Georgia to New England, make up the body. The message is clear: The Colonies must stick together or their revolt against tyranny would fail. At the Continental Congress (above) Thomas Jefferson presents a draft of the Declaration of Independence to John Hancock.

Abigail Adams

★ Speaking Out for Women ★

"I DESIRE YOU WOULD REMEMBER the Ladies, and be more generous and favorable to them than your ancestors," Abigail Adams wrote to her husband, future President John Adams. "All Men would be tyrants if they could," Abigail warned, and if men did not recognize greater liberty for women in the new country's laws, "we are determined to foment a rebellion" of our own.

Abigail Adams made this stunning claim for women's rights in an age when almost no one—man or woman—thought that women deserved any political consideration at all.

Abigail Smith was born into a prominent Massachusetts family. Though she would achieve a reputation as one of the most intelligent women of the age, she had no formal schooling. The education of girls was not seen as important in the 18th century.

In 1764, Abigail married John Adams, a young lawyer. Theirs was a famous union, and they cared deeply for each other. Because of John's career and ambitions, they were separated for much of their marriage. The letters that they wrote to each other spoke of love and children (they had five), as well as religion, philosophy, and, of course, politics.

John quickly became a leading figure in the American Revolution. When he was a diplomat in Paris and London, Abigail took in the glory of these cities but still made it clear that she much preferred her farm in Braintree, Massachusetts.

When John became George Washington's Vice President, Abigail was an avid supporter of the conservative Federalist party. Many men at the time were suspicious of her influence over her husband. One called Abigail "Her Majesty." But she refused to back down from political fights. In 1797, John became the second President of the United States. When the government moved to Washington in 1800, he and Abigail were the first occupants of the White House.

How did John respond to that famous letter, in which Abigail asked him to remember the ladies? His response made clear the limits of the Founders' democratic thinking. "Depend upon it, We know better than to repeal our Masculine systems." He added that men would never submit to the "Despotism of the Peticoat." John understood the real threat that Abigail's thinking represented. If women sought greater legal and political power, so would men without property and, perhaps, even children.

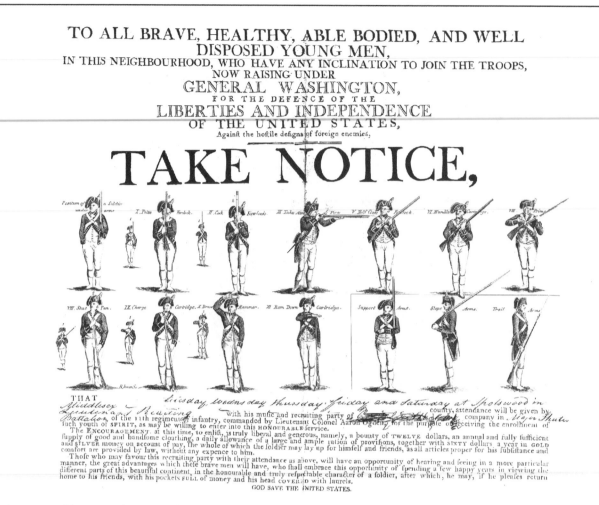

TO ALL BRAVE, HEALTHY, ABLE BODIED, AND WELL
DISPOSED YOUNG MEN,
IN THIS NEIGHBOURHOOD, WHO HAVE ANY INCLINATION TO JOIN THE TROOPS,
NOW RAISING UNDER
GENERAL WASHINGTON,
FOR THE DEFENCE OF THE
LIBERTIES AND INDEPENDENCE
OF THE UNITED STATES,
Against the hostile designs of foreign enemies,

TAKE NOTICE,

Most American soldiers were farmers and workingmen. This recruiting notice appealed to them to join the Continental Army. They would receive a $12 signing bonus, handsome clothing and good food, and $60 a year. The poster shows the many stages of proper musket use, from "Poise" through "Fire" to "Ram Down Cartridge." The soldiers would be sure to hear drums (below) in camp and in battle.

John Adams's answer to Abigail Adams illustrates that not all men received the fruits of democracy right away either. The drafters of the Declaration of Independence were wealthy and powerful men. All men might have been *created* equal. But according to most of the Founding Fathers, poor men were too dependent on the favor of others to be trusted with political power. The rich or the corrupt could bribe or threaten the poor into voting a certain way.

This failure to apply the principle of equality is

nowhere clearer than when we recognize how many of the nation's Founding Fathers were slaveowners. Only a few had begun to doubt the morality of slavery. During the Revolution, when the royal governor of Virginia offered slaves their freedom if they would fight for the British, the Virginia elite was furious at this attempt to upset the existing order. More than 800 slaves took Governor Dunmore up on his offer, wearing sashes proclaiming "Liberty to Slaves." During the rest of the war, roughly 50,000 slaves, or 10 percent of the country's total, fled their owners. The declaration planted the seeds of an entirely new political system based on equality, democracy, and citizenship. But those seeds bore fruit only in a limited way during the Revolution. It would take decades for a truer democracy to come to America.

No group was more trapped in the contradictions of the Revolution than Native Americans. Americans and British both had promised to preserve the lands of different Indian nations. Indians hoped to avoid choosing sides in the Revolution, though most decided to fight with the British. They did so for strong reasons. Despite the talk about equality, Americans represented a greater threat to Indian lands and livelihood. A Patriot victory, the British warned, would bring hordes of land-hungry farmers to Indian territory.

British predictions came true. At the end of the war, Americans claimed the right to push westward. They displaced not only those who had fought for the British, such as the Cherokee, but also allies such as the Oneida, who had fought

Native Americans played an important role in the war, fighting on both sides. Indians usually lost their land to American settlers after the war, even if they fought against the British. In this painting, titled "Wyoming Massacre," Loyalists to England, called Tory Rangers, and their Iroquois allies fight rebel colonists in the Wyoming Valley of Pennsylvania's Susquehanna River in July 1778.

alongside the revolutionaries. One American general summed up the country's thinking by proclaiming: "Civilization or death to all American savages." In many ways, Native Americans lost even more than the British in the Revolutionary War.

Others who lost were the large group of Americans who supported the British. Loyalists made up roughly one-fifth of the population and included colonial officials, such as Governor Thomas Hutchinson of Massachusetts, as well as Church of England clergy. The Loyalists, known as Tories after the conservative political party in England, included persecuted minorities such as Highland Scots and many poor southern whites who sought freedom from the slaveholding elite who controlled so much land.

Benedict Arnold was the most famous—and most hated—of the Loyalists. At the start of the war, Arnold was an American hero, but eventually he switched sides. First he spied for the British, then he became a general in the British Army. Many Loyalists were the target of mob violence. Upwards of 80,000 had fled the country by the end of the war. Most went north to Canada.

The fate of the Loyalists is just one example of the fact that the American Revolution was a war within American society as well as between the British and the Americans.

The war was a difficult one for the Americans to win. Not only were there Loyalists in their midst, but as much as one-third of the population remained neutral. This group was often known as the "disaffected." The Patriots had advantages, though, even against such a powerful empire as Great Britain. First, the Americans were fighting on their own turf. Local militias knew the terrain. They could live off the land and were used to working together.

The Continental Army also played a crucial role. George Washington commanded this army.

Battles of the Revolution

AMERICA'S WAR FOR INDEPENDENCE began on April 19, 1775, when the first shots were fired at Lexington and Concord, in Massachusetts. The retreating British rallied to claim a victory over the rebels near Bunker Hill just outside Boston. The following year, British troops attacked at Brooklyn Heights on Long Island, then swept into New York City, forcing General Washington to retreat to White Plains. From there, redcoats chased rebels into New Jersey. Patriot troops scored victories at Trenton and Princeton before wintering at Morristown.

In July 1777, Fort Ticonderoga on Lake Champlain fell to the British. In September and early October, Americans lost costly battles at Brandywine and Germantown, in Pennsylvania. But soon after, the tide of war shifted with a Patriot victory at Saratoga, in upstate New York.

Patriots suffered through a bitter winter at Valley Forge outside Philadelphia, but in spring cheered the news that France would join their cause.

In the west, George Rogers Clark led the capture of British-held posts at Cahokia, Kaskaskia, and Vincennes. By mid-1779, Americans controlled the area between the Appalachians and the Mississippi River.

In December 1778, the British captured Savannah, Georgia. In 1780, the war moved into South Carolina, where Charleston and Camden fell to the British. Patriots took revenge with victories at Kings Mountain and Cowpens and inflicted heavy casualties in North Carolina at the battle of Guilford Courthouse, pushing Lord Cornwallis into Virginia. At Yorktown, French and Americans closed in by land and sea, forcing Cornwallis to surrender on October 19, 1781.

It took 15 seconds for a Revolutionary War soldier to prime, load, and fire his musket (above, left to right).

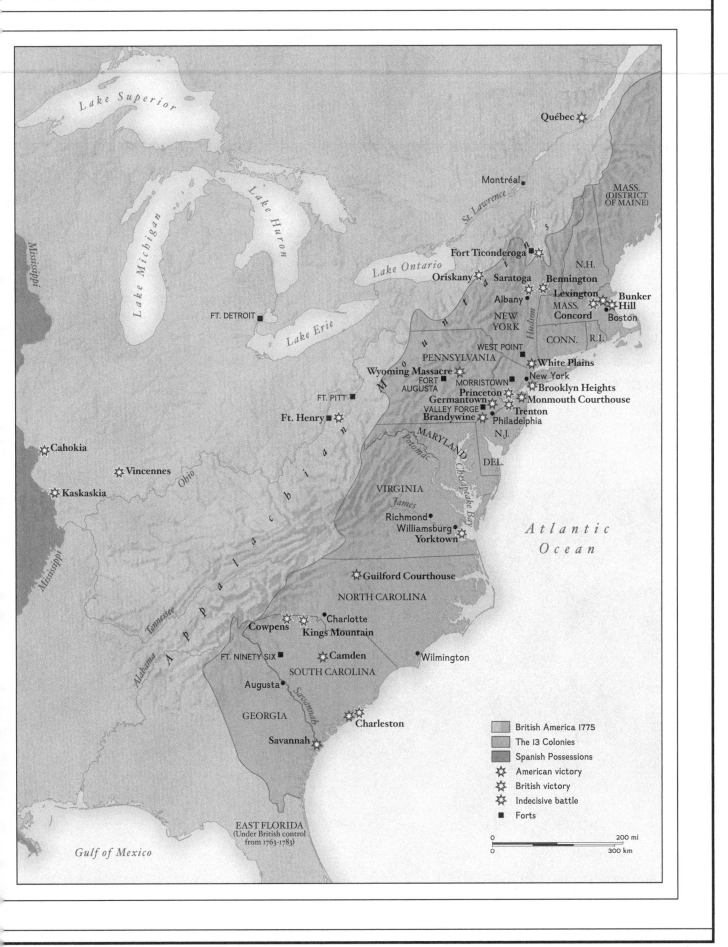

Lake Superior

Lake Michigan

Lake Huron

Lake Erie

Lake Ontario

St. Lawrence

Québec ✡

Montréal •

MASS.
(DISTRICT
OF MAINE)

Fort Ticonderoga ✡

N.H.

Oriskany ✡   Saratoga ✡   Bennington ✡

Albany •   Lexington ✡   Bunker
             MASS.   Hill ✡
             Concord ✡   Boston •

NEW
YORK   Hudson   CONN.   R.I.

WEST POINT ■

PENNSYLVANIA   White Plains ✡

FT. DETROIT ■

Wyoming Massacre ✡   New York •
FORT   MORRISTOWN ■   Brooklyn Heights ✡
AUGUSTA   Princeton ✡   Monmouth Courthouse ✡
FT. PITT ■   Germantown ✡
             VALLEY FORGE ■   Trenton ✡
Ft. Henry ■ ✡   Brandywine ✡   Philadelphia •
                                N.J.

✡ Cahokia   Ohio   DEL.

✡ Vincennes   MARYLAND   Potomac   Chesapeake Bay

✡ Kaskaskia

Mississippi   Tennessee   VIRGINIA

James
Richmond •
Williamsburg •
Yorktown ✡

Atlantic
Ocean

✡ Guilford Courthouse

NORTH CAROLINA

Appalachian   Alabama

Cowpens ✡ ✡   Charlotte •
         Kings Mountain

FT. NINETY SIX ■   ✡ Camden   Wilmington •

SOUTH CAROLINA

Augusta •   Savannah

GEORGIA

✡ Charleston

Savannah ✡

EAST FLORIDA
(Under British control
from 1763-1783)

Gulf of Mexico

□ British America 1775
□ The 13 Colonies
■ Spanish Possessions
✡ American victory
✡ British victory
✡ Indecisive battle
■ Forts

0 ————— 200 mi
0 ————— 300 km

He possessed considerable military genius and organizational skills, most of which he had learned from the British before the war. The French and Spanish joined in the fight against the British, sending troops and money to retaliate for their loss in the French and Indian War and to strengthen their claim to land in North America.

In the end, America won the war in part because its soldiers were inspired by the democratic dreams of the Revolution. This strength enabled them to survive such hardships as the winter at Valley Forge, during which nearly one-quarter of the Continental Army perished from disease and lack of food. In all, approximately 25,000 American soldiers died during a war that lasted for six years.

The final battle ended when British General Charles Cornwallis surrendered his army to Washington at Yorktown, Virginia, on October 19, 1781. Peace talks continued through 1782, and a final set of agreements, known as the Treaty of Paris, was signed on September 3, 1783.

Throughout the war, Americans had struggled over the type of government to create for their new nation. In 1777, the Continental Congress drafted the Articles of Confederation, which called for strong state governments and a relatively weak national government.

Once the war was over, though, Americans learned that developing a new country based on truly democratic principles was far from easy. By the mid-1780s, the economy was in shambles, and the government did not have the power to raise

The harsh winter at Valley Forge was deadly for many American soldiers. But it also provided an opportunity to learn discipline and new military skills. Soldiers who showed exceptional courage received the Badge of Military Merit, now known as the Purple Heart.

General Washington acknowledges cheering New Yorkers during a victory parade on November 25, 1783, that marked the official end of Britain's seven-year occupation of New York City. The treaty that ended the war (below) had been signed on September 3.

taxes in order to help citizens in financial trouble. The Continental Congress did pass two important laws that made it easier for people to settle in western lands, but it failed to tackle the national debt or even to pay its soldiers.

Shays's Rebellion dramatically illustrates the consequences of this inaction. In 1787, Daniel Shays, a popular Revolutionary War captain who was having a hard time paying his debts, led a band of 1,200 men to attack the local courthouse and attempt to seize the federal arsenal in Springfield, Massachusetts. They wanted government help in paying their debts, fair taxation, and a system of paper money that would meet the needs of farmers rather than those of merchants and bankers.

The movement quickly fell apart when four rebels were killed, but it sparked fear among the

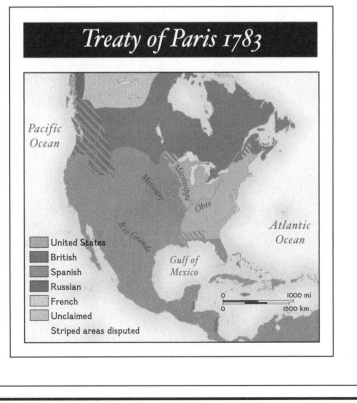

Treaty of Paris 1783

Pacific Ocean

Missouri

Mississippi

Ohio

Rio Grande

Atlantic Ocean

Gulf of Mexico

United States
British
Spanish
Russian
French
Unclaimed
Striped areas disputed

0   1000 mi
0   1500 km

"A little rebellion now and then is a good thing. It is a medicine necessary for the sound health of government. God forbid that we should ever be twenty years without such a rebellion."

THOMAS JEFFERSON

This engraving shows one of Daniel Shays's rebels getting the best of a government supporter. After the Revolution, Shays's followers tried to shut down local courthouses to keep from losing their farms as a result of being unable to pay state taxes.

wealthy that a weak federal government would encourage the poor to take power from the rich. This was a serious concern when delegates from all states (except Rhode Island) met several months later at the Constitutional Convention in Philadelphia. Their purpose was to revise the Articles of Confederation, but it soon became clear that the leaders had a much broader vision: to create an entirely new system, one with a stronger central government. All but two of the most distinguished members of the revolutionary generation attended. Thomas Jefferson was in Paris serving as minister to France, and Patrick Henry did not want to play a part in undoing the power of state governments.

George Washington led the meeting. Alexander Hamilton and James Madison set the tone for debate and were the most commanding members of the convention. Because they wanted to establish a federal—central—government that had more power than state governments, along with a strong President and the power to levy taxes and regulate commerce, these men and their followers were called Federalists.

Americans tried to use this paper money during the Revolutionary War, but it quickly lost its value. Foreign coins were a much more stable form of exchange.

From May to September 1787, the members of the convention argued over ways to accommodate the needs of states small and large, and over what to do about slavery. What became known as the Great Compromise solved these problems. The convention agreed that the federal government under this new Constitution would have two legislative bodies, or houses, known collectively as the Congress. Each state would receive equal representation in the Senate, or upper house of Congress. This meant states with small populations would have the same number of votes and the same power as states with more people.

The other chamber of the legislature would be based on the population of each state. The larger a state's population, the more representatives and the more votes it would have. When it came to figuring out population so that states would know how many representatives they would have and how much tax they owed to the federal govern-ment, the states agreed to count a slave as only three-fifths of a person. In effect, the delegates were endorsing slavery when they refused to pass a motion condemning this institution.

The convention's final act was to decide that the Constitution would take effect as the framework for the federal government when as few as nine states ratified it. Because the members of the convention had no legal authority to seek a change in the way Americans governed themselves, they were in essence declaring a coup—an illegal takeover of the government. Still, they advocated a peaceful overthrow, one that they hoped would result in a government with much firmer popular support.

Despite their divisions, the delegates agreed on who should be the first President. On April 30, 1789, George Washington, with great popular support, took the oath of office. Such unanimity of spirit would not last for long in the new Republic.

George Washington was a commanding presence at the Constitutional Convention in Philadelphia during the summer of 1787. The delegates argued fiercely about the kind of government the nation should have, but on September 17, all but three of the 42 men still present signed the document. Those staunchly opposed to it had gone home.

The Great Debate

TODAY ALMOST ALL AMERICANS honor the Constitution. Under its guidance, the American people have created a national government that has done a tremendous amount to promote freedom. Given the sad record of world history, with governments coming and going in many countries, often with brutal consequences for their citizens, this stable central government has proved to be a mainstay of our democracy.

The Constitution, though, almost did not become the law of the land. Its opponents had valid arguments that are still worth hearing. What were these Anti-Federalists concerned about?

First and foremost, Anti-Federalists believed in local control. They believed that if the government took power away from a city, a state, or a region, then it would be increasingly difficult to watch what government officials were doing. And since government officials often sought to enlarge their power, citizens had to keep an eye on them. Otherwise, taxes would be spent in unwise ways, fattening the wallets of the rich and well connected. Citizens' liberties would eventually decline, Anti-Federalists feared.

The Anti-Federalists also believed that the new government, with its President, Supreme Court, and two separate houses of the legislature, was far too complex. The simpler and more locally based the government was, they claimed, the more responsive it would be to the people.

These opponents of the Constitution believed that the middle class, made up of farmers, craftsmen, and others, should help run the government. They feared that the new government's size and complexity would benefit the rich and encourage the growth of corrupt special interest groups. A new aristocracy of government officials and the wealthy might even arise. This would re-create the oppressive British system.

To many Americans at the time, the Anti-Federalists seemed truer to the principles of the Declaration of Independence than the Federalists were, because they focused on equality. The

> "The people seldom judge or determine right. Give therefore to the first class a distinct permanent share in the government."
>
> ALEXANDER HAMILTON

defenders of the Constitution, by contrast, seemed to have become more interested in order than in the ideal of democracy.

The Federalists, though, declared that they were the rightful heirs to the Revolution. They argued that concentrating power at the national level enhanced rather than destroyed liberty. Anarchy—the chaos that would result from a weak and useless government—would not benefit anyone, rich or poor. They believed that by separating the powers of government among an executive branch to govern, a legislative branch to make laws, and a judicial branch to enforce those laws, they could prevent any one of these branches of the government from making rash decisions or gaining too much power.

A POLITICAL CARTOON shows Federalist and Republican congressmen fighting over issues of the time.

The vision of the Federalists is recorded in *The Federalist* (better known today as *The Federalist Papers*), a collection of essays by James Madison, Alexander Hamilton, and John Jay. This book contains some of the most important reflections on the American political experiment ever written.

Today, however, Americans take just as seriously the Anti-Federalists' most lasting creation: the Bill of Rights. If it had not been for the insistence of the Anti-Federalists, we would not have these first ten amendments to the Constitution. This list includes such basic rights as freedom of speech, freedom of religion, freedom of the press and assembly, and the right to a trial by a jury of one's peers.

The Federalists ultimately won most of the great debate, but it was a difficult struggle. Because of powerful Anti-Federalist opposition, the two largest and most powerful states, Virginia and New York, ratified the Constitution only after it was accepted by the ninth state, when the new government was formally in place.

The 13th, and last, state to ratify the Constitution—Rhode Island—did not do so until more than a year after the new government began operating. It did so only by a vote of 34 to 32 and only after the government of the United States threatened to stop trading with it.

This great debate between those who prefer a strong central government and those who want to protect the rights of the states and of individuals continues. Every day, in newspapers, on television, in offices and schoolrooms, we discuss ways to make our government more effective while preserving our liberties.

Being free to express different points of view about the way our nation should be run helps us resolve issues peacefully and keeps our government responsive to its citizens' needs. And if we can learn to see the wisdom in both sides of a debate, then we will be in a better position to work out solutions that can lead to better government and a better life.

The conflict of ideas between Federalists and Anti-Federalists during the 1780s grew into bitter struggles between different political parties during the next decade. Above, two opposing members of Congress fight each other on the floor of the House of Representatives.

CHAPTER THREE
THE NEW REPUBLIC

★ *1789-1848* ★

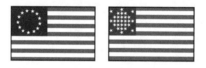

"We the People of the United States...do ordain and establish this
Constitution for the United States of America."

PREAMBLE TO THE CONSTITUTION

1790

This pitcher displays the results of the country's first census. Four million people lived in the United States in 1790. Virginia, with more than 474,000 people, was the most populous state, followed by Pennsylvania.

1800

In 1800, when the government moved to Washington, D.C., the Capitol was still under construction. At the time it housed the Congress and the Supreme Court. Today this building is part of the Capitol's north wing.

1803

In 1803 the United States purchased Louisiana from France. The Lewis and Clark expedition, which explored the new territory, was guided through the snow-covered Rockies by the Indian woman Sacagawea.

1807

Robert Fulton's Claremont made the first steam-powered voyage in America in 1807. Within 20 years, hundreds of other steamboats (above) were carrying passengers along the country's major inland waterways.

THE UNITED STATES OF AMERICA came into being amid great celebration. Yet Americans had concerns as they began their new experiment in liberty. According to 18th-century European political thinkers, a country as large as the United States simply could not survive without a king to hold everyone together. And these pronouncements were made when the new nation was settled only along the Atlantic seaboard!

People of almost all political views admired, even loved, George Washington. He was the one figure who could keep the United States united. But what would happen after he had passed from the political scene? What would happen when the country grew, when settlers pushed west beyond the Appalachian Mountains?

1812–15

The War of 1812 was the last time the United States fought Great Britain. In 1814 British soldiers set fire to Washington, D.C. The Capitol (upper right) was engulfed in flames. Even the White House was damaged.

1825

With the opening of the Erie Canal in 1825, goods could be transported from the Atlantic Ocean up the Hudson River to Albany, New York, which the canal linked to Buffalo, a port on the Great Lakes.

1830–40

The Shawnee Tecumseh (above) was killed early in the government's fight against eastern tribes. This campaign peaked between 1830 and 1840 with the forced march of the Cherokee along the Trail of Tears to Indian Territory.

1846–48

Texas adopted the Lone Star Flag when it became independent from Mexico in 1836. Ten years later a boundary dispute led to the Mexican-American War and the addition of several territories to the southwestern United States.

What would happen when political parties developed, or if slavery became a political issue? Would the United States simply vanish from the Earth, a noble but failed experiment?

In the decades after the setting up of the Constitution, our country had many gifted leaders, including George Washington, Alexander Hamilton, John Adams, Thomas Jefferson, and James Madison. By the end of the 1840s, eloquent senators such as Daniel Webster, John Calhoun, and Henry Clay made the era the golden age of congressional politics.

But for all the eloquence of its leaders, the nation's destiny was clearly in the hands of its ordinary citizens. These were the people who cleared forests, tended farms and factories, constructed new cities, and, with the help of the fed-eral government, built turnpikes and canals. These were also the people who launched full-scale efforts to exterminate Indians and engaged in a war of conquest against Mexico. A good number of them even helped extend the empire of slavery so that it began to threaten the Union.

While doing all these things, the American people passionately debated politics and created solid new institutions of government. In the process they were creating the world's first genuine mass democracy. The most important parts of the English political system, the monarch and the powerful aristocracy, were by now completely gone from American soil. Considering the number of European thinkers who were sure the United States would fail, it is quite appropriate to marvel at the many achievements of the new American nation.

HOW DEMOCRATIC would the United States be? The simple matter of what to call George Washington revealed tensions left over from the debate between the Federalists and Anti-Federalists. Federalist John Adams, who believed that the awe a monarch inspired was important for any country, suggested "His Highness the President of the United States." Most congress-men thought that this title was reminiscent of the monarchy they had just escaped. Washington agreed, though he enjoyed traveling around New York City, which was then the nation's capital, in an elegant horse-drawn carriage like that used by British royalty. Eventually people, whether high or low, addressed him simply as "Mr. President."

Today we are so used to the conflicts of a two-party system that it may be difficult to imagine that George Washington's presidency began without

George Washington (left) was a military hero. By universal acclaim, he was also the only political leader capable of uniting the new nation. One of the most important results of the American Revolution was that Americans could now settle west of the Appalachian Mountains. Families often traveled by flatboat (above). The boats could be taken apart and the lumber used for building a house.

political parties. Many politicians who vigorously disagreed with each other—and some who even disliked each other—served in Washington's Cabinet. The Cabinet was made up of the heads of the most important government agencies, and these men served as the President's closest advisers. But their political conflicts quickly became bitter.

Alexander Hamilton and Thomas Jefferson were the first to clash. Hamilton argued that the Constitution gave the federal government broad powers to strengthen commerce and industry. Jefferson held to a stricter interpretation of the new Constitution. He wanted the central government to be allowed to do only what the Constitution clearly and specifically allowed.

Jefferson and his followers were also enthusi-astic supporters of the French Revolution, which began in 1789. The French were experimenting with forms of democracy even more radical than those in America, and ultimately they executed their king. Jefferson believed that the United States should support freedom movements throughout the world, but he did not support French attempts to interfere in our government.

Hamilton, on the other hand, was suspicious of democracy even in America. He feared that the French Revolution would unleash anarchy across the globe. George Washington sided with Hamilton, pressuring Jefferson to resign from the administration.

During this time many pro-French and pro-Jeffersonian democratic societies were formed. These would grow into the first real political

The tax collector in this cartoon (top) risked being tarred and feathered by farmers who refused to pay taxes on the whiskey they produced. Meanwhile on the high seas, British officers seized American ships and impressed, or forced, the sailors into service to the Crown.

parties in our country's history. Soon the more conservative Federalists were battling it out with the Democratic Republicans, or Republicans, as they came to be known.

The Whiskey Rebellion of 1794 was the biggest conflict between the Friends of Order (Federalists) and the Friends of Liberty (Republicans) during Washington's presidency. One of Hamilton's economic policies involved a tax on whiskey. This tax was unpopular among poor farmers in the backcountry west of the Appalachians. They believed that rich landowners, including the President, should be taxed, but that farmers should not be taxed for the alcohol that they made, drank, and sold. A furious Washington described these settlers as "a parcel of barbarians."

Proclaiming themselves defenders of American liberty, militias made up of western Pennsylvania farmers attacked the local tax collectors. Bloodshed followed. Washington sent 13,000 men—a force larger than the Revolutionary Army—to subdue the mob.

Washington was successful in the short run. Many whiskey rebels were arrested, with two even sentenced to death for treason. But their cause remained popular, and Washington was pressured to pardon them. No significant money ever came from the tax on whiskey.

George Washington was quite shaken by the Whiskey Rebellion and other expressions of vio-

Americans burn an effigy of Supreme Court Chief Justice John Jay in 1795. They were upset that Jay had negotiated a commercial treaty with Britain that failed to respect international maritime law and the United States's neutrality in Britain's war with France.

lence during his administration. Before leaving office he gave a farewell address that focused on the new nation's problems. One goal of the address was to argue that Americans should have economic, but not military or political, alliances with foreign countries. On the domestic front, Washington asked for unity. "With slight shades of difference you have the same religion, manner, habits, and political principles," the beloved President told his fellow citizens. He asked them to banish "the baneful effects of the spirit of party."

His plea came too late to bring back political harmony. John Adams became the second President in 1797, narrowly defeating Jefferson, who, according to the rules at the time, became his Vice President.

Adams fanned the flames of political conflict and division. The threat of war with Britain and France was a strong possibility. Adams, a Federalist, was pleased when the Federalist Congress passed four laws that severely restricted political liberties. They were known as the Alien and Sedition Acts, and the strongest of them authorized stiff fines or imprisonment for anyone convicted of making statements against the government or its leaders. This in effect did away with First Amendment guarantees of freedom of speech and freedom of the press.

The Federalists' goal was to stamp out the Republicans. They did not yet recognize that

As President, John Adams was at the center of conflict between his Federalists and Thomas Jefferson's Democratic Republicans. On his last night in the White House, Adams signed papers appointing a large number of judges to new positions created by the Federalist-controlled Congress. They were known as midnight judges. Infuriated, the Democratic Republicans, party of the newly elected President Jefferson, eliminated the judgeships. One of the Federalist judges, William Marbury (on the left in this painting), sued James Madison, the Secretary of State, to get his job back. The resulting Supreme Court decision by Chief Justice John Marshall effectively gave the Supreme Court, rather than Congress or the President, final authority to declare laws constitutional or unconstitutional.

opposition to the government could be good. Instead, the Federalists believed that Jefferson and his supporters were dangers to the welfare of the nation—even traitors.

Adams and Jefferson ran against each other again in 1800. In spite of their bitter rivalry, Adams accepted the outcome when Jefferson won the election. This proved to be a landmark moment in American history. Instead of attempting to keep control of the government, those who had been in power peacefully turned the government over to the newly elected officials. This is just one reason why historians call this election

the Revolution of 1800. The other reasons have to do with one of the most important figures in all of American history, Thomas Jefferson.

As President, Jefferson worked to democratize the government—to make it more controlled by ordinary people—in the spirit of the Declaration of Independence. He walked to his Inauguration instead of riding in a carriage, as Washington and Adams had done. Whereas government policies of the 1790s had been designed to help bankers and rich merchants, Jefferson placed farmers and craftsmen at the center of his economic vision.

Thomas Jefferson

★ *Hero or Hypocrite?* ★

GENERATIONS OF AMERICANS have debated Thomas Jefferson's place in our country's history—and for good reason. He was one of the most influential Presidents in American history and one of the most complex men ever to hold the office. Jefferson still gets front-page headlines almost two centuries after his death.

Jefferson was a lawyer, a politician, an architect, an ambassador, an accomplished amateur scientist, and one of the most important political theorists in United States history. Since 1769, Jefferson had been agitating for American rights in Virginia's legislative assembly, the House of Burgesses. When the time came for the Continental Congress to declare independence, Jefferson was appointed head of a five-man committee to draft the document that would present the new nation's grievances to King George III. The result was the statement in the Declaration of Independence that speaks to equality: "All men are created equal." In Virginia, he drew up impressive legislation that made the inheritance of land fairer and ensured religious freedom.

Jefferson did not always practice the freedom he preached. He was a slaveholder. The 180 slaves he owned cared for his more than 10,000-acre estate, leaving him free to practice politics and engage in intellectual debates. Jefferson knew that his ownership of fellow human beings contradicted his principles. While refusing to grant freedom to his own slaves because they were a significant part of his wealth, he eloquently condemned slavery. Because of his work, Virginia became the first southern state to ban the slave trade, though not slavery itself. Yet Jefferson did not believe in racial equality. He thought blacks were intellectually inferior. Although he hoped for the gradual emancipation of slaves, he wanted blacks to go back to Africa.

These views made it all the more surprising when in 1998 the nation learned that Jefferson, after his wife died, had almost certainly fathered at least one child with his slave Sally Hemings, with whom he appears to have had a relationship that lasted many years. Does this news diminish Jefferson's status as an American hero? In some ways, yes, because it shows his hypocrisy—the gap between what he said and what he did.

But this discovery also makes us realize that our Founding Fathers were human like the rest of us. The message may be that we, too, can make major contributions, even if we are not perfect.

The Louisiana Purchase

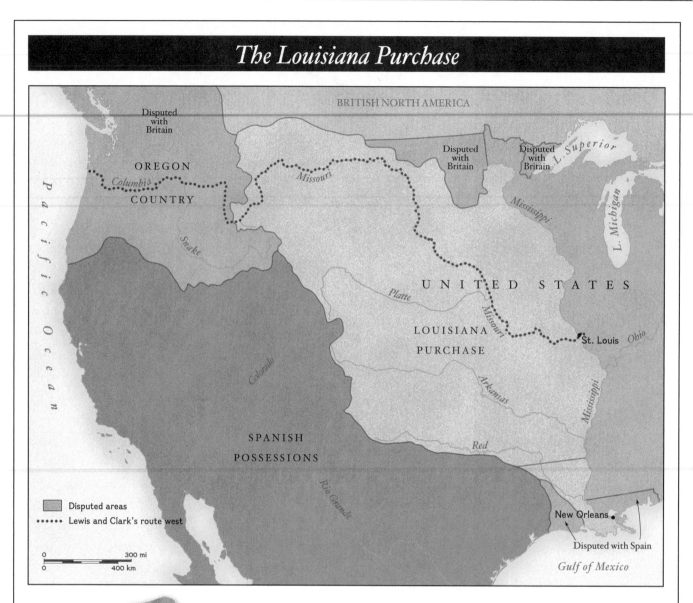

Disputed areas	
•••••• Lewis and Clark's route west	

THE LOUISIANA PURCHASE RAISED QUESTIONS FOR AMERICANS. What peoples and land lay in the newly acquired territories? Would the rivers lead them to the Pacific Ocean? Thomas Jefferson organized a Corps of Discovery, led by Captain Meriwether Lewis and Captain William Clark, to find the answers. In 1804, Lewis and Clark, along with about 40 comrades, departed from St. Louis. They followed the Missouri River and spent the winter at a Mandan village along its shore with friendly Mandan and Arikara Indians. When spring came, they pressed on in small boats to the foothills of the Rockies. Only one woman was part of the expedition. Her name was Sacagawea, and she helped forge friendly relations with her Shoshone people. The rapids along the Columbia River were among the most difficult challenges of the journey. After finally reaching the Pacific, Lewis and Clark built Fort Clatsop and spent the winter of 1805 there. They returned to St. Louis in 1806. The explorers recorded details of what they saw in their diaries. Clark was the expedition's artist and cartographer. The sage grouse (left) was one of the many drawings he made in his journal.

The British burning of Washington, D.C., during the War of 1812 inspired considerable patriotism among Americans. Edward Percy Moran's "By Dawn's Early Light" (right) captures the famous morning in 1814 that led to the writing of "The Star-Spangled Banner." Here Francis Scott Key sees that the American flag is still flying over Baltimore's Fort McHenry after an intense night of attack.

PERHAPS JEFFERSON'S MOST IMPORTANT ACT as President was the Louisiana Purchase in 1803. Bought from the French for $15 million, this new territory more than doubled the size of the country. The following year Meriwether Lewis and William Clark, at Jefferson's request, set out to explore the new land in the most famous expedition in American history.

The Louisiana Purchase was a great triumph, but the rest of Jefferson's foreign policy was less successful. In particular, the British harassed Americans on the western frontier and on the high seas. The British Navy seized American ships, accused thousands of American sailors of

> "And the rockets' red glare, the bombs bursting in air, Gave proof through the night that our flag was still there."
>
> FRANCIS SCOTT KEY, from "The Star-Spangled Banner"

desertion, and forced them to serve under harsh conditions in the imperial navy. Jefferson attempted to cut off trade with Britain, but this failed to stop British mistreatment of Americans.

Tensions between the United States and Britain boiled over into war several years after Jefferson left office. During the War of 1812 the British burned much of Washington, D.C., including the new Capitol building. In turn, Americans unsuccessfully invaded Canada, which was still a British territory. In the end, neither side really won the war, but it did put an end to British threats to the United States. The people who lost the most in the war were the Native Americans.

The Great Debate

★ *Assimilation versus Resistance* ★

MANY INDIAN TRIBES had allied with the British to fight against the Americans during the War of 1812. They had hoped to use the great power of the British empire to stop the westward movement of American settlers hungry for land. Instead, the war forced the British north to Canada, unleashing a flood of farmers into the West. In the decades that followed, this great human migration led to a debate among Native Americans: What was the best way to preserve their life and culture in the face of a rapidly growing nation? Would it be better to try to blend in with white society or to live apart from it?

Assimilation means that one group of people adopts the customs and laws of another group. In this case, Indians would adopt the ways of white Americans. Some Indians decided to fight the United States and live as they always had. Others decided that the best way to survive was to become as American as possible.

The tribe that assimilated most successfully in the decades before the Civil War was the Cherokee Nation. These Indians of the southeast became farmers, had an extensive system of slavery, and fought in the Civil War. (The last Confederate general to surrender in the Civil War was Cherokee Stand Watie.) Many Cherokees became Christians, and most learned to speak English. The great Cherokee scholar Sequoyah developed a system for writing the Cherokee language, which until then had been exclusively a spoken language. According to Sequoyah, "When a writing was made for the Cherokee, then...the Cherokee would be of equal understanding with the white man." The Cherokee created a government based on the United States Constitution. Most of them thought of themselves as loyal Americans and good, modern Cherokees.

Within the Cherokee Nation, a small group of young warriors was unhappy with this approach. They wanted to resist American ways, and they advocated the use of violence to protect their lands. Their voices became louder when all Cherokees—those who had tried to fit in and those who had resisted— were forced to leave their land. In 1838, the United States government moved them from their Georgia homeland to Indian Territory in what is now Oklahoma. Nearly one-quarter of the 16,000 Cherokee who were removed died during this brutal march, which we now call the Trail of Tears.

Many Native Americans resisted assimilation even before the War of 1812. Among them was a Shawnee warrior named Tecumseh. He and his brother Tenskwatawa, or the Prophet, wanted nothing to do with white ways. They launched a religious movement to boycott American trade goods, dress, and alcohol. Tecumseh drew together

> "These lands are ours.
> No one has a right to remove us....
> The Great Spirit above
> has appointed this place for us."
>
> TECUMSEH

many of the tribes of the Ohio River Valley into a confederacy that promised to fight the Americans. He proclaimed, "The white race is a wicked race....The only hope for the red man is a war of extermination against the paleface."

And fight to the death they did. Aided by the British, Tecumseh and his allies launched devastating attacks against settlers along the frontier, among them the future President, William Henry Harrison. By 1813, the tide had turned, and Tecumseh perished in battle. The Creek, who had put up the fiercest resistance in the South, met defeat the following year.

In the end, neither resistance nor assimilation prevented the mass destruction of Native American communities. So who was right in this great debate? As is true with most difficult questions in history, there is no single answer. The debate can be looked at from the point of view of political violence. Is using violence to accomplish a political end ever justified? Before we condemn the Native Americans who chose resistance, it is important to remember that Americans had resisted the tyranny of the British with violence, and lots of it. Today we celebrate that revolution.

What we can say with certainty is that both sides in this great debate had their eloquent and persuasive defenders. Perhaps the greatest tragedy is that Americans told Indians to become "civilized" and then drove them off their land anyway.

One of the great tragedies of U.S. history occurred in the 1830s when the government forced members of the Cherokee Nation to leave their homes in the Southeast and march to Indian Territory in what is now Oklahoma. This march is known as the Trail of Tears.

Railroads were at the heart of the industrial and transportation revolutions. Here a steam locomotive chugs along the Providence, Rhode Island, waterfront. Both freight and passengers could now be moved at previously unimagined speeds.

AS MORE AND MORE PEOPLE moved into lands made available by the removal of Native Americans, it became clear that the country needed a good transportation system. Most of the settlers were farmers. They cut down trees, pulled stumps and rocks out of the ground, and planted seeds, hoping that bad weather would not destroy their crops. They needed to be able to get to markets to sell their produce so they could buy plows and other manufactured goods. But at the time just getting from place to place was difficult, even in the East. It took at least two days to get from New York to Philadelphia, a trip that today takes less than two hours by car or train. On the frontier, travel took even longer in all the mud and muck.

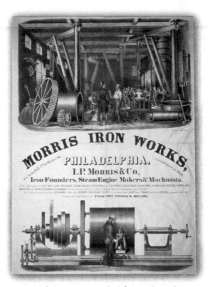

Most of the iron needed for railroads and other industries was produced in Pennsylvania, which had large deposits of coal and iron ore.

The transportation revolution that occurred between 1800 and 1840 was critical to the success of creating a truly "continental" nation, one that reached from the Atlantic to the Pacific. With the help of state governments and local communities, citizens established a new system of roads, often called turnpikes, that could carry people and goods. Next came canals, most notably the Erie Canal in New York State. A marvel of engineering, this canal took nine years of pick-and-shovel work to build. When completed, the canal, together with the Hudson River, provided a crucial link between New York City and the Great Lakes. About the same time, steamboats began chugging up and down the Mississippi and other big rivers.

Most notably during this era, the United States became a world leader in the development of railroads. These iron beasts went so fast—up to 20 miles per hour—that it seemed to some Americans that they violated the way God intended for humans to travel. But compared with today, travel took a long time. Not all the track was the same gauge, or width. This meant passengers had to get on and off eight trains to get from

Charleston, South Carolina, to Philadelphia, Pennsylvania. Freight had to be transferred each time, too.

The improvements in transportation benefited farmers isolated on the frontier and encouraged the rapid spread of factories. The best known factories were in New England, where mills depended first on waterpower and then on steam to operate. Processing cotton from the South, the mills produced cloth for sale at home as well as export to Britain and much of the rest of the world.

Even more groundbreaking than the size and output of the factories were the people who worked in them. During the 1830s and 1840s, mills employed young farm women from the surrounding countryside. Many people worried about young women living away from the watchful eyes of their parents. Few people during this era thought women should be independent, shaping their own lives. Mill owners created a sheltered environment, with plenty of supervision and some educational opportunities. The women who worked in Lowell, a well-known mill town in Massachusetts, enjoyed this limited freedom and three dollars a week in pay, which was considered a good salary at the time.

Roads, Canals, and Rails

WATERWAYS AND A GROWING network of railroads linked the frontier with eastern cities. Produce moved on small boats along canals and rivers from the farms to the ports. Large steamships carried goods and people from port to port. Railroads expanded to connect towns, providing faster transport for everyone.

On the frontier, stagecoaches continued to carry passengers over the growing number of roads. By 1840 the National Road stretched some 600 miles from Cumberland, Maryland, to Vandalia, Illinois.

Men, women, and children labored as many as 70 hours a week in the new factories. Child labor was a crucial part of the success of the industrial revolution. Children tended machines, like these in a Lowell textile mill (above) that combed fibers into loose coils that could later be spun into yarn or thread. Here a young girl helps pack the coils into canisters.

Traveling New England salesmen, known as Yankee peddlers, were common in the North. Riding in horse-drawn wagons, the peddlers sold cloth, candles, candy, and all kinds of other goods to rural families. Sometimes customers were grateful. Other times they were suspicious about the quality or price of the available products.

Mill owners soon faced competition from other mills. They cut wages and made women work longer and faster at the noisy and dusty machinery. The women responded by going on strike. They wanted more money for their increased output, and they wanted to regain the dignity they felt they had lost. The efforts of the strikers were unsuccessful, and many of the women were fired or quit. By the 1850s, the workers in the factories were mainly poor Irish women who had recently come to America because of a famine in their homeland. No one looked to the mills as a great place to work any more.

Many Americans marveled at the economic growth that resulted as the United States became a manufacturing powerhouse that rivaled Britain. Still, the dangers of the economy—unemployment, low wages, frequent depressions—taught Americans some difficult lessons during these

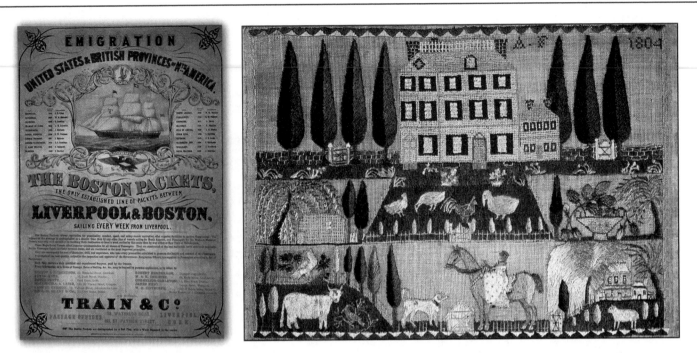

Immigrants poured into the United States during the 1840s after a famine in Ireland and a failed revolution in Germany. The poster on the left offers a transoceanic voyage for only $12.50. Samplers like the one on the right showed off a girl's skill with a needle. In days when clothing was often homemade, girls learned sewing at an early age. Stitched in fine detail, this sampler is signed only "AF 1804."

years. As the country became more and more industrialized, goods were no longer made by hand at home. They were machine-made in factories. Large businesses often provided dead-end jobs. Workers were required to put in 10- to 14-hour days, usually six days a week. Wages barely paid for food, much less shoes and winter coats.

It is not surprising, therefore, that the first labor unions, and the first wave of strikes, arose during the 1830s and 1840s. Workers banded together to try to improve their conditions. What many wanted was a chance to set up their own businesses. That was the American dream for much of the 19th century, and still is for many today. But the likelihood of workers achieving this goal was diminishing, even though America's economy was growing stronger.

The economic changes of this period often caused disappointment for ordinary people. But the political changes were beneficial to some, especially white males. In the decades after the Revolution, only one state, New Jersey, allowed women to vote, and then only until 1807. Native Americans could not vote either. The same was true for most African-American males, except in New England. New western lands such as Indiana and Oregon even attempted to deny the entry of any blacks into their territories.

What people today often do not remember is that many white men could not vote at our nation's beginning either. Men had to own property in most states in order to earn the privilege (not the right) of choosing their own political leaders. Finally, in the 1820s, state legislatures gave almost all white men the right to vote. This was a dramatic change not only in American history, but in world history. Nowhere else had so many people ever had the right to vote. Some wondered: Would this produce mob rule?

When Americans elected Andrew Jackson President in 1828, many wealthy citizens worried that "the reign of King Mob" had indeed come to Washington. In certain ways Jackson was a strange figure to represent the "common man."

Indian Removal

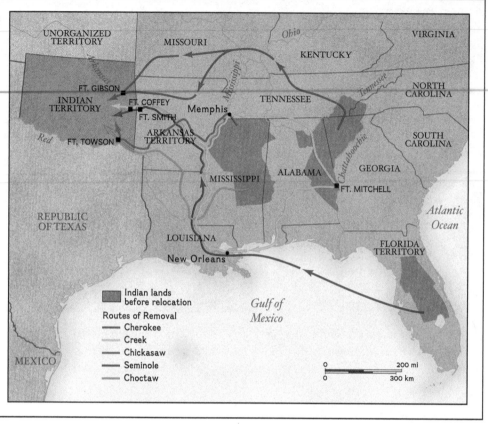

THIS MAP SHOWS the routes of the five southeastern tribes that were forced to leave their homelands in the Southeast and live in Indian Territory in what is now Oklahoma. A surprising number of Americans opposed Indian removal. (The first bill in Congress passed by only 103 votes to 97.) But the demand for new land was high, and former Army officers such as Andrew Jackson used their experiences as Indian fighters to gain political popularity and get elected to office.

Although born poor, he became a wealthy slave-owner in Tennessee. What made him popular with the masses was his success in conquering Indians and his dislike of rich Northerners, especially bankers. Showing his democratic instincts, Jackson opened up the White House to give ordinary folks the chance to have a say in their government. As he made clear in his first annual message, "The majority is to govern."

Jackson used his popularity to increase the power of the presidency. He forced South Carolina, and its powerful senator John Calhoun, to back down when that state tried, on its own, to declare a federal revenue bill unconstitutional. Jackson continued his ruthless campaign against the Indians. He refused to accept the authority of

> "There are no necessary evils in government. Its evils exist only in its abuses."
>
> ANDREW JACKSON

Chief Justice John Marshall, who tried to use the Supreme Court to keep the Cherokees from being removed from their land.

Jackson's opposition to the creation of a national bank run by the federal government nearly destroyed the economy. He feared that a big money-lending power of this kind might greatly harm American liberties. The "Bank War" helped throw the economy into a depression, a severe downturn that forced many businesses to close and put thousands out of work.

One of the most important events to occur during the "age of Jackson" was the Second Great Awakening. Energetic ministers such as Charles Finney offered many non-churchgoing people a highly emotional experience of Christianity. The major difference between the Second Great

Awakening and the religious revival of the 1700s (see Chapter One) was that the clergy now emphasized ways in which people might try to perfect themselves, instead of dwelling on the sinful side of human nature.

If people could become perfect, so could society—provided that everyone worked hard at it. That is why the Second Great Awakening encouraged the first big wave of social reform in American history. Evangelical women, especially, put their time into trying to make life better for the mentally ill, prisoners, and the poor.

Their ideas for making a perfect world were not always welcomed by others. Many reformers hoped to rid the world of alcohol. Such a plea for "temperance," as it was called, was not popular among workingmen who were used to drinking a couple of glasses of beer to relax after a hard day. However, those men's wives were often happy to have that beer-drinking money available for more necessary household purchases.

These Christian reformers were prominent figures in the new movement against slavery (see Chapter Four). They had to fight a formidable foe, for the empire of the slaveholder grew stronger during these decades. At the time of the Revolution, many Americans, Thomas Jefferson among them, believed that slavery would die out naturally. When the federal government outlawed the slave trade in 1808, it looked as if Jefferson's prediction might come true.

Everything changed when Eli Whitney's cotton gin (invented in 1793) came into use throughout the South. The gin separated the many little seeds in a cotton boll from the actual cotton fiber. Before Whitney's invention, this had taken a lot of time, making the process expensive. The new method was faster and highly profitable, and it freed up slave labor for planting, weeding, and harvesting. Rice and indigo (a plant that contained a blue dye) were other important crops worked by slaves. But cotton became king throughout much of the South, especially in states of the Deep South, such as Mississippi and Alabama. Southern slaveowners shipped their raw cotton to northern factories for processing into thread, yarn, and fabric. In many ways, the economy of the whole country depended on slave labor.

The combination of slavery and cotton placed the South in a unique position during these years. Two-thirds of all southern whites owned no slaves. This majority of small-scale, or yeoman, farmers often did not approve of what the slaveowners did. But slaveowners were so rich and politically powerful that they ruled the region. The South was just

Bales of cotton from a nearby plantation are loaded onto a Mississippi riverboat. Logs stacked on the shore will provide fuel to create steam to power the ship. Steamboats opened new ports along America's rivers by making the transport of goods and passengers upriver almost as easy as down and at far less cost than by land.

Slaves could be sold at auction at any time. Parents and children, husbands and wives would probably never see each other again.

content to accept his or her place in life.

Slaves' lives were completely controlled by their masters. At any moment a slave could be whipped—or have an ear or a toe chopped off—for the slightest disobedience. Even kind masters if they were in need of money sold brother away from sister or child away from parent.

But slaves were determined to live as decent a life as possible under these circumstances. They relied on one another, cultivating strong extended family networks of aunts, uncles, and cousins. They created their own strong culture. And they continued to develop their Christian faith as a way to survive hardships. Masters expected Christianity to make slaves "obedient." Slaves had a different idea of how to use their faith. Nat Turner is the most extreme example of a slave using the religion of his master as a force for rebellion, rather than subservience.

as Christian as the North, with evangelical revivals throughout the region. Many of the white ministers were slaveowners who were not about to give up their way of life, so they preached that every person—especially every slave—should be

Spread of Cotton

THIS MAP SHOWS HOW RAPID AND FAR-REACHING the spread of cotton was following the invention of the cotton gin by Eli Whitney. Prior to the cotton gin, only long-fibered "lowland" cotton could be grown economically, and it would grow only in a few hot and humid coastal areas. When Whitney's invention provided an easier way to remove seeds from the shorter fibers, huge new tracts of land were opened up for planting hardier, short-fibered "upland" cotton. Once the new technology was in place, however, enormous numbers of slaves were required to tend and harvest the cotton. Their numbers increased from 700,000 in 1790 to 2 million in 1830 and 4 million by 1860. The explosive growth and economic success of slavery ultimately led to the Civil War. By mid-1861, all of the cotton states would secede from the Union.

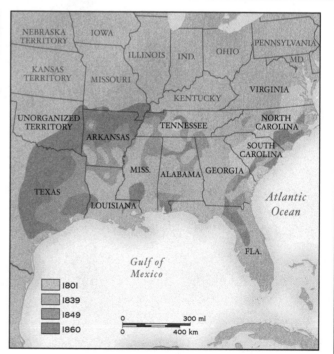

Nat Turner

★ *Slave Rebel* ★

IN AUGUST 1831, NAT TURNER led the most deadly slave revolt in all American history. Turner began by murdering his master, Joseph Travis, and Travis's family. After killing Travis, Turner and his allies went from plantation to plantation in his home of Southampton County, Virginia. There is no official record of how many people died in the uprising. More than 50 whites were killed, and the state executed as many blacks, including Turner himself.

What led to such murderous acts? Even Turner later stated that Travis "was to me a kind master, and placed great confidence in me; in fact I had no cause to complain about his treatment."

Nat Turner had been treated badly by other masters and knew firsthand the cruelties of slavery. When he was 22, his master, Samuel Turner, died. Nat, his wife, Cherry, and his mother were all sold to different plantations.

Many slaves experienced similar fates. What made Nat Turner react as he did? Before his execution, Turner dictated a confession in which he tried to explain his ideas. A longtime preacher, Turner thought himself "ordained for some great purpose in the hands of the Almighty." He experienced a religious vision in which "white spirits and black spirits engaged in battle." The spirit of the Lord told him that he should "arise and...slay my enemies with their own weapons." Statements such as these suggest that he was influenced by the religious fervor of the time.

The majority of slaves did not revolt because whites simply held too much power. Still, Nat Turner's rebellion terrified whites throughout the South. One Virginia state legislator spoke of "the suspicion that a Nat Turner might be in every family, that the same bloody deed could be acted over at any time in any place, that the materials for it were spread through the land and always ready for a like explosion."

Nat Turner left an important legacy for our own time. Since 1831 Nat Turner has served as an example of the American tradition of fiery rebellion against racial injustice.

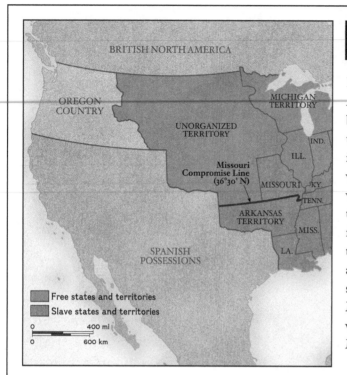

Missouri Compromise 1820

IN THE DECADES BEFORE THE CIVIL WAR, many Americans began to view as inevitable a bloody conflict between slave states and free states. Congress constantly tried to work out compromises that would prevent fighting between the North and the South. The first of these was the Missouri Compromise of 1820. The main issue was how to deal with the spread of slavery into western territories. Would the new western states allow slavery or forbid it? The Missouri Compromise divided the lands of the Louisiana Purchase into two parts. Slavery would be allowed south of latitude 36°30'. But north of that line, slavery would be forbidden, except in the new state of Missouri. Maine (previously a part of Massachusetts) would enter the union as a free state, balancing out Missouri's pro-slavery senators.

FACED WITH THE THREAT of slave uprisings, southern slaveholders recognized that they needed to offer some kind of moral justification for their "peculiar institution." Today it is difficult to imagine justifying the enslavement of four million human beings. But rich Southerners believed that slavery was not only a necessary way to grow cotton but also a good, kind, and decent way of life.

Southerner George Fitzhugh compared the lives of slaves to those of factory workers in the North. He claimed that southern slaves worked fewer hours, had more to eat, had better clothes and housing, and were not cast out when they became too old to work. According to him, old workers in the North simply starved if they had no family to support them. Factory owners felt no responsibility for the welfare of their workers.

Fitzhugh, of course, overlooked the cruel and brutal qualities of slavery. His reasoning, though, helped convince many Southerners that by defending slavery, they were defending a wonderful way of life. Meanwhile antislavery thinking was gaining

power in the North. Battle lines between the North and the South were being drawn.

After 1820, congressmen continued trying to prevent slavery from destroying the Union. Some believed they had put the issue of slavery's expansion to rest with the passage of the Missouri Compromise of 1820 (see map box above). But Thomas Jefferson knew better. He wrote: "This momentous question like a fire bell in the night, awakened and filled me with terror. I considered it at once the [death] knell of the Union."

Jefferson was correct. Westward expansion proved to be the primary reason that Americans could no longer compromise over slavery. The more Americans triumphed in bringing land into their nation, the more they disagreed about what to do with it. This was particularly the case when the United States acquired much of the American Southwest from Mexico between 1846 and 1848.

War between Mexico and the United States had been brewing since shortly after Texas declared independence from Mexico in 1836. The

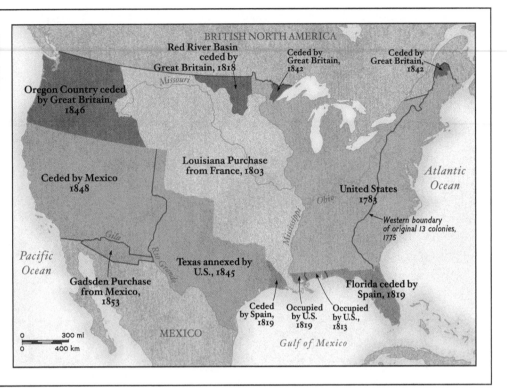

Territorial Gains

IN LESS THAN 50 YEARS, the United States grew from the Mississippi River to the Pacific Ocean, starting with the Louisiana Purchase and ending with the territories gained from Mexico in the Mexican-American War. Spain gave up its claims to Florida and the northeastern Gulf Coast, and agreements with Great Britain established the boundary with Canada by 1846.

Map labels:
- BRITISH NORTH AMERICA
- Red River Basin ceded by Great Britain, 1818
- Ceded by Great Britain, 1842
- Ceded by Great Britain, 1842
- Oregon Country ceded by Great Britain, 1846
- Ceded by Mexico 1848
- Louisiana Purchase from France, 1803
- United States 1783
- Atlantic Ocean
- Western boundary of original 13 colonies, 1775
- Pacific Ocean
- Gadsden Purchase from Mexico, 1853
- Texas annexed by U.S., 1845
- Florida ceded by Spain, 1819
- Ceded by Spain, 1819
- Occupied by U.S. 1819
- Occupied by U.S., 1813
- MEXICO
- Gulf of Mexico
- 0 300 mi / 0 400 km

Mexican government did not recognize Texas's independence and continued to claim the area between the Nueces River and the Rio Grande. In 1845, despite opposition from antislavery Northerners, Texas was admitted to the Union as a slave state. President James Polk sent a military force to defend its borders. When U.S. soldiers crossed into the disputed area, the Mexicans fired on them. Polk blamed Mexico for the resulting war.

Not all Americans supported the war. A young congressman from Illinois named Abraham Lincoln spoke out eloquently against it. But America's victory brought with it new lands for settlement. California, Utah, Nevada, most of New Mexico and Arizona, and portions of Colorado and Wyoming all became part of the United States. The question of whether the new lands should permit slavery was immediately raised. David Wilmot, a congressman from Pennsylvania, introduced a legislative amendment that would have made the Missouri Compromise of 1820 null and void by banning slavery from all territory seized during the Mexican-American War. The "Wilmot Proviso" did not become law, but it was a sign of just how powerful antislavery opinion had become in the North. The measure's defeat ensured that the 1850s would see fights over the question of slavery in the territories.

The real question, though, was whether the Union could survive half slave and half free.

U.S. troops scale the walls of Chapultepec Castle, outside Mexico City, in the last major battle of the Mexican-American War.

CHAPTER FOUR

A NEW BIRTH OF FREEDOM: CIVIL WAR AND RECONSTRUCTION

★ 1848–1877 ★

"A house divided against itself cannot stand."

ABRAHAM LINCOLN

1848

The discovery of gold nuggets at Sutter's Mill in California touched off a stampede of people from across America and around the world, all hoping to get rich. Some died just trying to get there; others went home penniless.

1851

The Fugitive Slave Act of 1850 inspired Harriet Beecher Stowe to write Uncle Tom's Cabin. Her story about the cruelty of slavery helped spread antislavery sentiment in the North in the years leading up to the Civil War.

1858

The now classic debates between Stephen A. Douglas and Abraham Lincoln during their campaign for the U.S. Senate brought Lincoln to national attention and paved the way for his election as President in 1860.

1859

In this painting, John Brown holds a Bible in one hand and a gun in the other as he implores Americans to rise up against slavery. His raid on the federal arsenal at Harpers Ferry failed in its goal to start a slave revolt.

BY THE MID-1840S SLAVERY was clearly an issue that needed to be addressed. At the time, though, Americans did not realize that slavery would embroil them in a bloody civil war that would divide families and threaten the existence of the United States. People continued to go about their lives. Gold had just been discovered in California, and the whole country had gold fever.

Another kind of fever was spreading, too. Women were beginning to realize that the Constitution had overlooked their rights. In 1848, women gathered in Seneca Falls, New York, for a meeting that would transform world history. There, women's rights activists changed forever the way we think about a woman's place in American society.

1861–1865

On April 12, 1861, the bloodiest conflict in American history began when Confederate forces fired on Fort Sumter. More than a half million Americans would die over the next four years in the Civil War.

1865

Just five days after the Civil War ended, John Wilkes Booth, actor and Southern sympathizer, assassinated President Lincoln at Ford's Theatre. His death threw the nation into confusion over how to deal with the South.

1865–1877

The carpetbag, carried by Northerners who worked to establish democratic reforms in the South, became a symbol of Reconstruction. But in reality, southern blacks were the key players during this period.

1870

The 15th Amendment to the Constitution, which was ratified on March 30, gave black men the right to vote. The sight of freed slaves casting their ballots showed what a revolution Reconstruction was.

BEFORE THE 1840S American women, and women throughout the world, were generally told to remain in the background while men took care of the affairs of the world. Americans believed that men and women were meant to live in "separate spheres." Men would earn money to provide for their families, and women would take care of the house, the children, and to a large extent the church. Women's work was strenuous and time consuming. They didn't have the modern conveniences of electric stoves, washing machines, microwaves, vacuum cleaners, or running water. If a woman needed water for cooking, she had to carry it in from an outdoor well, then build a fire to boil it. A wood stove, and even a well, were luxuries.

Some women began to realize that they had no say in their own lives. Abigail Adams's plea to "Remember the Ladies" had been ignored by her husband and the other Founding Fathers. Nothing had been written into the Constitution guaranteeing women any rights. Women were especially displeased with their legal "disabilities." They could not serve on juries, and often they couldn't even testify in court. Colleges were closed to women, so they could not get an advanced education. Married women could not own property. Upon marrying,

they were obligated to transfer ownership to their husbands. Any wages they earned became the property of their husbands. It was extremely difficult for a woman to obtain a divorce, even from an abusive husband. Most important, women could not vote. Without representation in government they had no way to get laws passed that would improve their situation in society.

Elizabeth Cady Stanton helped change all this. When she found out that she couldn't go to college, Elizabeth did what most women of the time did: She married. Although her husband allowed her to accompany him to his political meetings, he made it clear that her main responsibility was taking care of the household, which eventually included seven children.

This was tolerable for Elizabeth so long as she lived in an exciting place like Boston. But when the family moved to Seneca Falls, a quiet town in the Finger Lakes region of upstate New York, she felt trapped in her duties as housewife and mother and later wrote, "I now fully understood the practical difficulties most women had to contend with in the isolated household." Her determination to free herself and women everywhere from this bondage gave birth to the women's rights movement.

Searching for gold was hard work (left). Prospectors had to swirl pans of dirt or shovel it into strainers in order to sift out the gold. Few miners found enough gold to become wealthy. Many gold seekers followed the Oregon Trail (above) before turning off to head across the Sierra Nevada to California. River crossings could be dangerous, but traveling together in wagon trains helped reduce the risk.

Elizabeth Cady Stanton

★ Crusader for Women's Rights ★

BORN INTO A WEALTHY FAMILY in 1815, Elizabeth Cady was a bright child, eager to please her father, a powerful judge. When Elizabeth's brother died, Judge Cady was grief-stricken, so Elizabeth resolved to take her brother's place. She became a good student, studying Greek from an early age. This was almost unheard of, since girls usually studied only the Bible and the "domestic arts," such as knitting and cooking. Elizabeth's father loved her. But he broke her heart when he refused to let her go to college. She was, after all, a young woman, and in those days only men went to college.

Two events dramatically changed her life in 1840. She married the abolitionist Henry Stanton and traveled with him to London to attend the World Antislavery Convention. There she befriended Lucretia Mott, a radical Quaker and nationally known antislavery agitator. When the male delegates refused to allow the women to participate—even making them sit behind a curtain—Elizabeth and Lucretia realized they had a lot in common with slaves. Then and there they decided to launch the women's rights movement.

The first formal meeting was held eight years later in Seneca Falls, New York, where the Stantons lived. There, more than 200 women (and 40 men) debated Stanton's Declaration of Sentiments. In words that echoed the sentiments of the Declaration of Independence, it said in part: "The history of mankind is a history of repeated injuries and usurpations on the part of man toward woman, having in direct object the establishment of an absolute tyranny over her." Also included were a list of 15 grievances—made to sound like the grievances the Continental Congress had leveled against King George III in 1775. Ultimately all the demands of Stanton's declaration were accepted by the women in attendance, even the most radical—the right of women to vote. Thus was born the women's suffrage movement.

Elizabeth Cady Stanton, along with her dear friend Susan B. Anthony, crusaded for the vote until Stanton's death in 1902. Sadly, she lived only long enough to see a handful of territories and states—beginning with Wyoming in 1869—grant the vote to women. It would be 1920 before Congress passed the 19th Amendment to the Constitution, giving all women in the country the right to vote.

Stanton is one of the great heroines of our history. It is important to appreciate her efforts to win for women what we now consider a basic civil right.

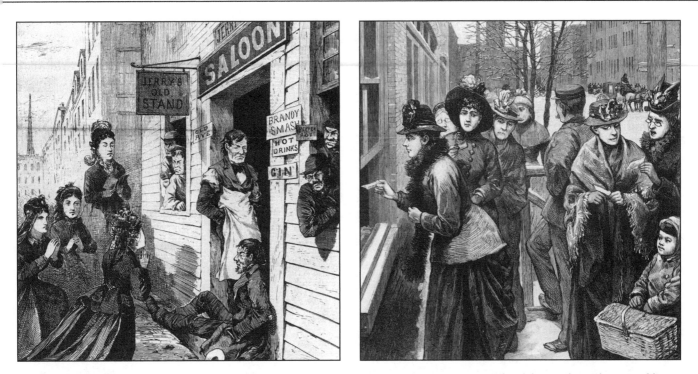

American women launched great crusades during the 19th century. In many communities, women closed down saloons that served liquor (left), concerned that husbands and fathers were spending too much of their small incomes on beer, while their families often went hungry. They first won the right to vote (right) in Wyoming Territory in 1869, but American women as a whole did not gain the vote until 1920.

THE OTHER EARTHSHAKING EVENT of 1848 took place clear across the country from Seneca Falls. The California gold rush began that year when James Marshall discovered gold at Sutter's Mill. Sutter tried to keep the discovery a secret, but within a few months the whole world had learned the news. Then it seemed as though everyone was taking off for the foothills of the Sierra Nevada. Many of these early prospectors struck it rich. The work was hard, but it did not take much skill to sift heavy flakes of gold from the dirt and minerals that came out of a stream.

By the following year, miners from around the globe had come to make their fortunes. Some of these "forty-niners" (named for the year 1849) did well, but most did not. The legend we have of the gold rush is just that—a legend. We still think of this event as a great adventure, with more than

> "Boys, by God
> I believe
> I have found a gold mine."
>
> JAMES MARSHALL

enough gold to go around. In reality the easiest gold to find was near the Earth's surface, and that was quickly taken. As time went on, miners had to dig deeper and deeper to find their treasure. This took huge equipment, which in turn required a lot of money. Most miners worked as employees of others, not as rugged individualists. In the end, miners were lucky to go home without losing too much money. The people who did get rich were the merchants who provided goods and services. The most famous was Levi Strauss, who brought along enough denim and copper rivets to outfit an army of miners in blue jeans.

From the outset the gold rush was one of the most multicultural events in the history of the world. Yet for the Indians and many of the Chinese, Chileans, and other foreigners who came to California, the gold rush was a tragedy. The

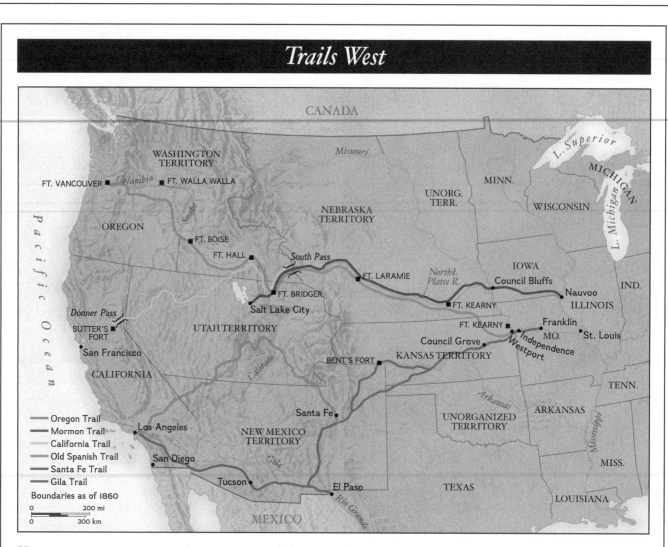

Trails West

Oregon Trail
Mormon Trail
California Trail
Old Spanish Trail
Santa Fe Trail
Gila Trail

Boundaries as of 1860

0   200 mi
0   300 km

HUNDREDS OF THOUSANDS OF AMERICANS traveled westward during the great migration of the 1840s and 1850s. This was one of the epic migrations of people in all of history. Pioneers had a choice of trails, but none was easy. The Oregon Trail alone claimed some 34,000 lives—most from accidents or cholera. About one grave was dug for every hundred yards. The biggest fear was not finishing the journey before winter with its deadly storms. Those who were successful could claim inexpensive, fertile land and had an excellent chance of carving out a good life for themselves.

Indians lost their land, and as the gold became harder and harder to extract, whites turned against the foreigners, especially the Chinese, who worked for low wages, and the Mexicans, whom America had just defeated in war. When extra taxation did not work to drive out these foreigners, whites turned to violence.

Those who traveled on to the Northwest along the Oregon Trail, rather than branching off to head southwest to California, generally prospered

much more than the gold seekers. Life on the trail wasn't easy, however. It usually took seven months to make the 2,000-mile trip from Missouri to the West Coast. Many people died of disease. Children sometimes fell out of wagons and were crushed. If a sudden winter storm came up, everyone was in danger of perishing. But at the end of the trek, many settlers were able to claim much more farmland than they could have imagined in the Midwest. Women often suffered great isolation in the early years of their life in Oregon, but in the end, women and men were proud of their achievements as pioneers.

Why did Americans feel compelled to head west? For many, it was a simple economic decision. They were in debt, or else they believed they could live a richer and more independent life beyond the Mississippi River. They could start fresh by claiming free or cheap government land.

For others it was more than thinking about their pocketbooks. Historians call the force behind their decision "Manifest Destiny." This term was taken from a quote by journalist John L. O'Sullivan, who said it was "our manifest destiny to overspread the continent." Many Americans of the time believed it was clear that God planned for the country to expand from sea to sea. People felt it was their sacred duty to yoke up oxen and take their families in covered wagons along the Oregon Trail.

This family is probably "nooning," as the midday rest was called. Their faces carry expressions of exhaustion and determination. Their wagons carried all their supplies and clothes, plus provided shelter and a place to sleep. Children often had fond memories of the westward trek. Although they worked hard, kids usually had many playmates and enjoyed listening to stories by the fire.

As more and more Americans settled in the West, the nation's politics became more complicated. Slavery remained a big problem. What would become of the western territories? As in previous decades, Congress tried to reach compromises on the issue of admitting new slave states and free states, but by the end of the 1850s, almost everyone knew that Congress had failed. Southerners and Northerners had come to dis-

trust each other so much that it would take only a few sparks to ignite a huge conflict.

The Compromise of 1850 was the most significant attempt to keep the North and South together in the same union. The compromise was made up of several parts. First, California was admitted as a free state. As for the rest of the land won from Mexico, each territory's citizens would vote on whether or not that territory would become a slave state or a free state. This method of deciding statehood was known as "popular sovereignty." Congress also banned the slave trade—but not slavery itself—from the nation's capital. That was at least a small triumph for people in the North. But the most controversial victory—the passage of a stronger Fugitive Slave Act—was won by the South.

The Fugitive Slave Act of 1850 infuriated most Northerners. The basic principle of the law was that northern state governments and northern citizens were legally required to cooperate with the federal government in catching and sending escaped slaves back to the South.

The danger of being caught and sent to the South existed for free blacks, too. Slave catchers could come north and grab free American citizens simply because they were black. Most of the time they would get away with it. Northerners became increasingly convinced that the federal government

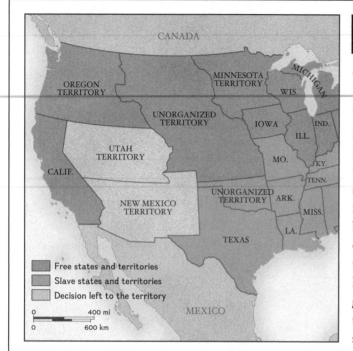

Free states and territories
Slave states and territories
Decision left to the territory

0   400 mi
0   600 km

CANADA

OREGON TERRITORY

MINNESOTA TERRITORY

MICHIGAN

WIS.

UNORGANIZED TERRITORY

IOWA

IND.

ILL.

UTAH TERRITORY

MO.

KY.

CALIF.

TENN.

NEW MEXICO TERRITORY

UNORGANIZED TERRITORY

ARK.

MISS.

LA.

TEXAS

MEXICO

Compromise of 1850

THE POLITICS OF SLAVERY had reached a fever pitch by 1850. When California asked to be admitted to the Union, the question of whether slavery would be allowed in the new state touched off a new debate in Congress. Lawmakers patched together another compromise, this time in several parts. California would enter the Union as a free state. It would be up to the citizens in the territories of Utah and New Mexico to decide the slavery issue by vote. Congress outlawed the slave trade, but not the ownership of slaves, in the nation's capital. The most controversial part of the Compromise of 1850 was the Fugitive Slave Act. It required citizens to help the federal government not only catch runaways but also return them to their owners. Those who ignored the law faced severe penalties if caught.

was on the side of what they came to call the "Slave Power." In turn, resistance to the law made the South more certain that all Northerners were intent on destroying slavery.

The next important episode in the slavery crisis was the 1854 Kansas-Nebraska Act. Stephen A. Douglas, the U.S. senator from Illinois who introduced the legislation, thought he could win political popularity by applying the idea of popular sovereignty to Kansas and Nebraska. Allowing people in these territories to decide the slavery question overturned part of the 1820 Missouri Compromise. Pro- and anti-slavery forces rushed into each territory to try to stack up votes at the polls. The greatest battle came in Kansas. The two sides terrorized each other so much that the territory became known as Bleeding Kansas. Eventually the anti-slavery forces won, but not without the slaughter of many on both sides.

These conflicts strengthened support for the

Dred Scott

new Republican Party in the 1856 presidential election. Republicans were insistent on stopping slavery in the territories. By 1860, they would win the presidency, the most rapid rise to power of any political party in U.S. history.

The years between 1856 and 1860 were filled with several other important events. Two in particular—one involving Dred Scott, the other John Brown—make it possible to understand why so many Southerners and Northerners began to hate each other as the 1850s came to a close.

Dred Scott was a slave, yet he had as great an impact on the fate of the nation as any politician. Scott was the property of an Army surgeon, Southerner John Emerson, who had taken Scott with him to Illinois and Wisconsin. Did Scott's time in these northern areas, both of which outlawed slavery, mean that he was free? In 1846, Dred Scott sued for his freedom, arguing that his time on free soil indeed made him permanently free. Eleven years later, his

Kansas-Nebraska Act

THE KANSAS-NEBRASKA ACT of 1854 was the brainchild of Illinois Senator Stephen A. Douglas. It applied the idea of popular sovereignty to Kansas and Nebraska. Since these new states were north of 36° 30', they should have been admitted as free states according to the Compromises of 1820 and 1850. By allowing popular sovereignty in Kansas and Nebraska, the 1854 act overturned the previous compromises and increased tensions, especially in Kansas. There, pro-slavery forces from Missouri swarmed in to try to sway the vote. For a while Kansas had two governments, one for and the other against slavery. Ultimately the anti-slavery forces won in Kansas, but the fighting that had taken place there foreshadowed the Civil War that would engulf the country in the next decade.

Free states
Slave states
Territory closed to slaveholding
Territory open to slaveholding

case finally reached the Supreme Court. On March 6, 1857, Chief Justice Roger Taney declared that Scott had no right even to sue. Not only were slaves not citizens of the United States, *no* black people anywhere in the country were. Taney wrote in his decision that African Americans were "beings of an inferior order [who] had no rights which white men were bound to respect." The Court ruled that Congress could not ban slavery in any territory, effectively undoing the doctrine of popular sovereignty.

The decision was a tremendous blow to African-American freedom. Frederick Douglass, the most prominent and eloquent African-American opponent of slavery, stated that the *Dred Scott* decision was "a most scandalous and devilish perversion of the Constitution." Historians today generally agree that the decision was the worst ever handed down by the Supreme Court. At the time, Northerners viewed the ruling as proof that the national

John Brown

government had been captured by the Slave Power.

John Brown was another person who, at first glance, seemed unlikely to become an important historical figure. Brown was a hard-working white farmer and craftsman who was almost always in debt. His Protestant religion, however, required that he put aside his own concerns to purge sin and evil from the world. Brown's Christianity inspired him to fight for the end of slavery and for equality of all races. This was a radical position to take. At the time, most white Americans did not want racial equality even if they opposed slavery.

Brown had actively participated in Bleeding Kansas, where he and his sons had killed five Southern settlers in what became known as the Pottawatomie Massacre. Three years later, in 1859, Brown decided to raid the federal armory, where guns were manufactured and stored, at Harpers Ferry, Virginia. He and 22 comrades, including several free blacks, believed that once they took over

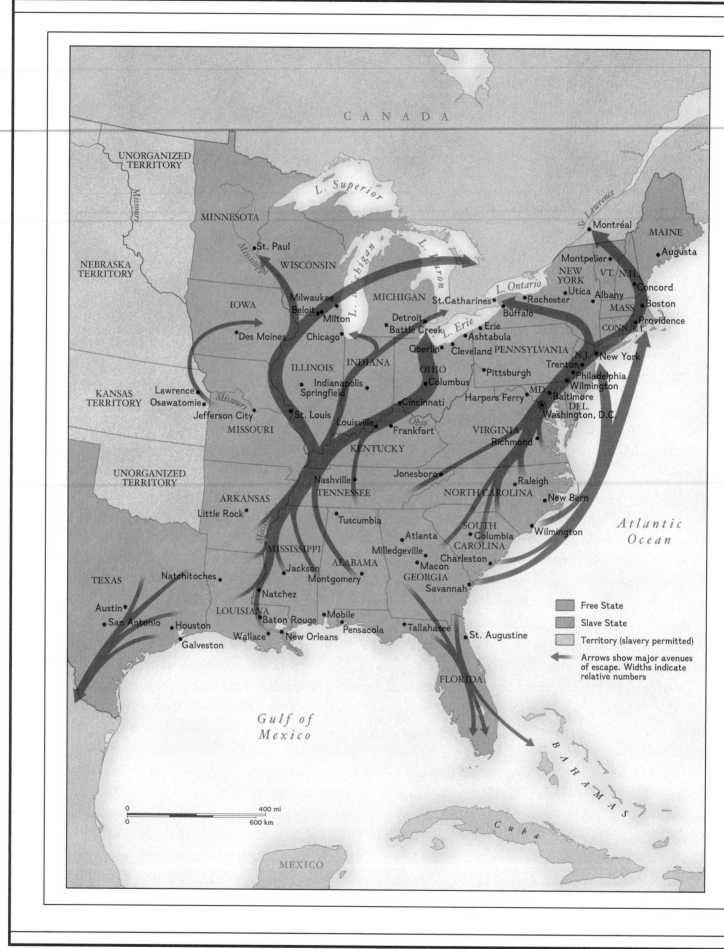

CANADA

UNORGANIZED
TERRITORY

NEBRASKA
TERRITORY

MINNESOTA

L. Superior

St. Paul

WISCONSIN

IOWA

Milwaukee
Beloit
Milton

L. Michigan

MICHIGAN

Detroit
Battle Creek
Oberlin

L. Huron

St.Catharines

L. Ontario

Rochester

Buffalo

L. Erie

Erie
Ashtabula
Cleveland

St. Lawrence

Montréal

Montpelier

NEW
YORK

Utica

VT. N.H.

Albany

MAINE

Augusta

Concord
Boston
MASS.

Providence

CONN. R.I.

KANSAS
TERRITORY

Des Moines

Chicago

ILLINOIS
INDIANA

PENNSYLVANIA

N.J. New York

Lawrence
Osawatomie
Jefferson City

Missouri

St. Louis

Indianapolis
Springfield

OHIO

Columbus

Cincinnati

Pittsburgh

Trenton

Harpers Ferry

MD.

Philadelphia
Wilmington
Baltimore
DEL.

MISSOURI

Louisville
Frankfort

Ohio

Washington, D.C.

KENTUCKY

VIRGINIA

Richmond

UNORGANIZED
TERRITORY

ARKANSAS

Little Rock

Nashville
TENNESSEE

Jonesboro

Raleigh

NORTH CAROLINA

New Bern

Tuscumbia

SOUTH

Atlantic
Ocean

Atlanta

Columbia

Wilmington

TEXAS

Natchitoches

Mississippi

MISSISSIPPI
Jackson

ALABAMA

Montgomery

CAROLINA

Milledgeville
Macon

Charleston

GEORGIA

Savannah

Austin

San Antonio

LOUISIANA

Houston

Natchez

Baton Rouge
Wallace

Mobile

New Orleans

Pensacola

Tallahasee

St. Augustine

Galveston

Gulf of
Mexico

FLORIDA

Free State

Slave State

Territory (slavery permitted)

Arrows show major avenues
of escape. Widths indicate
relative numbers

BAHAMAS

Cuba

MEXICO

0   400 mi
0   600 km

Underground Railroad

THE UNDERGROUND RAILROAD provided a means for slaves to free themselves in the years before the Civil War. Conductors on the Underground Railroad were either blacks who had gained their freedom by successfully traveling along the Underground Railroad or whites, mostly Northerners, who were against slavery. Passage of the Fugitive Slave Act of 1850 increased Northern support for the Underground Railroad. Arrows on the map show major avenues of escape, and the width of the arrows gives some indication of which routes carried the most people. The goal of most fugitive slaves was Canada, but some found freedom in Mexico and on islands in the Caribbean Sea. After the Civil War many returned to the United States. This chapter in American history is full of amazing tales of bravery and ingenuity.

One such legendary figure was Henry Brown, who became known as Box Brown (below). With the help of his white friend the Reverend Samuel A. Smith, Brown arranged to have himself shipped from Richmond to Philadelphia in a wooden crate. The trip took 26 hours, much of which Brown spent upside down. Brown gained his freedom, but Smith was sent to prison for his work with the Underground Railroad. John Fairfield, a master of disguise, posed 28 slaves as a funeral procession and marched them to freedom. Former slave Harriet Tubman helped lead so many slaves to freedom that she was called Moses.

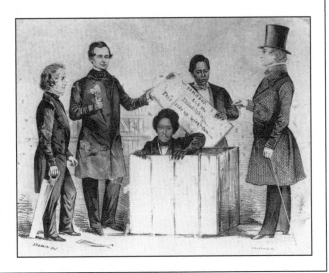

the armory—strategically located along two railroad lines where the Shenandoah and Potomac Rivers flow together—slaves throughout the South would rise up in revolt. Brown had not planned the rebellion well, however, and soon he and most of his followers were either killed or captured by government troops.

The state of Virginia speedily tried and convicted Brown of murder and treason. Sentenced to die, Brown gave an eloquent and dignified speech at his trial. "If it is deemed necessary that I should forfeit my life for the furtherance of the ends of justice, and mingle my blood further with the blood of my children and with the blood of millions in this slave country whose rights are disregarded by wicked, cruel, and unjust enactments, I say, let it be done."

Brown became a hero throughout much of the North. The writer Ralph Waldo Emerson declared that Brown made "the gallows as glorious as the cross," and fellow author Henry Thoreau called him "an angel of light." This Northern reaction made white Southerners extremely fearful. Many came to believe that all Northerners, not just a tiny band of fanatics, wished to inspire deadly slave revolts.

With such suspicion on both sides, it was just a matter of time until war came. Many Southerners remained moderates, if only because they knew that the South had a much weaker military than the North. But after John Brown's raid, those who advocated taking a strong stand against the North—known as the Fire Eaters—became increasingly powerful, especially in the states of the Deep South, including South Carolina and Alabama.

The two things that all Americans could agree on were that the 1860 election would focus on slavery and that the outcome of that election would determine the fate of the Union.

The Great Debate

★ *How to Rid the Country of Slavery* ★

FEARFUL SOUTHERNERS were correct in thinking that the number of people in the North who detested slavery was growing rapidly, and these abolitionists had a strong influence on Northern culture. Still, many Northerners simply wanted the problem to go away. Others were actively hostile to African Americans and to the abolitionists.

Abolitionists were determined to fight against the odds to rid the country of slavery, which they believed was morally evil. The question was: What was the best way to accomplish their goal?

For three decades, beginning in the 1830s, a vigorous debate had divided antislavery activists. Some argued that the easiest way to rid America of the evil of slavery was to rid America of black people. The advocates of this position, who were often as racist as Southerners, wished to ship all blacks to Africa. They did not even try to understand that almost all black people, even those who were slaves, had long before truly become Americans of African descent. They had been born in the United States, and they did not want to leave even if they met discrimination everywhere they went.

"The only way to make the Fugitive Slave Law a dead letter is to make a half dozen or more dead kidnappers."

FREDERICK DOUGLASS

Other abolitionists chose to use moral persuasion to convince their fellow citizens that slavery was evil. William Lloyd Garrison, their eloquent leader, fought for full social and political equality for blacks even though sometimes he personally was guilty of discriminating against African Americans. Through his Boston newspaper, *The Liberator,* in fiery speeches, and especially in sermons in Quaker and other Protestant churches, Garrison and his allies found every opportunity to oppose slavery and slaveholders. He called for an immediate end to slavery, even though it caused him to be attacked by pro-slavery mobs.

Garrison opposed the use of politics because he believed that the governing system favored the interests of slaveowners. In his most controversial statement, he proclaimed that the United States Constitution itself was "a covenant with death—an agreement with hell." Garrison even burned a copy of the Constitution to show his scorn for the "enslaving" government under which he lived.

Other antislavery activists believed that the only way to end slavery was through the political system. By the 1840s, antislavery parties had presidential candidates in every election. And they were making it much more difficult for politicians of all parties to ignore this issue.

Finally, there were advocates of violence. John Brown was the most extreme, but others more quietly shared his views. The most famous abolitionist of the age, an ex-slave named Frederick Douglass, counted himself a close friend of Brown, and he knew the potential value of violence. But in the end he did not support John Brown's raid on Harpers Ferry because he felt Brown had not thought out the attack well. By traveling around telling how he had suffered as a slave, Douglass convinced more and more Northerners of the horrors of slavery and the need to get rid of it. African Americans therefore actively took part in the debate—openly in the North, secretly in the South.

Harriet Tubman

While white abolitionists argued about how to rid the country of slavery, other people—blacks and whites— were bravely involved in the highly dangerous work of trying to smuggle slaves to freedom along escape routes that became known as the Underground Railroad.

Harriet Tubman was the most famous conductor, or escort, on this route to freedom. An escaped slave, she risked her life again and again by returning to the South to bring her entire family and several hundred other blacks to freedom.

Traveling at night, following the North Star toward Canada, chased by bounty hunters, facing extreme punishment if caught, slaves themselves proved, in their courage, that they were the anti-slavery activists who most consistently put their lives on the line.

This painting is based on an actual event in Plymouth Meeting, Pennsylvania, a well-known stop on the Underground Railroad. As slave catchers on horseback search for fugitive slaves, this slave family finds temporary safety in a snow fort built by Quaker children.

THE GREAT DEBATE finally engulfed the nation after the 1860 presidential election. Candidates ran from four different parties. The South held one election, with Vice President John C. Breckinridge, a southern Democrat, running against John Bell of the Constitutional Union Party. Meanwhile in the North, Democrat Stephen A. Douglas, the chief advocate of popular sovereignty, squared off against Republican Abraham Lincoln, who promised to end the extension of slavery in the territories (but not end slavery itself). By sweeping the more densely populated North, Lincoln rolled to victory in the electoral college *(see the Constitution Article II and Amendment XII in the Historical Documents)*. But he won only 40 percent of the total number of popular votes, because his name had not appeared on the ballot in most southern states.

After the November election, Americans watched and waited to see what the South would do. They did not have to wait long. Six weeks after the election, before Lincoln took office, South Carolina held huge ceremonies to celebrate its secession, or withdrawal, from the Union. Six more states in the Deep South, fearing an all-out attack on slavery from Lincoln, soon joined South Carolina. Still, many citizens hoped that the destruction of the Union, and the likely war, might

Abraham Lincoln (shown doffing his hat to the crowd) rides up Pennsylvania Avenue to his Inauguration on March 4, 1861. President James Buchanan is at his side. Lincoln's name had not appeared on the ballot in ten slave states, making him the first President to take office as the leader of a sectional party. Lincoln spoke on behalf of unity in his Inaugural Address, saying, "We must not be enemies."

Cannon blaze as Confederates fire at Fort Sumter, a federal installation in Charleston harbor manned by about 75 U.S. troops. More than 3,000 shells were fired before the fort surrendered and the Union flag was replaced by the Confederate banner (opposite, top right). No one died in the opening battle of the Civil War.

be prevented if the eight other slave states (Arkansas, Delaware, Kentucky, Maryland, Missouri, North Carolina, Tennessee, and Virginia) remained in the United States.

The Confederate States of America began its life when the seven secessionist states met in Montgomery, Alabama, in February 1861 to establish a government. Its president, Jefferson Davis of Mississippi, a skilled former U.S. senator and secretary of war, gave an inaugural address that quoted from the Declaration of Independence. He focused on "the American idea that governments rest on the consent of the governed...and that it is the right of the people to alter or abolish them at will whenever they become destructive of the ends for which they were established."

What would Abraham Lincoln do? After taking office on March 4, 1861, he took a moderate course, calling on "the better angels of our nature" to preserve the Union peacefully. Lincoln's hopes of avoiding war, however, ended at Fort Sumter, located in the strategically important harbor of Charleston, South Carolina. Lincoln considered all southern forts, customs houses, and federal buildings to still be property of the United States. When Fort Sumter began to run low on supplies,

Union/ Confederacy

SOUTH CAROLINA left the Union first. Other states in the Deep South (dark gray) seceded next. The debate in the Upper South (light gray) lasted longer, but by the middle of 1861, they, too, seceded. Lincoln knew that the Border States (light blue), where slavery was permitted, were crucial to the Union cause. To keep them in the Union (dark blue), he initially refused to free slaves as part of the war effort.

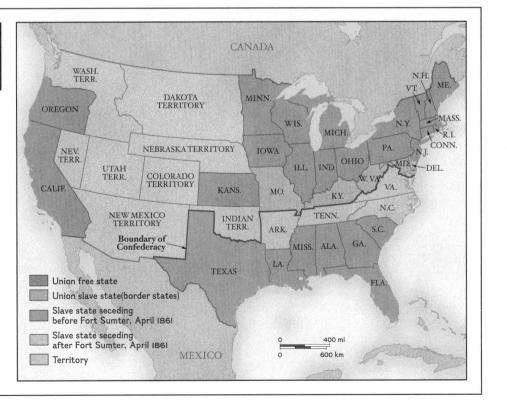

Union free state
Union slave state(border states)
Slave state seceding before Fort Sumter, April 1861
Slave state seceding after Fort Sumter, April 1861
Territory

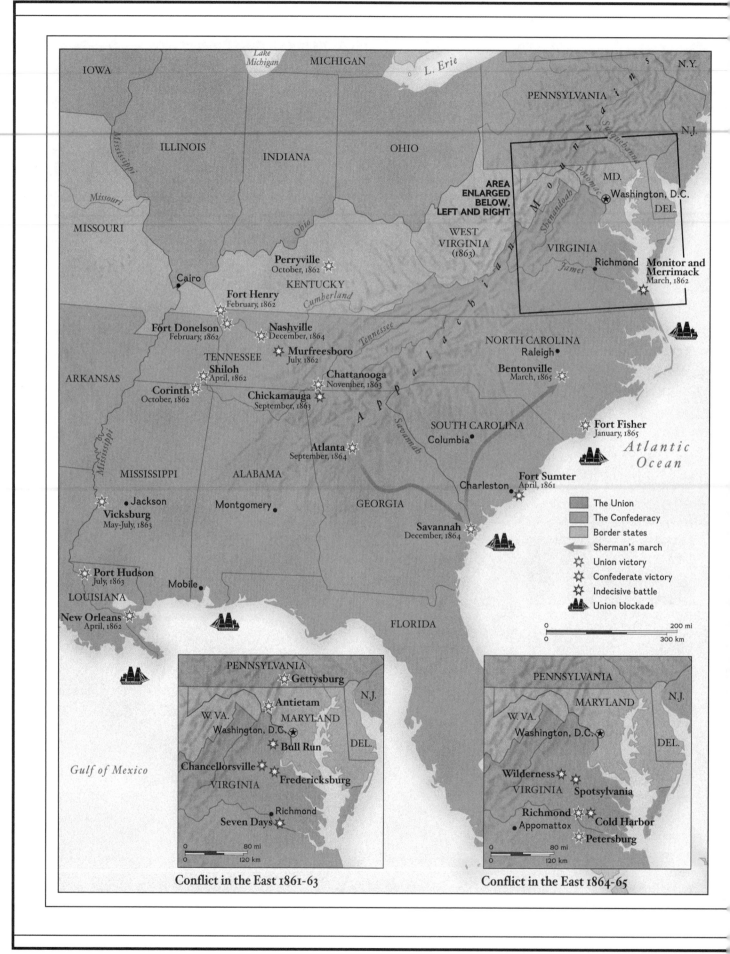

IOWA

Lake Michigan

MICHIGAN

L. Erie

N.Y.

ILLINOIS

INDIANA

OHIO

PENNSYLVANIA

N.J.

Mississippi

Missouri

MISSOURI

Ohio

WEST VIRGINIA (1863)

AREA ENLARGED BELOW, LEFT AND RIGHT

MD.

⊛ Washington, D.C.

DEL.

VIRGINIA

Shenandoah

Potomac

James

Richmond •

Monitor and Merrimack
March, 1862

Cairo •

Perryville
October, 1862 ☆

KENTUCKY

Cumberland

Fort Henry
February, 1862 ☆

Tennessee

NORTH CAROLINA

Raleigh •

Fort Donelson
February, 1862 ☆

Nashville
December, 1864 ☆

Appalachian

Bentonville
March, 1865 ☆

TENNESSEE

Murfreesboro
July, 1862 ☆

ARKANSAS

Shiloh
April, 1862 ☆

Chattanooga
November, 1863 ☆

Corinth
October, 1862 ☆

Chickamauga
September, 1863 ☆

Savannah

SOUTH CAROLINA

Columbia •

Fort Fisher
January, 1865 ☆

Atlantic Ocean

Atlanta
September, 1864 ☆

MISSISSIPPI

ALABAMA

GEORGIA

Charleston •

Fort Sumter
April, 1861 ☆

• Jackson

Montgomery •

The Union

The Confederacy

Border states

Vicksburg
May-July, 1863 ☆

Savannah
December, 1864 ☆

Sherman's march

☆ Union victory

☆ Confederate victory

☆ Indecisive battle

⛵ Union blockade

Mississippi

Port Hudson
July, 1863 ☆

Mobile •

0   200 mi

0   300 km

LOUISIANA

New Orleans
April, 1862 ☆

FLORIDA

Gulf of Mexico

PENNSYLVANIA

☆ **Gettysburg**

N.J.

W. VA.

Antietam ☆

MARYLAND

Washington, D.C. ⊛

DEL.

☆ **Bull Run**

Chancellorsville ☆

☆

Fredericksburg

VIRGINIA

Richmond •

Seven Days ☆

0   80 mi

0   120 km

Conflict in the East 1861-63

PENNSYLVANIA

MARYLAND

N.J.

W. VA.

Washington, D.C. ⊛

DEL.

Wilderness ☆ ☆

VIRGINIA

Spotsylvania

Richmond ☆ ☆

• Appomattox

Cold Harbor

☆ **Petersburg**

0   80 mi

0   120 km

Conflict in the East 1864-65

Civil War Battles

FROM THE FIRST BATTLE OF THE CIVIL WAR, at Fort Sumter near Charleston, South Carolina, on April 12, 1861, to the Confederate surrender at Appomattox Courthouse, in Virginia, on April 9, 1865, the Civil War lasted four years.

On land, the fighting began with a surprise Confederate victory at Bull Run, in Manassas, Virginia. Then, Union forces stopped the Rebels at Antietam, in Maryland. Back in Virginia, Confederate General Robert E. Lee won victories at Fredericksburg and Chancellorsville. Another attempt to penetrate the North was stopped at Gettysburg, in Pennsylvania.

In Tennessee, General Ulysses S. Grant won the nickname "Unconditional Surrender" Grant after capturing Forts Henry and Donelson. These victories were key to breaking the Confederate defense along the Mississippi and other western rivers. At Shiloh he battled back after a surprise attack to beat the Rebels. The surrender of Vicksburg and Port Hudson gave the Union control of the entire Mississippi River.

A string of battles from Tennessee (Murfreesboro and Chattanooga) through Georgia (Atlanta and Savannah) tore the South apart. The surrender of North Carolina's Fort Fisher completed the Union blockade of the South's Atlantic and Gulf ports. The final series of battles took place in Virginia *(map inset),* where Grant and Lee battled each other's troops from the Wilderness to Cold Harbor and Richmond, which fell on April 2, 1865. Lee surrendered a week later.

Bodies of Confederate soldiers lie in Bloody Lane after the Battle of Antietam. Such photographs clearly showed the horrors of war.

Lincoln notified the governor of South Carolina that the United States would be sending in food—but no weapons—to relieve the federal soldiers stationed in the fort. Four days later, Jefferson Davis ordered General P. G. T. Beauregard to take over the fort before it could be resupplied. Beauregard opened fire on April 12, beginning the bloodiest war in all of American history, a war that pitted brother against brother and father against son. Ironically, during this 33-hour artillery duel, the only casualty was a Confederate horse.

Soon after the South took Fort Sumter, Arkansas, Tennessee, North Carolina, and Virginia joined the Confederacy. Four slave states remained in the Union: Missouri, Kentucky, Maryland, and Delaware. Because of their strong economies and strategic location, these Border States made the Union much more powerful. But they made fighting against slavery—still not the goal of Lincoln and most Unionists (those dedicated to preserving the whole United States)— much more difficult.

Northerners called this the War of the Rebellion. Southerners named it the War of Northern Aggression. Whatever its label, no one expected the conflict to continue for long. Southerners expected Northerners to have no stomach for war and to let the South go its own way, perhaps after a few months. Northerners, in turn, were certain that their overwhelming advantage in population (22 million to 9 million) and firepower would subdue the rebellious states quickly. Both were tragically wrong.

The Union and the Confederacy first learned how unpredictable the war would be at the Battle of Bull Run in July 1861. Here, at Manassas, Virginia, not far outside Washington, D.C., 36,000 Union troops prepared to fight 34,000 Confederates. Unexpectedly, many untrained volunteer Northern troops broke and

"Watch Meeting—Dec. 31st 1862— Waiting for the Hour," a painting by William Tolman Carlton, shows a gathering of slaves anxiously anticipating the stroke of midnight, which would herald the enactment of the emancipation on January 1, 1863. The painting was delivered to the White House in early July 1864 by several leading abolitionists. There is no record of Lincoln's reaction to it. His wife apparently took the original when she left the White House after her husband's assassination. The painting that now hangs in the Lincoln Bedroom in the White House (the one shown here) is a copy.

For blacks, the Civil War was always a war to end slavery. But for most whites, the goal of abolishing slavery came slowly and only after much bloodshed.

ran. During the first year of the war, the South would outmaneuver the North on several occasions. Then, in September 1862, the Union won a horribly bloody but crucial victory at Antietam, in Maryland.

The South's defeat at Antietam, where nearly as many Americans died in one day as died during the Revolutionary War's entire six years of combat, persuaded Britain and France not to open diplomatic relations with the Confederacy. Antietam, along with an earlier victory at Shiloh, in Tennessee, gave the Union a significant military advantage in the East and the West. However, the Union naval blockade of Confederate ports, designed to keep Britain and France from sending weapons to the South in exchange for cotton, was not working as well as Lincoln had planned. The Union was also discovering just how difficult it was to defeat a people fighting for—and on—

> "If I could save the Union without freeing any slave, I would do it; and if I could save it by freeing all the slaves, I would do it...."
>
> ABRAHAM LINCOLN

their own land, people worried that their slaveholding way of life and what they saw as their political freedoms would vanish forever. As long as the Confederacy could simply hang on and wear down the North, Southerners believed that they would win.

The military stalemate forced Lincoln to rethink the aims of the war. Originally the objective was to preserve the Union. The longer the war dragged on, the less eager Northerners were to sign up to fight. Members of his own party, responding to growing abolitionist sentiment, were beginning to demand that Lincoln start using the powers of the Union Army to free slaves. This is something that Lincoln had refused to do, fearing that it would anger the Border States loyal to the Union. As Lincoln put it, "What I do about Slavery and the colored race, I do because I believe it helps to save this Union."

Finally, the President decided that freeing slaves would gravely weaken the Confederacy. On January 1, 1863, he issued the Emancipation Proclamation, which formally committed the U.S. government to freeing slaves. It did so in a strange way, though. Only slaves in areas that the Confederacy controlled—and thus were off-limits to the Union—were officially declared emancipated. Border State slaves still remained in bondage, as did those under Union control in the South.

So the Emancipation Proclamation did not immediately free a single slave. As the Union took the war farther into previously Confederate-held territory, though, military officials did free slaves. And many slaves freed themselves by fleeing their owners. Lincoln rapidly came to agree with those who wished to abolish slavery completely. With his encouragement, Congress passed a constitutional amendment to outlaw slavery everywhere in the nation. With the South out of the Union, this was ratified quickly by the northern states. The 13th Amendment became law in 1865.

After the Emancipation Proclamation, Lincoln also agreed to admit African-American soldiers into the Union Army. Many blacks had been disappointed at not being allowed to serve. They now flocked to join, eager to help free their brethren and preserve their own liberty. In turn, the Confederates vowed to execute any captured black soldiers.

African-American volunteers launched a brave attack on the Confederate stronghold of Fort Wagner, near Charleston, South Carolina, in the summer of 1863. Although nearly half the soldiers were killed or wounded, their actions helped begin the 22-month siege of Charleston. Led by white abolitionist Col. Robert Gould Shaw (with saber in hand), the men of the 54th Massachusetts Infantry are today memorialized in the movie Glory. In 1865, Charleston surrendered to another black regiment that proudly took control of the city.

Many whites greeted black soldiers with great kindness. "We are cheered in every town we pass through," wrote one black soldier. But African Americans continued to meet discrimination. They could only serve in segregated, or separate, regiments, which they were not permitted to command, and they received less pay than white troops. To protest this discrimination, they boycotted their meager pay. In the end, one in five black men served in the Union Army, with 37,000 bravely dying for the cause of freedom.

Soldiers, whether black or white, Rebel (Confederate) or Yankee (Union), faced horrifying conditions in battle. The rifled muskets developed in the 15 years before the war were much more accurate from much greater distances than the ones that had been used in the Mexican War. Generals on both sides continued to mass their soldiers together and charge, leading to huge numbers of casualties.

Disease was a more frequent killer than battle. Despite dedicated service by nurses such as Clara Barton, infection frequently claimed the lives of the wounded. Illnesses ranging from malaria to cholera swept through the ranks.

Desertion was common, especially among the poorly fed and clothed Confederates. Patriotism fired up many "Johnny Rebs" and "Billy Yanks," but that was not enough to keep millions in the field as the war ground on.

The war was growing more and more unpopular in both the North and the South. The most

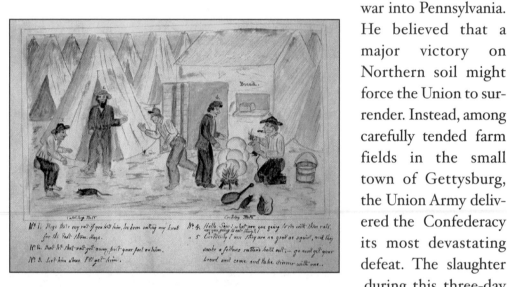

Conditions in both Confederate and Union prisons camps were horrid. In this sketch, drawn by a Rebel prisoner at Point Lookout, Maryland, starving inmates catch, skin, and cook rats to eat.

dramatic explosion came in July 1863. That month poor Irish laborers in New York City rioted against the Union's draft laws, which made it easy for the rich to escape military duty. Bitterly racist, the rioters targeted blacks, whom they blamed for the war and their poverty. They killed 105 people.

The New York City draft riots occurred only days after the greatest Union victory of the war. In May, General Robert E. Lee, fresh from a significant victory at the Battle of Chancellorsville, in Virginia, had decided to take his troops and the war into Pennsylvania. He believed that a major victory on Northern soil might force the Union to surrender. Instead, among carefully tended farm fields in the small town of Gettysburg, the Union Army delivered the Confederacy its most devastating defeat. The slaughter during this three-day battle, which took place from July 1 to July 3, and especially during Pickett's Charge, was almost beyond belief. A third of Lee's army lay dead.

On July 4, the news came that Union General Ulysses S. Grant had captured Vicksburg, Mississippi, taking control of the Mississippi River and cutting off the Confederate states to the west. If the Confederates had won at Gettysburg, it is likely that they would have won the war. Instead, they lost. Never again would the South launch another major offensive. The Confederates now decided to fight a defensive war. Rather than hoping to win a decisive military victory, they simply wanted to exhaust the North.

Abraham Lincoln

★ *Savior of the Union* ★

SEVERAL MONTHS after the Battle of Gettysburg, Abraham Lincoln came to the battlefield to participate in a memorial ceremony honoring the Union dead. Lincoln began his short speech: "Fourscore and seven years ago our fathers brought forth on this continent a new nation, conceived in liberty and dedicated to the proposition that all men are created equal. Now we are engaged in a great civil war, testing whether that nation or any nation so conceived and so dedicated can long endure."

Lincoln asked his listeners to dedicate their lives to the Union for which so many soldiers had died and to the even greater task of ensuring that "this nation, under God, shall have a new birth of freedom—and that government of the people, by the people, for the people shall not perish from the earth." Arguably, the Gettysburg Address is the most important speech in all of American history because it states so clearly and eloquently the enduring national values of equality and democracy.

Abraham Lincoln was our country's leader during its worst crisis. With his assassination just days after the war ended, he became one of America's greatest national heroes. Without him, we might have a very different United States. Slavery might have lasted decades longer, and our nation probably would have split into two parts.

Unlike George Washington, America's other great national hero, Lincoln was not born to a wealthy family. Lincoln was raised on the Kentucky and Indiana frontiers. His parents, Nancy and Tom, were illiterate, and young Abe could go to school for only a few weeks or months at a time when a school was even available. Yet he hungered for books.

When Lincoln was 21, the family moved to Illinois, where he studied law and eventually became a successful lawyer and politician. Stopping the spread of slavery, which he viewed as a cruel and immoral denial of human rights, became his chief political goal. A series of debates with Stephen Douglas catapulted Lincoln to national prominence and led to his election as President in 1860.

As President he continued to voice the moral goals that inspired millions of Northerners and eventually saved the Union. In his Second Inaugural Address, Lincoln spoke of his desire for a peace "with malice toward none; with charity toward all." But he warned: "...if God wills that [the war] continue, until all the wealth piled by the bondsman's two hundred and fifty years of unrequited toil shall be sunk, and until every drop of blood drawn with the lash, shall be paid by another drawn with the sword," then the Union would continue to fight in the cause of the Lord.

Ghostly figures walk through the burned-out remains of Richmond, capital of the Confederacy. Fleeing Rebel soldiers set fire to factories and warehouses on April 3, 1865, to prevent Union troops from using the supplies that were made and stored there. When Lincoln toured the rubble the next day, he was called "Messiah" by some African Americans.

The fighting after Gettysburg was much more intense than Lincoln had expected. In 1864 Union General William Sherman marched through Georgia. He spared civilians but burned as much property as he could, destroying a great deal of the South's agricultural heartland.

Atlanta, an important rail center, fell in September 1864, disrupting the South's transportation system. By early 1865, the Virginia city of Petersburg, close to the Confederate capital of Richmond, was locked in a deadly siege. General Grant sent waves of fresh Union soldiers against increasingly desperate Confederate forces. Lee

and his troops fled Petersburg on April 2, and the Union took Richmond.

After four bloody years of fighting, the Confederates finally surrendered on April 9, 1865, at the town of Appomattox Courthouse, Virginia. More than 620,000 Americans lost their lives in the Civil War—a greater number of deaths than our country has suffered in any other war.

Abraham Lincoln lived only five days longer. His assassination by John Wilkes Booth, part of a general conspiracy to overthrow the United States government, sent much of the nation into mourning. Once again it was time for great worry. Now

This painting re-creates the parlor of the Wilmer McLean home in Appomattox Courthouse, where on April 9, 1865, General Robert E. Lee (seated, left) surrendered to General Ulysses S. Grant (seated, right). Lee's secretary, Lt. Col. Charles Marshall, said of Grant's liberal surrender terms, "He triumphed...without exultation, and with a noble respect to his enemy."

that Lincoln was dead, what should the United States do with the rebellious Confederacy?

The next 12 years, from 1865 to 1877, came to be known as the period of Reconstruction. The United States had many different ideas about how to reconstruct, or transform, the South. How should the leaders of the Confederacy be treated? Should ordinary Southerners be punished? Should the southern states have to do anything in order to be readmitted to the Union? And most pressing, what should be done about the millions of former slaves, freed by the 13th Amendment? Should they vote? How would they earn a living now that slavery was gone forever?

Lincoln had, during the war, expressed his desire to be as friendly as possible to his former adversaries. When Vice President Andrew Johnson took over as President after Lincoln's assassination, he adopted a conciliatory approach.

> "The whole fabric of southern society must be changed."
>
> THADDEUS STEVENS

A Southerner from a modest background, Johnson hated the rich slaveholders of the region but believed fully in white supremacy. Congress at the time was controlled by a powerful group, the Radical Republicans. The Radicals included many abolitionists, who hoped for revenge against the Confederates and full justice for African Americans. Above all, they insisted on equal legal and political rights for blacks. They wanted much of the land of rich slaveholders given to the slaves who had worked the land. The Radicals, led by Pennsylvania Representative Thaddeus Stevens, wished to imprison and strip away the property of a number of the rebellion's leaders.

White Southerners, especially the rich and powerful former slaveowners, were not happy about any of the plans for Reconstruction. They hoped to keep their power. Soon after the war a number of southern states passed "black codes,"

Congress set the goals of Reconstruction, but millions of citizens—black and white—decided how it would really work. One of the most important tasks was education. Many of the first teachers of illiterate former slaves were white women from the North, sent by the government and church groups. By 1870, though, blacks themselves filled half the teaching jobs.

In this sketch, the soldier—an agent of the government's Bureau of Refugees, Freedmen, and Abandoned Lands—tries to prevent violence between southern whites and newly freed blacks.

designed to take away the economic and political rights of African Americans. If slavery could no longer legally exist, white Southerners figured they could restrict the movement of blacks so much that they could not work for anyone but their old masters. This was designed to be slavery in all but name.

For a good part of Reconstruction, the Radical Republicans got most of what they wanted. The United States Army conducted a military occupation of the South. The southern states would not be readmitted to the Union until they agreed to

three constitutional amendments (the 13th, 14th, and 15th) that ended slavery, established equality before the law for all citizens, and guaranteed black men the right to vote.

The United States created the Freedmen's Bureau to build schools, train teachers, and help protect the rights of blacks. Blacks gained considerable power under these laws, and ex-slaves such as Robert Smalls of South Carolina even began to represent southern states in Congress.

President Johnson fought the Radical Republicans on almost every front. In response, they passed the Tenure of Office Act in 1867, which took away the President's power to fire members of his Cabinet without Senate approval. When Johnson challenged this, the Radical Republicans accused him of breaking the law and decided he should no longer be President. They began the process of removing him from office by impeaching him—formally accusing him of serious legal misconduct.

Impeachment is the first step Congress must take to remove a President or a federal judge from office. To impeach Johnson, the U.S. House of Representatives needed to determine what "high crimes and misdemeanors" the President had committed. Then a majority of House members had to decide that the Senate should put him on trial for these crimes.

Once the House had formally brought charges against President Johnson by impeaching him, his case went to the Senate. A President is removed from office only when the Senate votes to convict him. In the case of Andrew Johnson, the Senate voted 35 to 19—one vote short of the two-thirds majority required by the Constitution to remove a President from office. Johnson was able to finish his term, though his power was significantly reduced. Andrew Johnson would remain the only President ever impeached until Bill Clinton more than a century later.

Ulysses S. Grant, the great Union war hero, was elected President in 1868. Grant was more sympathetic to the Radical Republicans. As a result, the opposition of white Southerners to black equality became increasingly violent. The Ku Klux Klan, which had its beginnings in Tennessee in 1866, was a terrorist organization that tortured and murdered many blacks as well as their white Republican supporters. Blacks fought back, sometimes with guns, but much more often by speaking out for themselves and by refusing to be treated as slaves any longer.

When former masters and mistresses begged former slaves to come back to work for them,

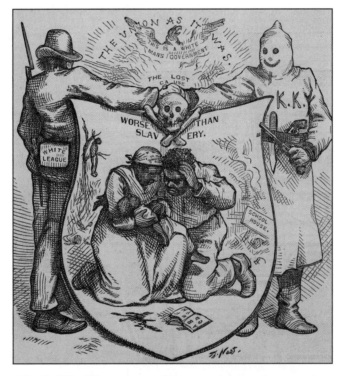

The Ku Klux Klan was one of the most violent racist groups in American history. Founded in Pulaski, Tennessee, in early 1866 by former Confederate soldiers, the Klan murdered and threatened blacks and their white allies and burned schoolhouses.

blacks made sure to let them know they now had a choice about how to run their lives. One South Carolinian politely told her old mistress: "No, Miss, I must go. If I stay here I'll never know I'm free." Black family members did all they could to find one another, even if it took years of searching. Most African Americans wished to own their own farms, and a significant minority was able to do so. But whites still owned most of the land in the South. So most blacks were forced to become sharecroppers. This meant they had to share a large portion of their harvest with white landowners. As difficult as this was, blacks viewed it as a great improvement over slavery.

For many years, northern whites continued to hate the Southerners who had provoked the Civil War. But their own commitment to racial equality was limited. For example, between 1865 and 1868, voters in eight northern states went to the polls to decide if their own black citizens could vote. Only two states, Iowa and Minnesota, said yes. The longer Reconstruction dragged on, the more powerful the Democrats, who had always been opposed to Radical Reconstruction, became in both the North and the South. Finally, through the use of violence and economic intimidation of voters, the Democrats began to regain political control of much of the South.

The conflicts over Reconstruction came to a head on election day in November 1876. A great economic depression had hit the country three years earlier, and voters were ready for a change. Democrat Samuel J. Tilden received 51 percent of the popular vote. But because of disputes over who should receive 20 electoral votes in Louisiana, South Carolina, Oregon, and Florida, neither Tilden nor Republican Rutherford B. Hayes had a clear majority in the electoral college. Never before had such an elec-

toral crisis hit the country, and some spoke of a renewed civil war. Congress appointed a special commission to solve the problem. All the members of the commission voted for their own party's candidate, so the Republicans won eight to seven. This infuriated the Democrats, who threatened to prevent Congress from counting the electoral votes.

Rather than see this episode turn into a full-scale national crisis, the Democrats and Republicans made a deal. The Compromise of

The 1897 photograph (top), taken in Virginia, shows how even decades of freedom brought little change in economic conditions for blacks. Whites continued to control land, jobs, and politics. But the gains made by African Americans during Reconstruction were real. The sketch from the cover of Harper's Weekly *shows a black man proudly casting his first vote as a free American citizen.*

Despite their overall defeat during Reconstruction, African Americans could—and did—celebrate the freedom that they had gained. In this painting, a family welcomes a minister to their modest household. No longer did whites control the way blacks practiced their religion. And perhaps most important of all, no longer did they have to worry that family members would be sold away into slavery.

1877 gave Rutherford Hayes the presidency by the tiniest margin—185 to 184 electoral votes. In return, Hayes agreed to appoint a Southerner to his cabinet, give the South money for economic development, and, most important, pull all remaining federal troops out of the region. The Republicans also agreed to let white Southerners have their own way on racial matters. It would take almost a century before the national government once again decided that it should safeguard the voting rights, or even the human rights, of southern blacks.

Besides, Northerners reasoned, those troops were needed in the North to deal with growing labor unrest. In 1877 a series of strikes involving railroad workers broke out. In what became known as the Great Strike of 1877, railroad workers refused to let trains move until their demand for higher wages was met.

The strikes became especially violent in Pittsburgh, St. Louis, and Chicago, and President Hayes decided to use federal troops to end the strikes, put men back to work, and get the trains moving again. The strikes produced a growing fear that labor tensions would lead to rebellion. It soon became clear that concern over the conflict between workers and their employers had replaced Reconstruction as the most pressing issue of the age. A Republican announced the new era when he said, "The overwhelming labor question has dwarfed all other questions into nothing."

CHAPTER FIVE

INDUSTRY AND EMPIRE

★ *1876–1900* ★

"The day of combination is here to stay.

Individualism has gone, never to return."

JOHN D. ROCKEFELLER

1876

People from all over the world attended America's 100th birthday celebration in Philadelphia. Exhibits showed off America's industrial might and inventions such as the telephone.

1879

In 1879, inventor Thomas Edison presented America with the first incandescent electric light bulb. Within three years, America and the world moved from the age of steam into the age of electricity.

1880s

The availability of canned food helped raise the standard of living for the nation's poor. This can of condensed soup sold for ten cents. Taking the water out made it lighter and cheaper to ship.

1886

The Statue of Liberty was unveiled on October 28, bearing poet Emma Lazarus's words on its base:. "Give me your tired, your poor / Your huddled masses yearning to breathe free...."

IN CELEBRATION OF THE 100TH ANNIVERSARY of the Declaration of Independence, the country held a festive Centennial Exposition in Philadelphia, the city where the declaration had been signed. This gathering showed off the new technology of the age. Nothing inspired so much pride as the invention of the telephone, patented that very year by Alexander Graham Bell.

Not all the news was cause for celebration, however. Just days before the centennial, Americans learned that Native Americans in the West had delivered a stunning defeat to the U.S. Army at the Battle of the Little Bighorn on June 25, 1876. The trouble began when gold was discovered in the Black Hills of South Dakota. These mountains were sacred to the Lakota people.

1889

On April 22, 50,000 settlers swarmed into Oklahoma to stake claims to former Indian lands, touching off the last series of such land rushes in the United States. Each homesteader got 160 acres.

1892

The Ellis Island reception center opened in New York Harbor. Health officials examined each immigrant. Those found unfit (about 2 percent) were refused entry and were sent back home.

1896

In Plessy v. Ferguson the Supreme Court upheld creating "separate but equal" schools and other facilities for blacks and whites. In reality, most facilities for blacks were inferior.

1898

The acquisition of Cuba, Puerto Rico, the Philippines, and several small islands in the Pacific as a result of a war with Spain marked the beginning of U.S. control over other nations.

Lieutenant Colonel George Armstrong Custer, following U.S. Army policy, decided it was his duty to push the Indians off the land so that whites could get to the goldfields. The flamboyant Custer was so confident of success that he invited newspaper reporters along to witness his triumph. Instead, at a place the Lakota called Greasy Grass, along what whites called the Little Bighorn River, in what is now Montana, Custer made his last stand. The Lakota and their allies, the Cheyenne, brilliantly led by warriors Crazy Horse and Sitting Bull, surrounded Custer and his troops and killed all who were under his direct command. The news shocked the nation.

Lingering tensions over Reconstruction, the defeat at the Little Bighorn, and growing labor unrest were among the pressing problems facing Americans as they entered the late 19th century.

Just as in 1776, Americans wondered whether democracy could really work. Many believed that immigrants streaming in would dilute the country's "racial purity" and weaken the nation.

Extraordinary technological advances had taken place in the hundred years since the country's independence, and the industrial revolution that occurred after the Civil War created a class of millionaires, but workers in the vast new factories were by no means happy. By the end of the 1800s, the question of whether or not the United States should be an imperialist nation, ruling over other countries, also led to bitter divisions.

Authors Mark Twain and Charles Dudley Warner named this era the Gilded Age because on the surface the country glowed like bright gold-leaf decoration. But beneath the surface most of the nation was not experiencing a golden age at all.

IN THE 21ST CENTURY, we learn of new technology almost every month. Computers get more powerful, cell phones seem to be in everyone's hands, and the launch of a space shuttle is almost routine. In the technological revolution of the late 19th century, each invention was seen as equally momentous. Indeed, it is nearly impossible for us now to imagine life without the telephone, without electricity, refrigerators, canned food, steel, or cars.

Americans were responsible for developing most of the great inventions of the Gilded Age, and they were proud of their country's accomplishments. They were proud also of the economic

Immigrants, mainly from southern and eastern Europe, poured into the United States during the late 19th century (above). Most were poor, unskilled laborers who ended up working in coal mines, steel mills, or the garment industry. These children (left) lived in Homestead, Pennsylvania, site of Andrew Carnegie's steelworks, where a deadly strike brought attention to the need for labor reform.

growth that resulted from combining the country's nearly boundless natural resources with new technology. During this period, American manufacturing took off like never before. Between the end of the Civil War and 1900, the United States multiplied its annual output of goods by six. America became the leading industrial nation, supplying a full one-third of the world's manufacturing output.

Increasingly, the wealth from these economic gains went to a new class of powerful and rich businessmen. New and gigantic corporations gobbled up their smaller competitors. People who ran these corporations were called captains of industry by their supporters, and robber barons by their critics. John D. Rockefeller was the most famous, or perhaps infamous, of these men. Rockefeller's Standard Oil Company gained control of more than 80 percent of the country's oil refining. General Electric, Nabisco, and Kodak are just a few of the other companies that came to dominate the late 19th-century economy. All of these companies are still in business today.

Many Americans feared these corporations and the men who ran them. But the corporate bosses believed they were doing the Lord's work in bringing prosperity to themselves and to the United States. Rockefeller, for example, was so sure of the virtue behind his hard work that he remarked: "The good Lord gave me my wealth....I believe it is my duty...to use the money I make for the good of my fellow man according to the dictates of my conscience." This kind of thinking became known as the Gospel of Wealth, after an influential book by the "Richest Man in the World," Andrew Carnegie.

In this cartoon, Rockefeller's Standard Oil is shown as a giant octopus reaching out to strangle opposition to its practices. The Supreme Court would eventually rule that the oil monopoly had to be broken up so that competition could be restored.

Andrew Carnegie

★ *Industry's Generous Baron* ★

ANDREW CARNEGIE did not begin his life surrounded by wealth—far from it. He came to the United States from Scotland as a poor boy of 13. He completed only four years of schooling, but he was very bright. Carnegie worked during the day in a textile mill and studied bookkeeping at night. He then got a job with the busiest telegraph company in Pittsburgh.

The young Carnegie became such a fast telegraph operator that a superintendent of the Pennsylvania Railroad hired him as his personal secretary. By the age of 23, Carnegie had taken over his boss's job.

This new position gave Carnegie access to important professional connections and financing for his next business venture. He dreamed of making the steel industry as important as the railroads that depended on it for material to make rails and engines. Within just a few years, he accomplished his goal. His steel mills became the largest and most efficient in the country, perhaps even the world.

Carnegie was ruthless in dealing with his competitors, and even more so in dealing with his workers, who were primarily immigrants from southern Europe. Their wages were so low that many felt the only course of action was to go on strike. When Carnegie's workers did walk off the job—as thousands did in 1892 at his huge Homestead steelworks—his top aide was willing to use deadly violence in order to break the union and show who was boss.

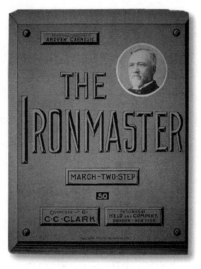

By the time Carnegie sold his vast steel mills to financier J. P. Morgan in 1901, he was a multimillionaire a hundred times over.

The characteristic that distinguished Carnegie from most of his fellow "robber barons" was his humility. Carnegie believed that the wealth he had earned was not really his. He was only God's trustee, and he had the responsibility to give back to the community some of what he had earned. He funded cultural and educational institutions such as New York City's Carnegie Hall, one of the nation's great concert halls, and Carnegie-Mellon University in Pittsburgh. He was also responsible for the establishment of many public libraries in the United States.

So, next time you are in a public library, you might think of Andrew Carnegie—and perhaps his workers, too.

After leaving business at the age of 66, Andrew Carnegie became famous for sharing his wealth with others. A march titled "The Ironmaster" (above) was written as a sign of appreciation for his generosity.

An immigrant family looks past the Statue of Liberty to the skyline of their new nation, uncertain of what lies ahead (left). Many, like the children playing in front of rundown tenement houses on New York's Lower East Side (right), never went farther west than that. Others, especially Swedes and Norwegians, were attracted by posters they had seen in Europe (below) that promised cheap farmland in the West.

The increasing prominence of rich men like John D. Rockefeller and Andrew Carnegie stirred up considerable opposition. Many Americans believed that it was not right for the rich to possess so much money while others lived in poverty. Some used religious arguments, saying that Jesus Christ favored the poor and suffering. Others appealed to wealthy people's sense of fairness. These crusaders greatly influenced the labor movement. To fight the growing economic and political power of big business, many workers threw themselves into organizing unions. Unions during this period represented a small part of the workforce, but they challenged big business and provided many ways for workers to preserve their dignity.

Before the Civil War, people who lived in cities worked mostly in small shops that had a handful of employees each. With the growth of industry after the war, a single factory could employ thousands of workers. Most of these industrial workers were immigrants. Before 1865, most people arriving in America came from northern Europe, especially from Ireland, Great Britain, and Germany. Beginning in the 1870s, this immigration changed dramatically. Southern and eastern Europeans such as Italians, Greeks, Lithuanians, Hungarians, Poles, and Jews (many from Russia) flocked to big cities hoping to find employment.

It wasn't easy. Those lucky enough to find work at all had to start at the bottom—with low wages and in difficult, sometimes dangerous, working conditions. For example, machines with sharp knives generally had no safety guards. Workers often lost fingers, arms—even their lives. If workers got hurt, they rarely received money from their employers, and if they died, their survivors were seldom compensated. Children suffered alongside their parents. Many workers in the mills and mines were as young as eight years old.

Unions were formed to try to improve these

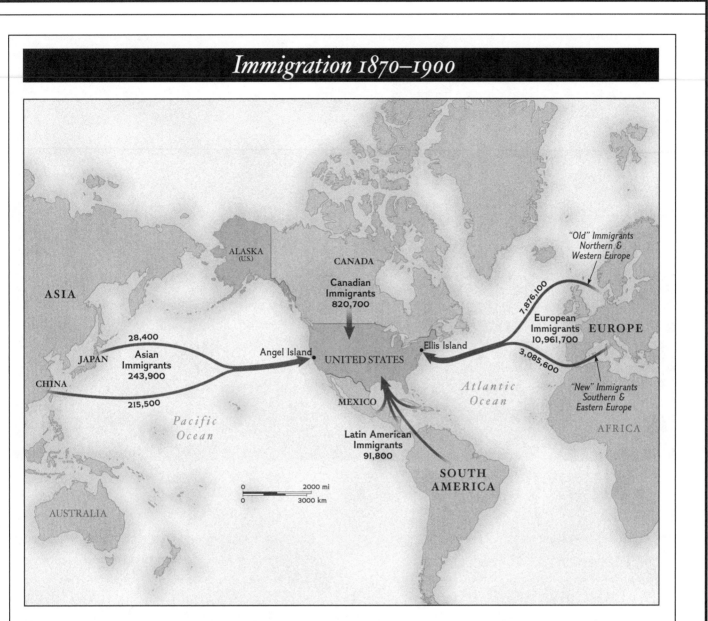

BETWEEN 1870 AND 1900, the largest number of immigrants continued to come from northern and western Europe including Great Britain, Ireland, and Scandinavia. But "new" immigrants from southern and eastern Europe were becoming one of the most important forces in American life. Sicilians from Italy, peasants from Greece, and Jewish villagers from western Russia all looked upon the chance to come to the United States as a golden opportunity. More controversial, and much more limited, was immigration from Asia and Latin America.

conditions. The first successful national union was the Noble and Holy Order of the Knights of Labor. Started in 1869, the Knights of Labor grew dramatically during the 1880s. It fought for an income tax that would help equalize wealth, free land on the frontier so that workers could escape from oppressive jobs, and the abolition of child labor. And, at a time when workers were lucky to work only 10 hours a day—14 hours during busy seasons—the union believed employees should work only eight hours a day.

The Knights generally did not like to strike, but in 1886 more than 200,000 members across the nation walked out on their jobs. Many gathered

Employers needed child labor because it was cheap, and immigrant families needed their children to work to help put food on the table. Many found jobs in textile factories (above). Most worked 10- and 12-hour shifts, seven days a week (below) often without a lunch break.

in Chicago, where they demonstrated for an eight-hour workday and against police brutality. Some workers who participated were anarchists, who wished to overthrow the existing government. When police tried to break up a protest rally in Haymarket Square, a bomb was tossed into the crowd, touching off riots. Anarchists were blamed for the riots, although there was no evidence linking them to the bomb. Many newspapers claimed that the riots showed that labor leaders were planning a bloody revolution. Unions in general and the Knights in

IF YOU DON'T COME IN SUNDAY DON'T COME IN MONDAY.

THE MANAGEMENT

particular were seen as a threat to law and order, and membership declined.

The organization that took off after 1886 was the American Federation of Labor (AFL). The AFL was begun by printers, machinists, cigar makers, and other craft workers. Samuel Gompers, a cigar maker and Jewish immigrant from England, was its leader for many years. He believed that labor conditions could best be improved by organizing workers against their employers without promoting broader political goals. This philosophy led the AFL to great power. Indeed, the AFL survives today as part of the powerful AFL-CIO (Congress of Industrial Organizations).

The AFL's success came at a cost. The Knights of Labor had generally tried to organize all workers: women and men, immigrants and those born in the United States, and blacks and whites together. The AFL, on the other hand, excluded blacks and women and was suspicious of many immigrants, especially the "new" immigrants from southern and eastern Europe. Gompers was able to get higher wages for the skilled, white, male workers he represented. But while AFL membership grew, unskilled workers—those who could have benefited most from union help—got no relief.

The tension between rich and poor, employer and employees, capitalists (investors and company owners) and labor, affected many areas of life, even baseball. In the decades after the Civil War, the national pastime captured the imagination of people from all walks of life. Today we think of baseball as good clean fun. A century ago most people thought it was a rather rowdy sport. Many team owners also owned breweries, and they made much of their money from selling beer. Drunken fans, and sometimes drunken players, would get into fights—even in the middle of an inning!

The leaders of the newly organized National League wanted to clean up the image of the game. They outlawed the sale of alcohol at games. To attract more prosperous, well-mannered fans, they increased the price of tickets. Starting in the 1880s, black players generally were banned from baseball to satisfy the racist sentiments of whites. African Americans ended up forming their own "Negro League," which eventually produced some of baseball's most important stars.

The owners' strategy worked. Along with steel, oil, and railroads, baseball became a big business. Baseball players, like many other workers, thought that they were underpaid. The players were so unhappy that in the 1880s they organized their

own league, the Brotherhood of Professional Base Ball Players. This new league ultimately could not compete against the larger, stronger National League. It did, however, leave a legacy of conflict between owners and players that continues today. Indeed, baseball may show better than anything else that, as much as Americans came together during the Gilded Age to enjoy leisure activities and wonderful new technological marvels, significant social divisions remained.

Many individuals believed that they could escape the growing social conflicts of the Gilded Age by seeking their fortune on the frontier. So did at least one group, the Mormons—members of the Church of Jesus Christ of Latter-day Saints. Mormonism is a truly American religion, born in a vision that Joseph Smith had in the 1820s during the Second Great Awakening.

Persecuted where they settled in Missouri and then Illinois—where Smith was murdered—the Mormons, now under the leadership of Brigham Young, moved to the barren desert of what is now Utah. They called their settlement Deseret and set up their own government. The Mormons figured

Banned from playing on Major League baseball teams until 1947, black players formed their own clubs. The St. Paul Gophers (above) played out of Minnesota.

By the late 1800s, consumers no longer had to go to stores to buy goods. Even farmers in isolated homesteads could buy almost anything they needed through mail-order catalogs (above, left). In 1892 Alexander Graham Bell (above, right) made the first phone call between New York and Chicago, opening a permanent long-distance network that gradually came to link the entire country. Thanks to the genius of Thomas Edison, the phonograph (below) brought music into American homes.

that the United States would not care about this forsaken land.

By the 1850s, President James Buchanan made it clear that no people could set up their own government in any place formally claimed by the United States. Buchanan sent in the Army to take control of the area. Still, the Mormons continued to prosper.

They set up communal agricultural settlements, in which everyone worked the land together instead of as individuals. Church leaders even went so far as to prohibit the sale of land. The church owned all Mormon property.

Most controversially, the Mormon Church approved of polygamy, or the taking of more than one wife by the same husband. Approximately one out of every five Mormon families was polygamous. Mormon women defended this institution, saying that polygamy gave them more time for themselves because there were more wives to take care of one husband.

Faith and perseverance got the Mormons across the Great Plains to set up a religious colony in what is now Utah. Mormon settlers were unable to afford ox-drawn carts to carry them to their promised land, so they used handcarts, which they pulled from Iowa City to Salt Lake City. One of the last groups to leave was caught in a blizzard (left) in which some 200 Mormons died. About 600 reached their goal, however, and the colony flourished. Mormonism became the most successful new religion in American history.

Polygamy was unacceptable to most Americans, who believed it violated their own religions. The price the Mormon Church had to pay for the admission of Utah as a state in 1896 was the official prohibition of polygamy. Private ownership soon replaced church ownership of property. Mormons continued to practice their religion, and the Mormon Church still had great power. Mormon culture continued to develop and expand, but by the end of the 19th century, Mormons had become much more like other Americans in their everyday lives.

Farming families also sought refuge on the Great Plains and beyond. They were encouraged by railroad companies and by the Homestead Act of 1862. The Homestead Act allowed individuals to settle on, or buy at a low price, 160 acres of western government land. These farmers, though, never attained the prosperity of their midwestern neighbors. The soil was poor. The weather was brutal, with hailstorms and dust in the summer and blizzards in the winter.

When times got tough in the city, workers turned to unions. When times got tough for farmers, they turned to politics. In 1892, rebellious farmers organized the People's Party. They were known as Populists. They denounced banks that cheated them when loaning them money, railroads that overcharged them to transport their crops to markets, and the government for being taken over by the rich.

The Populists' Omaha Platform made it clear what the problems of the country were: "We meet in the midst of a nation brought to the verge of moral, political and material ruin....The fruits of the toil of millions are boldly stolen to build up colossal fortunes...." The Populists were clear about who should be in charge: "We seek to restore the government of the Republic to the hands of 'the plain people' with which class it originated." Their platform included direct voting on issues by the whole people; an income tax; and ownership of railroads and other industries by the government, rather than by robber barons.

For a few years, the Populists made great strides toward gaining power. They sent members to Congress, elected governors in states such as Kansas and Washington, and mobilized thousands

Farmers on the Great Plains built houses with any material available. Here, pioneer Sylvester Rawding and his family pose for a photographer in 1886. Their Nebraska house was made primarily of strips of sod. We can tell that this family was relatively prosperous by the wooden doors and the glass windows. Sod houses were cool in summer and warm in winter, although often leaky when it rained. They were also often infested with rodents, snakes, and all kinds of insects.

of members in the largest third-party movement since the Civil War. However, the party collapsed after the 1896 presidential election.

At the time, the debate over whether U.S. currency should be backed by gold or silver split the political parties. Both Populists and the pro-silver Democrats nominated William Jennings Bryan, an evangelical Christian from Nebraska who believed switching to silver would help farmers by raising farm prices. Bryan agreed with the Populists on many issues, but he refused their support because he saw them as too radical. Southern Populists ran the risk of being targets of terror and violence for daring to challenge the power of traditional Democrats.

When the votes were counted, both the Populists and Bryan went down to defeat. With the election of Republican William McKinley in 1896, the great age of protest among workers and farmers came to an end.

> From the same...governmental injustice we breed two great classes—paupers and millionaires.
>
> THE POPULISTS' OMAHA PLATFORM

Farmers were not the only people to suffer in the West. Chinese immigrants traveled across the Pacific to discover a "golden mountain" in places ranging from California to Wyoming Territory. Life in China during the 19th century was difficult. As was true in much of Europe, peasant farmers in China found it increasingly difficult to make a living, and their emperor could not maintain social order. Many Chinese came to America where they worked as miners, as cooks, and as laundry owners. These immigrants also supplied much of the backbreaking labor that built the transcontinental railroad in the 1860s.

Despite their great contributions to America's economy, the Chinese were disliked to a degree that would shock us today. Other workers feared that the Chinese would take their jobs, and politicians claimed that the Chinese would establish an alien and anti-Christian culture. As a result, Congress cut off almost all immigration from

Railroads

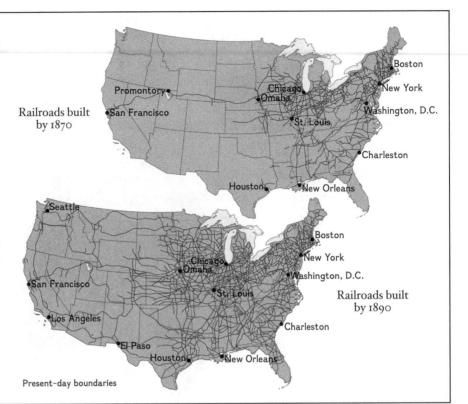

Between 1870 and 1890 the number of miles of railroad track in the United States tripled, dramatically changing the United States during the 19th century. Although trains traveled slowly by today's standards, they sped along tracks more quickly than anyone alive a century before could have imagined. Trains brought products made in the factories of the East and Midwest to the rest of the country and carried farm produce and livestock to market. They carried masses of people to new homes in thousands of towns that sprang up along the rails.

Railroads built by 1870

Railroads built by 1890

Present-day boundaries

China by passing the Chinese Exclusion Act of 1882.

This was also the period of the last Indian Wars. As more settlers moved into their land and prospectors hunted for gold, various western tribes fought to keep their lands and way of life. In response to Indian attacks, the military turned its attention to the frontier. The goal was clear. As General William Tecumseh Sherman declared: "The more I see of these Indians the more I am convinced that all have to be killed or maintained as a species of pauper."

Most fighting took place on the Great Plains and in the Southwest. The Army was quick to retaliate after Custer's defeat at the Little Bighorn in 1876. In the following years it quickly subdued the Lakota. The stiffest resistance over the next decade came from the Apache who, with their leader Geronimo, continued to elude the Army until a lack of food forced them to surrender.

By the end of the 1880s, the government had brought all Indian nations under its control.

Chinese workers were crucial to the building of the railroads. But only rarely were women allowed to come to the United States, so Chinese families were scarce here during the 19th century.

Chief Joseph

★ *Defender of His People* ★

MOST OF THE INDIAN TRIBES who conducted the last wars against the United States government had long opposed American expansion. But even Native Americans who had tried to assimilate became victims of America's lust for gold and land.

Chief Joseph of the Nez Perce found this out the hard way. His people had been kind to Lewis and Clark, saving them from starvation nearly a century before. They liked to trade with whites, and many of them—including Chief Joseph's father Tukekas—adopted Christianity. The Nez Perce even allied with the United States Army to fight other Indians.

But none of this helped the Nez Perce in 1860, when gold was discovered in their territory, the high mountainous area where Oregon, Washington, and Idaho come together. The government forced the tribe to sell 90 percent of its land—some six million acres—and move to a reservation in Idaho. Some of the Nez Perce went along with this treaty, but Chief Joseph protested, and his band was allowed to stay. Soon, however, the government changed its decision and told Chief Joseph that his people must leave or be attacked.

Chief Joseph agreed to go peacefully, but when his band of Nez Perce left their territory in the Wallowa Valley of Oregon, the Army came after them, and fighting broke out. The Indians killed one-third of the soldiers. Realizing that they had no choice but to flee, the Nez Perce began an epic trek. With the Army in pursuit, Joseph and his fellow chiefs shepherded as many as 800 Nez Perce, including children and the elderly, more than a thousand miles. Like slaves two decades earlier, they hoped to find freedom in Canada.

The Nez Perce almost made it. They battled the Army 18 times. Each time they successfully fought and fled. General Sherman even grudgingly admired the Nez Perce leaders for their military genius. Finally, the Army surrounded the hungry and freezing Indians at a camp in the Bear Paw Mountains of Montana. They were less than 40 miles from freedom. Chief Joseph decided it was time to surrender: "Hear me, my chiefs. I am tired; my heart is sick and sad. From where the sun now stands I will fight no more forever."

When the Nez Perce were captured in Montana, generals promised to return them to Oregon. The government did not keep that promise. Instead, the Nez Perce were sent to Kansas, then to Oklahoma. In a speech before Congress in 1879, Chief Joseph noted this unjust action when he pleaded: "Treat all men alike. Give them all the same law. Give them all an even chance to live and grow. All men were made by the same Great Spirit Chief."

NOT ALL THE ASSAULTS ON THE INDIANS were part of the Indian Wars. In 1887, Congress passed the Dawes Act. This law took large amounts of land away from Indians and required them to hold property as individuals, not as tribes. Poverty eventually drove individual Native Americans to sell large amounts of land to whites. During the mid to late 1800s, the reservations that the government had created to serve as Indian homelands continued to shrink.

Well-meaning Christians sought to educate Native Americans, but many of these missionaries thought of the Indians as savage heathens. At their boarding schools, they, like the government, prohibited traditional Indian religious ceremonies. Indians were not allowed to use their own languages, clothing, or hair styles. Many whites believed they had to "kill the Indian" in order to "save the man."

The ongoing assault on their culture led many

George Armstrong Custer was the most controversial military officer of the post-Civil War era. Undefeated at the age of 36, he and approximately 260 of his men died while attacking the Lakota and Cheyenne Indians in June 1876.

Army vs. Indians

AFTER CUSTER'S DEFEAT at the Battle of the Little Bighorn (known to the Lakota as Greasy Grass), the U.S. Army stepped up its campaign against western tribes. In a series of military engagements as well as massacres, the Army defeated powerful tribes such as the Lakota and Apache. By the time of the massacre at Wounded Knee in 1890, on the Pine Ridge Reservation in South Dakota, violent Native American resistance had almost completely ended.

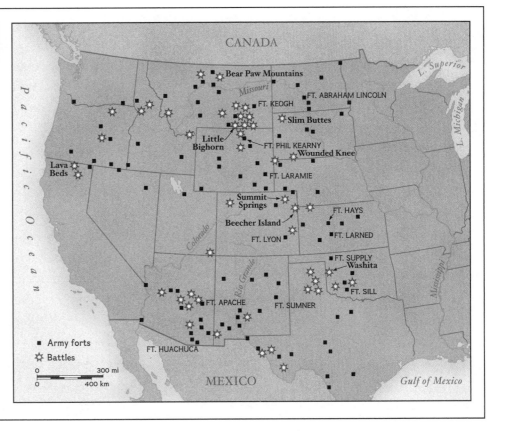

Indian Reservations

AFTER THEIR DEFEAT by the Army, most Indians lived on reservations established by the United States government. These were generally small parcels of land that were in undesirable locations. Yet when there was pressure from the white population for more land, the size of the reservation would generally be cut even further. With little good land, poor transportation links with the rest of the country, and little cash support from the government, the reservations became some of the poorest places in the nation.

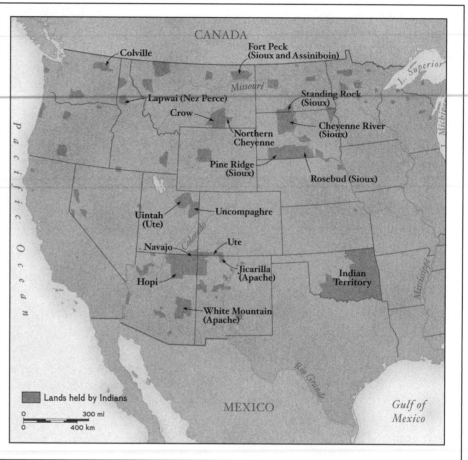

CANADA

Colville
Fort Peck (Sioux and Assiniboin)
L. Superior
Missouri
Lapwai (Nez Perce)
Crow
Standing Rock (Sioux)
Northern Cheyenne
Cheyenne River (Sioux)
Pine Ridge (Sioux)
Rosebud (Sioux)
Uintah (Ute)
Uncompaghre
Colorado
Navajo
Ute
Jicarilla (Apache)
Indian Territory
Hopi
White Mountain (Apache)
Rio Grande
Mississippi
Pacific Ocean

Lands held by Indians

0   300 mi
0   400 km

MEXICO

Gulf of Mexico

As Indians turned to religion rather than violence, one of the most popular spiritual movements was the Ghost Dance. Ghost Dancers believed shirts like this one protected them from bullets.

Indians to turn to religious practices such as the Ghost Dance to maintain their dignity. The Ghost Dance was an attempt to bring back their ancestors and the lost buffalo. Especially powerful among the Lakota, the Ghost Dance scared whites. The Army ordered the Lakota to stop doing the Ghost Dance.

The final tragedy of this era came in 1890 when the Army fired on a band of Lakota Ghost Dancers who were attempting to surrender. Two hundred women, children, and men were slaughtered in this massacre at Wounded Knee, on the Pine Ridge Reservation in South Dakota. Years later the prophet Black Elk sadly noted: "I can see that something else died there in the bloody mud, and was buried in the blizzard. A people's dream died there. It was a beautiful dream."

According to the U.S. Census, 1890 marked a

significant turning point for whites as well as Indians. The government officially declared the frontier closed.

With the nation "full," many whites—such as influential historian Frederick Jackson Turner and future President Theodore Roosevelt—came to believe that America must continue moving, continue pushing, continue seeking new lands to conquer. By the end of the century, the answer to this restlessness was overseas expansion.

Empire building usually starts with a feeling of superiority over other people, countries, and races. For the United States the attitude of "empire" took over where "frontier" left off. For America to become an empire it had to take control of other countries.

Ever since the Puritans and John Winthrop's "City on a Hill" sermon, Americans had believed themselves to be a chosen people. Americans, especially the rich and powerful, became more and more convinced over the course of the 19th century that their white, Protestant civilization was superior to any other. This attitude was held by Josiah Strong, a Congregational minister who was one of the most powerful advocates of American overseas expansion. Strong argued that "the rest of the world" needed to "be Christianized and civilized."

Senator Albert Beveridge of Indiana declared, along the same lines, that God "has made us adept in government that we may administer governments among savages and senile peoples....He has marked the American people as His chosen nation to finally lead in the regeneration of the world."

In 1893, the government opened up six million acres of the recently purchased Cherokee Outlet in the Panhandle of Oklahoma for white settlement. At noon on September 16, 1893, more than 100,000 settlers raced to claim land for homesteads.

Along with Europeans, Americans were urged to take up what British writer Rudyard Kipling called "The White Man's Burden."

Most Americans had long thought of the territories near their homeland as part of their "manifest destiny." In 1867, Secretary of State William Seward leaped at the opportunity to purchase Alaska from Russia for only $7.2 million. Critics called this "Seward's Icebox" or "Seward's Folly," seeing little of value in the vast Arctic wasteland. No one knew then about the vast oil reserves that lay beneath its frozen surface.

Seward hoped that eventually the United States would control Canada and Mexico, too. That never did happen, but in the 1890s the United States took advantage of opportunities to obtain lands overseas. In 1898, the United States annexed Hawaii. The American government, responding to pressure from American pineapple and sugar corporations, had already helped overthrow one king and one queen there earlier in the decade. Now, without any consultation with the native people, the United States brought Hawaii under its formal control.

Events that same year in Cuba involved the United States in a war with Spain. Cubans had begun a revolt against their Spanish rulers. Many Americans sympathized with Cuba, but Republican President McKinley was careful to avoid war. Recognizing the strength of anti-imperialist sentiment in the country, he stated, "We want no wars of conquest; we must avoid the temptation of territorial aggression."

Then the U.S.S. *Maine*, a ship McKinley sent to Cuba to protect U.S. citizens and their property, blew up in Havana harbor, killing 260 American sailors. A government commission declared the explosion an accident. However, newspapers had already concluded that Spain was responsible for the blast. Raging headlines inflamed public opinion, and the nation went to war.

The Spanish-American War was, in the words of Secretary of State John Hay, "a splendid little war." It lasted only a few weeks. Cuba, like Hawaii,

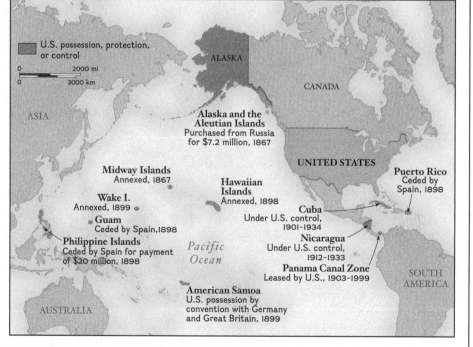

Growth of Empire

IN THE LATE 19TH CENTURY, and into the 20th, the United States gained an overseas empire. Americans gave various justifications for their control over new lands: the benefits of trade, the need for military bases, and the desire to convert native populations to Christianity and bring democracy to supposedly backward countries. But the empire brought much discord and disadvantage, as well as power and prosperity.

U.S. possession, protection, or control

0   2000 mi
0   3000 km

ALASKA

CANADA

ASIA

Alaska and the Aleutian Islands
Purchased from Russia for $7.2 million, 1867

UNITED STATES

Puerto Rico
Ceded by Spain, 1898

Midway Islands
Annexed, 1867

Hawaiian Islands
Annexed, 1898

Wake I.
Annexed, 1899

Guam
Ceded by Spain, 1898

Cuba
Under U.S. control, 1901-1934

Philippine Islands
Ceded by Spain for payment of $20 million, 1898

Pacific Ocean

Nicaragua
Under U.S. control, 1912-1933

Panama Canal Zone
Leased by U.S., 1903-1999

SOUTH AMERICA

American Samoa
U.S. possession by convention with Germany and Great Britain, 1899

AUSTRALIA

Americans were outraged when the battleship U.S.S. Maine *blew up in Havana harbor in 1898. Although the explosion was probably an accident, Americans believed Spain had caused the death of the ship's 260 sailors. The nation went to war and four months later took control of an empire made up of Cuba, Puerto Rico, Guam, and the Philippines.*

became an American protectorate, which meant that Cubans were in charge of their day-to-day affairs, but they could not make important policy changes without the permission of the U.S. government. Cuba remained a protectorate until 1934. Like much of the rest of the Caribbean, it fell increasingly under the domination of American big-business interests. The United States formally took control of Puerto Rico and the island of Guam in the South Pacific.

The United States also gained the Philippines in the treaty that ended the Spanish-American war. These islands proved much more difficult to control than Cuba. Filipinos, who had been ruled oppressively by the Spanish for centuries, at first welcomed American help in throwing off the Spanish yoke. When the Americans made it clear that they considered the islands to be strategically important and had no intention of giving up their control, Filipino rebels turned their guns on the United States. The result was a bloody war spread across the nation's 7,000 islands. In places, fighting continued for three decades, though most of it ended by 1902.

American soldiers committed atrocity after atrocity and slaughtered many civilians. In the end, one out of every eight Philippine citizens died. American sugar companies took over much of the island nation's economy, and the Philippines remained an American territory until just after World War II.

> "The American people, intrenched in freedom, take their love for it wherever they go."
>
> WILLIAM MCKINLEY

The Great Debate

★ Should the United States Become an Imperialist Nation? ★

MOST AMERICANS WERE SATISFIED with their new prominent role in world affairs. After all, European powers had spent much of the late 19th century acquiring colonies in Asia and Africa, so wasn't it the United States's turn? Imperialists believed that the U.S. economy would benefit from colonies to trade with, that security would be improved with the establishment of military bases abroad, and that they could spread Christianity among the "heathens."

Critics argued that Americans should not follow Europe's lead. These anti-imperialists echoed Thomas Paine's sentiments of a century earlier when they pointed out that the continent of Europe was beset with conflict, tyranny, and warfare. America believed in freedom. That meant not just freedom for citizens of the United States, they argued, but for citizens of the entire world. Therefore the United States had no business ruling over other countries or people.

The anti-imperialist cause never gathered many followers, but it was influential because it

appealed to America's democratic principles, and its supporters were often quite wealthy and powerful. Andrew Carnegie, who believed that commerce rather than conquest was the best way to tie nations together, was an anti-imperialist. So was the writer Mark Twain, the philosopher William James, and the black activist W. E. B. Du Bois. Politician William Jennings Bryan counted himself part of the cause, as did a number of labor leaders and Populists.

Unfortunately, many (but not all) anti-imperialists shared the racist views that imperialists used to justify their cause. They simply reached opposite conclusions. The anti-imperialists claimed that those who had dark skin were ignorant, uncivilized, and thoroughly unfit for democratic self-government, and that the United States should stay as far away from them as possible. AFL leader Samuel Gompers, for example, called Filipinos "perhaps nearer the condition of savages and barbarians than . . . any other civilized nation on earth."

Americans have always vigorously debated their role in world affairs. These important arguments continue today. For example, there are ongoing discussions about which influences foreign policy more: big oil and banking interests or the spread of democracy? As we debate these issues, it is important to remember more than the arguments of those who claimed victory in what many historians now call the Spanish-Cuban-Filipino-American War. We must also keep in mind those who so powerfully declared their concerns about American intervention overseas. Here is one eloquent statement of the anti-imperialist perspective, a poem called "The Real 'White Man's Burden'":

Take up the White Man's burden.
Send forth your sturdy kin,
And load them down with Bibles
And cannon-balls and gin.
Throw in a few diseases
To spread the tropic climes,
For there the healthy niggers
Are quite behind the times.
They need our labor question, too.
And politics and fraud—
We've made a pretty mess at home,
Let's make a mess abroad.
—Ernest Howard Crosby

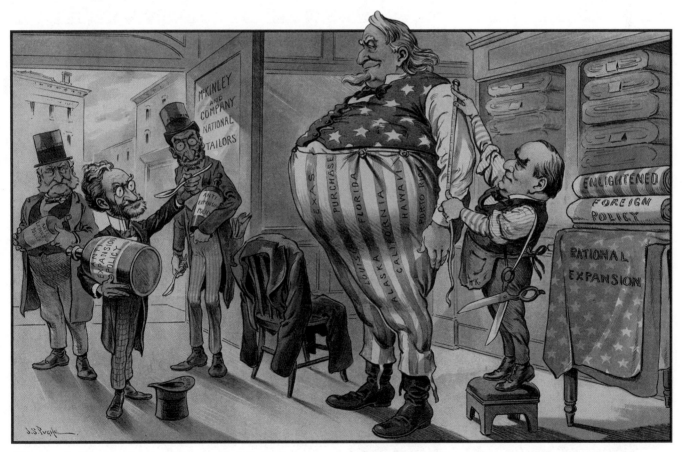

The spread of the American empire was one of the most controversial issues of the era. Here a cartoon from 1900 shows President William McKinley trying to fit an overgrown Uncle Sam with bigger clothes for the new empire. Note the list of American acquisitions on Uncle Sam's pants. They include the Louisiana Purchase, California, Alaska, Florida, and Hawaii. The men on the left seek to give Uncle Sam a dose of "Anti-Expansion Policy" medicine. Samuel Gompers (opposite), the most prominent labor leader of the day, was one of the most important anti-imperialists.

During the late 19th century, African Americans experienced massive educational, economic, and cultural discrimination. Their schools (above) were generally inferior to those of whites; southern blacks were usually limited to the most menial agricultural labor, such as cotton picking (left); and whites wearing black makeup made fun of black culture (opposite).

NONAMERICANS WERE NOT THE ONLY PEOPLE to suffer from the increasing power of 19th-century racism. As the 1800s drew to a close, African Americans living in the South learned what life would be like after the federal government abandoned them. Lynchings—mob hangings and other murders—skyrocketed. If an African American, particularly a man, became too well-off as a farmer or businessman, he risked being lynched by whites who felt threatened by his economic success. Sometimes the police lynched blacks; other times it was an unruly crowd that included cheering women and children. Torture, especially burning, was frequently part of the lynching. Railroads had special rates so that as many whites as possible could travel to watch this most sick form of "entertainment."

The courts did little to protect the rights granted to blacks by the 13th, 14th, and 15th Amendments to the Constitution. During the late 19th century the Supreme Court upheld a host of discriminatory pieces of legislation. The most damaging was *Plessy* v. *Ferguson*. In that 1896 ruling, the Court ruled that "separate but equal" waiting rooms, schools, and other public accommodations were legal.

Separation really meant segregation—the forced separation of the races. And equality never occurred: schools, public health facilities, and parks for blacks didn't receive anywhere near the funding as those for whites.

Separate but equal laws represented the worst of Jim Crowism. The term "Jim Crow" came from a kind of theater known as minstrel shows, in which white performers painted their faces black. The character Jim Crow was stupid and helpless. Jim Crow laws, which kept blacks separate from whites, were no laughing matter, though. They affected daily life by dictating what blacks could and could not do. They affected political activities too. Throughout the 1880s and 1890s, southern whites stripped blacks of their right to vote, either by threatening them with violence or by passing laws that allowed only men whose grandfathers had voted to vote. Since blacks didn't gain this right until after the Civil War, these laws kept them from voting.

Blacks would not approach full political equality until the Voting Rights Act of 1965. Arguably the Civil War was fought for more than a century before its highest ideals won the day.

CHAPTER SIX

PROGRESSIVISM AND THE NEW DEAL

★ 1900–1941 ★

"The only thing we have to fear is fear itself."

FRANKLIN DELANO ROOSEVELT

1903

Orville Wright piloted the first successful airplane above the sands at Kitty Hawk, North Carolina, on December 17. This achievement revolutionized transportation worldwide.

1911

The tragic Triangle Shirtwaist Company fire in New York City that killed 146 garment workers—mostly young Jewish and Italian women—made people realize the need for laws to protect workers.

1917–18

This image of Uncle Sam urged young Americans to fight the Germans in 1917. President Wilson's efforts to keep America out of World War I ended with the sinking of U.S. ships by German submarines.

1920

On August 18, 1920, 72 years after Elizabeth Cady Stanton's Declaration of Sentiments, the 19th Amendment gave women the right to vote.

SCHOLARS HAVE CALLED THE LATE 19TH CENTURY an age of excess. During this time some people became extremely rich and powerful while others sank to the depths of poverty and powerlessness. The first decades of the 20th century, in contrast, were an age of reform in reaction to the extremes of the Gilded Age. Throughout the country, Americans tried to figure out ways to make society work better for all. They asked: Was a business too big? If so, the courts could break it up. Were politicians too corrupt? Citizens could make them more honest by threatening to vote them out of office. Was immorality growing? Lawmakers could pass legislation to reform behavior. Was unemployment too high? The government could find ways to put people to work.

1928

Mickey Mouse starred in the first motion picture cartoon to use sound. The rise of "talkies" made movies the most popular form of entertainment in America, even at the height of the Depression.

1929

The worst economic depression in American history occurred with the crash of the stock exchange in October. Millions of people were thrown out of work. Thousands became homeless and relied on bread and soup lines for meals.

1933

The creation of murals like this one was part of President Franklin D. Roosevelt's New Deal, launched in 1933. The government put people to work in a variety of jobs, from building bridges to planting forests.

1930–1940

The Dust Bowl was perhaps the greatest ecological disaster in American history. Thousands of farmers were forced to abandon their land. New farming and conservation methods helped prevent future abuse of the soil.

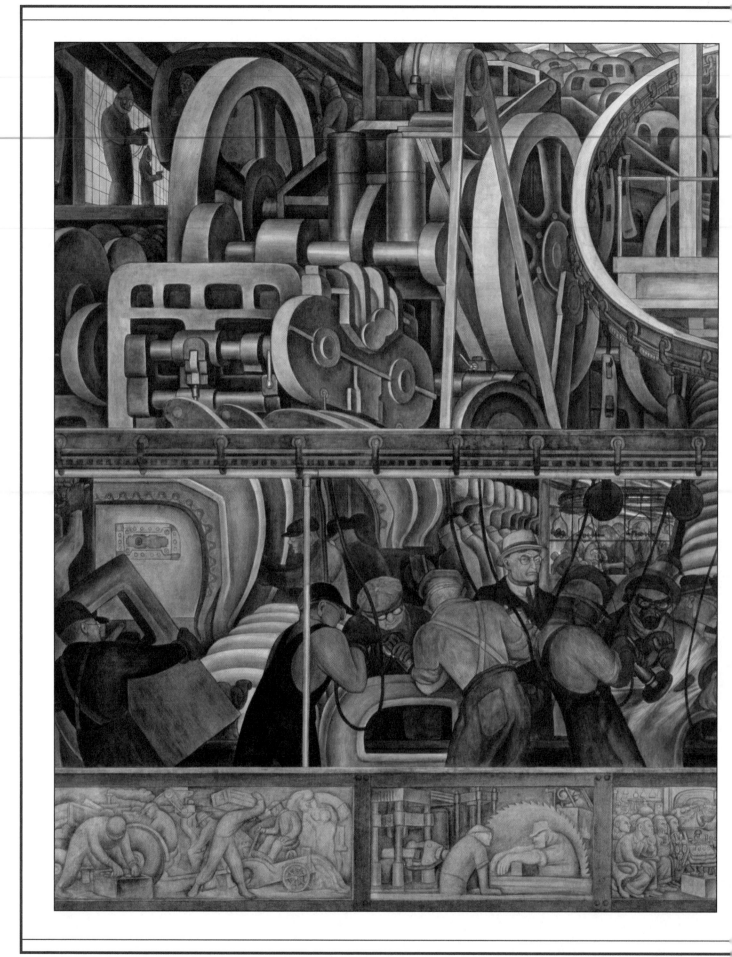

This spirit of reform was expressed in two major movements: Progressivism and the New Deal. Much of what Progressives and New Dealers worked for is reflected in present-day government programs. Other parts of the reform program have been rejected.

During the early 20th century, Americans argued passionately about how to make America a better place. Reformers wanted government to play a bigger role in coming up with legislation that would improve life for everyone, not just the favored few. Conservatives, often known at the time as standpatters, felt government should stay out of the way and let big business create prosperity.

This, in turn, would put money in people's pockets and make it possible for them to take care of their own lives.

The ultimate legacy of the Age of Reform may be continued disagreement over whether government or big business should have more influence in improving life in America. Vigorous debate is not only a good thing. It is the American way. Our democratic political structure allows individuals and groups to get involved in the way government works. There can never be agreement on everything. But through free and open debate of many points of view, people can discover ways to create a better world.

THE ENTIRE PERIOD from 1900 to 1941 was an age of reform. But the years 1900 to 1914 were especially intense politically, and it is this age that is commonly called the Progressive Era.

What was Progressivism in action? It was mothers going to city hall to make sure that public health officials had inspected milk to ensure it was safe for their children to drink; magazines screaming about the dirty deals that rich bankers made; citizens complaining when a city council gave a trolley company permission to use a busy street

where children played; and Congress trying to figure out how to regulate United States Steel so that the giant company could not run its competitors out of business. Progressivism was also African Americans, Latinos, and Native Americans using the spirit of reform to move toward equality.

For thousands of years men had been in charge of politics. By contrast, women were responsible for much of Progressivism. Settlement house workers such as Jane Addams and Lillian Wald were among the most prominent. These women were

The 1930s brought both hope and despair to millions of Americans. Wonderful artistic efforts graced post offices, ski lodges, and even factories. The murals on the left were painted by Diego Rivera. Commissioned by Edsel Ford, they show the industrial power of Ford's massive River Rouge automobile plant. Yet the basic fact of life for Americans during the Depression was economic suffering. Above, jobless people wait in line for a loaf of bread or a can of soup being handed out by a few prosperous New Yorkers.

born to middle-class, sometimes wealthy, families. After getting more than a high school education— a rare thing before World War II—they chose to devote their lives to helping others. They worked at "settlement houses," large community centers paid for by philanthropists—people like Andrew Carnegie who gave large sums of money to charity.

Jane Addams lived at Hull House in Chicago, and Lillian Wald moved to the Henry Street Settlement House in New York. At these places, they sought to help poor residents, especially recent immigrants. If a mother from Romania had a sick child, Wald and her comrades would make sure a nurse came to visit. If a construction worker from Italy broke his leg on the job and could not work, Addams and her co-workers would help him get insurance money from the state government.

The settlement house workers quickly moved beyond such one-on-one help. They testified in front of legislative committees about the problems immigrants had getting housing. They wrote letters to public health officials telling them how many babies were dying of preventable diseases.

They campaigned with labor unions to outlaw child labor and to win the eight-hour workday.

Almost all of the legislators, city council members, and health commissioners who had the real power were men. Increasingly, they understood the rising popular sentiment and came to agree with the women reformers: Americans had to take better care of the poor and less fortunate.

The Progressives' reliance on government to help people and improve the country was a very big change from the late 19th century. Then, the most influential thinkers, from industrialists like John D. Rockefeller to sociologists such as William Graham Sumner, believed that the government should stay out of people's lives and, especially, out of the economy.

The Progressives believed that in order for government to take on such big tasks, it needed to be free of all corruption. Progressives feared, with good reason, that city councils, state legislatures, and even the halls of Congress had been taken over by wealthy special interest groups that often used their power illegally.

Legislators passed laws that were favorable to big business; in return, big business financed their campaigns and got them reelected. Large corporations became known for bribing and intimidating politicians. Crusading journalists, known as muckrakers (for the "muck" they found) discovered these dirty deals and brought them out in the open. When this muck was printed in newspapers, the

The Progressive Era saw many attempts to make life better for all Americans. Visiting nurses offered help to sick children in disease-ridden slums (above). The Food and Drug Act focused on the problem of impure food. This cartoon (right) shows a grocer putting sand into sugar, parts of an animal carcass into butter, and dust into coffee.

public was moved to action. Citizens pressed hard for laws that would prevent the rich and the powerful from using their influence in the political process. They wanted to bring ordinary people closer to their governments.

Starting in Oregon, Progressives changed the constitutions of many western states so the people themselves could vote directly on laws, overturn the laws passed by their legislatures, or throw officials out of office if they did something wrong or unpopular. This kind of "direct democracy" was in many ways a challenge to the system of representative government that the Federalists had fought for in the Constitution.

Progressives were among the first to care about the environment. Americans created the first national parks, including Yellowstone and Yosemite, in the late 19th century. The concept that the government should take care of scenic places, and not allow them to be developed, was a relatively new idea in American history, even in world history. Early environmentalists such as John Muir believed deeply in the spiritual powers of nature, and they wanted the wilderness to be available for all Americans to enjoy.

Other Progressives were more interested in combining wilderness and development. Conservationists like Gifford Pinchot, head of the National Forest Service under President Theodore Roosevelt, were convinced that business and environmental values could be harmonized. Pinchot and Roosevelt believed that programs such as tree replanting would allow lumber companies to cut trees without destroying forests.

The most powerful Progressives were white, and they were often racist. President Woodrow Wilson, a Southerner and a Progressive, supported the segregation of government offices in Washington, D.C. Race was the Progressives' biggest blind spot. In spite of this, many minorities took up the Progressives' cause. They saw in the new progressive

The protection of wilderness areas was one of the triumphs of the Progressives. Here, John Muir (right), the staunchest American advocate of wilderness preservation, shows off the wonders of California's Yosemite Valley to President Theodore Roosevelt (left). Yosemite was made a national park in 1890.

attitude an opportunity to get government involved in helping to bring about racial equality.

Carlos Montezuma and other Native Americans believed that Indians could preserve their traditional cultures yet accept the best of modern American life. Mexican Americans had their first important political experiences of the century using progressive ideas to fight for voting rights and against school segregation in Texas and California. Still, the question remained of how much to confront the power of whites head-on.

The Great Debate

★ *How to Achieve Racial Progress* ★

AFRICAN AMERICANS carried out a great debate about how this energetic political environment might finally bring about their dream of genuine equality. Booker T. Washington was the most influential African American in early 20th-century America, but his origins could not have been more humble. His autobiography, *Up From Slavery,* tells how he was born a slave a few years before the beginning of the Civil War. He did not know the exact date of his birth or who his father was except that he was white. Although his mother was illiterate, young Booker showed an intense interest in reading from an early age.

At Hampton Institute, a school for blacks in southeastern Virginia, Washington learned agriculture and brickmaking. Soon after graduating, he founded the Tuskegee Institute to give black students a place to get a higher education at a time when they were barred from attending southern white universities. Under Washington's leadership, this Alabama school became one of the leading African-American colleges in the nation.

Instead of history and mathematics, blacks at Tuskegee concentrated on learning a trade, such as carpentry or farming, that would be useful in establishing a small business or in running their own households. Tuskegee also focused on building character, making sure that students knew the value of hard work, cleanliness, and thrift. The talented all-black faculty that Washington hired included the renowned scientist George Washington Carver.

In time, Washington became known as the Wizard of Tuskegee. His success there made him a popular lecturer around the nation, and whites in both the North and South flocked to hear what he had to say. Above all, Washington preached racial compromise. He argued that blacks had to earn their rights through hard work rather than through politics, and that they should tolerate segregation as long as they had the ability to start small businesses, hold property, and get a decent education. In an 1895 speech in Atlanta he said, "In all things that are purely social we can be as separate as the fingers, yet one as the hand in all things essential to mutual progress." In Washington's view, only at some time in the unforeseen future would black Americans be in a position to gain basic political rights.

> "The wisest among my race understand that the agitation of questions about social equality is the extremest folly."
>
> BOOKER T. WASHINGTON

W. E. B. Du Bois believed that Washington's slow, accommodating approach to racial equality was hogwash. Du Bois did not want to wait. Blacks were humans, blacks were Americans, and blacks deserved their rights *now*.

Unlike Booker T. Washington, William Edward Burghardt Du Bois was a Northerner. He was born free in Great Barrington, Massachusetts. One of his ancestors had even fought in the American Revolution. Du Bois graduated from all-black Fisk College in Tennessee before enrolling at Harvard. Intellectually brilliant, he became the first African American to receive a Ph.D. at that prestigious university. Du Bois went on to a long and distinguished career as a scholar, writer, and editor. In his classic *The Souls of Black Folk* (1903), he wrote: "The problem of the twentieth century is the problem of the color line."

Du Bois soon became an increasingly radical, or extreme, political activist. Initially he supported Washington and even praised Washington's speech in Atlanta. In time, though, Du Bois came to disagree with Washington's approach to race relations. In 1905, he and some other highly educated blacks formed the Niagara Movement, named for the city in Ontario, Canada, where the first meeting was held after discrimination forced the group to leave Buffalo, New York.

In Niagara Falls, Ontario, they issued the statement: "Any discrimination based solely on race or color is barbarous." A complete break with Washington's philosophy came when Du Bois and his colleagues declared: "Persistent manly agitation is the way to liberty." Washington was no "agitator"; Du Bois was a proud one.

"One feels his two-ness — an American, a Negro;...two unreconciled strivings;"

WILLIAM EDWARD BURGHARDT DU BOIS

Four years later, Du Bois helped found the NAACP, the National Association for the Advancement of Colored People. For many years he was the editor of the organization's journal, *The Crisis*. Throughout the 20th century and up to the present day, the NAACP has been the most effective agitator for the legal and political rights of blacks in America.

Eventually, Du Bois became disillusioned with the slow progress of racial equality. He became a member of the Communist Party, which believed in the overthrow of capitalism, the equalization of wealth, and the elimination of poverty. Near the end of his life, he moved to Ghana, then a newly independent country in Africa, because he believed that black people could gain true freedom only in their own countries.

Booker T. Washington died in 1915, nearly a half century before Du Bois's death. Historians looking through Washington's letters have uncovered an interesting fact. Washington and Du Bois may have disputed with each other intensely in public debate, but they sometimes supported each other in private. Out of public view, Washington funded civil rights organizations that fought for desegregated schools, for the right of blacks to serve on juries, and for the vote. Washington even secretly supported the NAACP on certain issues.

So the debate between Washington and Du Bois was great in public. In private, though, African Americans came to agree that the only way to achieve true justice was by struggling for full political equality.

Theodore Roosevelt's energetic prodding of Congress resulted in a 1903 treaty that allowed the U.S. to build a canal across Panama.

ONE OF BOOKER T. WASHINGTON'S claims to power within the African-American community was his close connection with President Theodore Roosevelt. TR, as Roosevelt was known, even invited Washington to dine at the White House— although only once, because afterward the President received so much criticism from white Southerners.

That episode captures Theodore Roosevelt well. TR did much that was daring in politics, even if in the end he usually took a moderate course. TR, who had gained national prominence as the leader of the "Rough Riders" during the Spanish-American War, was the most colorful and powerful Progressive of the period.

Elected in 1900 as William McKinley's Vice President, Roosevelt became President in 1901 when an anarchist assassinated McKinley.

Roosevelt was an avid outdoorsman and helped establish many national parks, monuments, and forests. Roosevelt gained a reputation as a trust buster. A "trust" is a large group of companies that dominate a certain kind of business, such as oil or steel. TR wanted to break apart some of the biggest trusts to make industry more competitive. He proposed legislation that would have regulated business more than at any other time in the nation's history.

TR's Vice President, William Howard Taft, became President in 1909. At first the two men were close allies. But Taft was more conservative, and soon they became political enemies. In 1912, TR left the Republican Party and created the Progressive Party to fight for his liberal policies while Taft ran as the more pro-big-business Republican candidate. The Democrats nominated New Jersey Governor Woodrow Wilson, who was a strong supporter of small businesses.

The 1912 presidential election was one of the most exciting and important races in our history because of the very different economic philosophies of the candidates and because it was not just a two-way race between Democrats and Republicans. It was actually a four-way race, with TR, Taft, Wilson, and Socialist Eugene V. Debs all serious candidates. Debs got nearly a million votes, or 6 percent of the total, running on a platform that called for government ownership of big business. This showed how dissatisfied many Americans were with the economics and politics of the day. In the end, Roosevelt took votes away from Taft, and Wilson swept to victory.

Although Wilson ran as a Democrat, he supported many Progressive programs. He succeeded in getting Congress to pass a graduated federal income tax in 1913. This helped equalize wealth by taxing rich people at a higher rate than the poor. He created a new national bank (the first since before the Civil War) that was designed to make the economy run more smoothly and fairly. He also cautiously supported labor unions. Increasingly, though, Wilson's time was taken up with World War I. The war began in 1914 when a Serbian assassinated Archduke Franz Ferdinand, heir to the throne of Germany's ally Austria-Hungary. During the next four years, Europe was engulfed in bloody, seemingly endless, trench warfare. Britain and France were the main allies on one side, with Germany as the primary enemy on the other. In the first two years of the war, it was clear that almost all Americans wanted to stay out of the conflict. Although Wilson did send troops to Mexico in 1914 to take part in a revolution to overthrow dictator General Victoriano Huerto, Wilson was reelected in November 1916 largely on the strength of the slogan "He Kept Us Out of War."

Events moved quickly soon after Wilson's re-election. In February 1917 Germany announced it would engage in unrestricted submarine warfare, meaning that it would attack even the ships of neutral nations without warning. Wilson broke off diplomatic relations with Germany. He then told a shocked nation that the German ambassador had offered to help Mexico win back New Mexico, Texas, and Arizona if Mexico would ally with Germany.

After German U-boats, or submarines, sank several American merchant ships, Wilson finally asked Congress for a declaration of war. Despite eloquent opposition led by Wisconsin's Robert La Follette, Wilson won the way with his message: "The world must be made safe for democracy."

Most Americans responded enthusiastically to the call for war. But German and anti-British Irish immigrants tended to oppose the conflict, as did many Socialists, who believed the war would benefit only the wealthy. The government launched a

During World War I, the government used patriotic posters (left) and young women (above) to sell liberty bonds and savings stamps to raise money to help pay for the war. A "thrift card" full of 25-cent stamps could be traded in for a $5 savings certificate.

propaganda campaign to win the hearts and minds of all American citizens. The Committee on Public Information produced more than a hundred million copies of books, articles, and pamphlets. When persuasion did not work, the government used new sweeping wartime powers to arrest those who opposed the war. It was a very shaky time for freedom of speech.

American soldiers did not go into battle in large numbers until the beginning of 1918, nearly a year after the U.S. declared war. In the remaining months of the conflict, Americans played an important role in pushing the Germans out of France and, ultimately, ending the war in November. Over 110,000 Americans died in that short time, more than half from influenza and pneumonia.

Most African Americans supported the war, though recruits had to fight in segregated units. On returning home, they hoped to be rewarded with greater political rights. As one black editor put it: "The colored soldier who fights side by side with the white American will hardly be begrudged a fair chance when the victorious armies return." They were to be bitterly disappointed.

Between 1913 and 1919, the importance of cotton to the South's economy declined. Thousands of blacks no longer employed in the cotton fields moved north to Chicago, Detroit, and New York. Known as the Great Migration, this movement freed these blacks from many restrictions, especially those against voting. However, as the northern black population grew, northern whites—who now had to compete with blacks for jobs—showed that they could be just as racist as southern whites. Few northern neighborhoods welcomed African Americans. Almost all showed some hostility, which eventually erupted in riots.

Meanwhile, life for southern blacks continued to get worse. State legislatures finished stripping them of their rights during this period, and lynchings reached horrifying new levels.

Battles of World War I

WORLD WAR I BEGAN when Austria-Hungary attacked Serbia shortly after a Serbian assassinated the heir to the Austro-Hungarian throne. Russia immediately came to Serbia's aid. Through an earlier treaty, France was obligated to fight with Russia. Germany united with Austria-Hungary to form the Central Powers. When Germany marched through Belgium to France, Britain and France joined forces. For more than three years, the two sides fired at each other from trenches, using periscopes (above) to keep an eye on enemy movements.

On the eastern front, the Germans beat back the Russians at Tannenberg in 1914, then moved deep into Russian territory. Russia, weak from an internal revolution, made peace with Germany in 1917. With fighting halted in the east, Germany could again turn its attention to the western front.

In April 1917 the United States joined the war, reaching the battlefields in France in time to help block the last great German offensive. American troops had no idea of the horrors that awaited them, including poison gas and the dampness and stench of the trenches where thousands of men became trapped and died. The first American victory came at Cantigny, in France (map inset). The Second Battle of the Marne halted the German advance. Nearly 120,000 Americans died in fighting in the Argonne Forest, but not in vain. Germany surrendered. The armistice ending the war was signed on November 11, 1918.

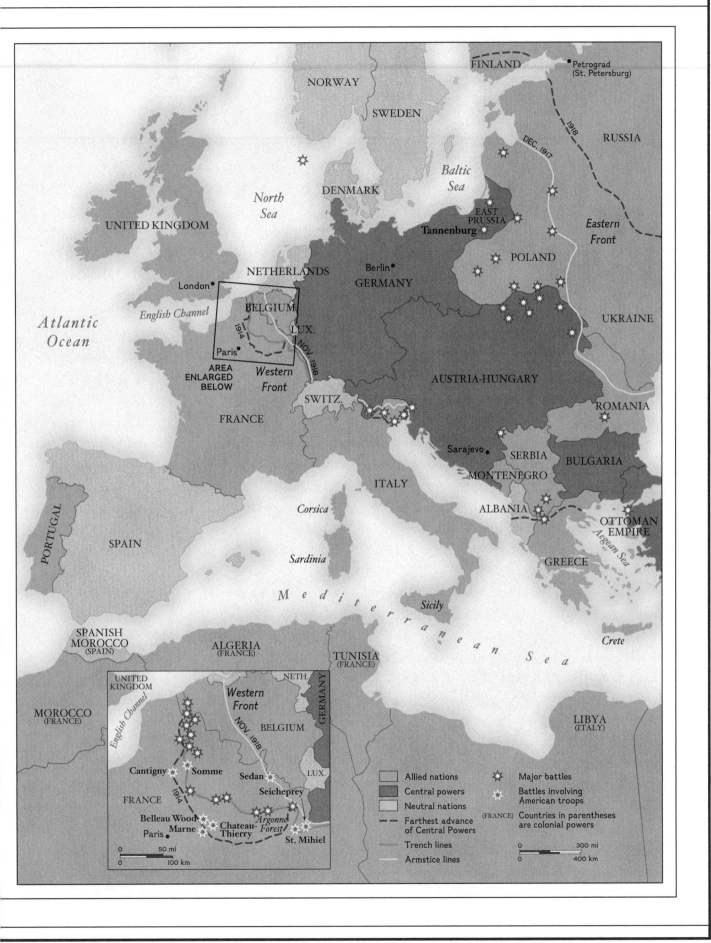

NORWAY

SWEDEN

FINLAND

Petrograd (St. Petersburg)

RUSSIA

North Sea

Baltic Sea

DENMARK

EAST PRUSSIA

Eastern Front

DEC. 1917

1918

UNITED KINGDOM

Tannenburg

POLAND

London

NETHERLANDS

Berlin

GERMANY

UKRAINE

English Channel

BELGIUM

LUX.

Atlantic Ocean

Paris

1914

NOV. 1918

AREA ENLARGED BELOW

Western Front

AUSTRIA-HUNGARY

SWITZ.

FRANCE

ROMANIA

Sarajevo

SERBIA

BULGARIA

MONTENEGRO

ITALY

Corsica

ALBANIA

OTTOMAN EMPIRE

Aegean Sea

PORTUGAL

Sardinia

SPAIN

GREECE

Crete

Mediterranean Sea

Sicily

SPANISH MOROCCO (SPAIN)

ALGERIA (FRANCE)

TUNISIA (FRANCE)

MOROCCO (FRANCE)

LIBYA (ITALY)

Inset map:

UNITED KINGDOM

NETH.

Western Front

GERMANY

NOV. 1918

BELGIUM

English Channel

LUX.

Cantigny

Somme

Sedan

1914

FRANCE

Seicheprey

Belleau Wood

Argonne Forest

Paris

Marne

Chateau-Thierry

St. Mihiel

0   50 mi
0   100 km

Legend:

☐ Allied nations
☐ Central powers
☐ Neutral nations
- - - Farthest advance of Central Powers
—— Trench lines
—— Armistice lines

☆ Major battles
☆ Battles involving American troops
(FRANCE) Countries in parentheses are colonial powers

0   300 mi
0   400 km

Ida B. Wells-Barnett

★ *Uncompromising Crusader* ★

ONE BOLD WOMAN made it her job to bring the issue of lynching to the conscience of the nation. Born into slavery, Ida B. Wells began her crusade in 1892 when she was a young editor of a black newspaper in Memphis, Tennessee. Three business-men—friends of Wells—were lynched in the city that year. Wells made it clear through arti-cles in her paper that the three men were innocent of any crime. She accused white businessmen of plot-ting their deaths because they did not like the competition that black people presented. In response, whites destroyed her printing press while she was traveling up North.

Undaunted, Wells began a full-scale inves-tigation of as many lynchings as she could uncover. The common reason that whites gave for lynchings was that the accused black men had attacked white women. Wells showed the falsehood of these charges. She began lectur-ing around the country and the world to get support for her cause so that this crime against humanity would end.

She fought other forms of racial prejudice, too. She bit a railroad conductor in Memphis when he tried to force her to leave the whites-only "ladies' car" and sit in the colored car. Her suit against this discrimination was successful until the state supreme court overturned the lower court's ruling. She continued her activism after marrying Ferdinand Barnett in 1895 and while raising four children. Wells-Barnett worked with W.E.B. Du Bois and the NAACP to launch the militant Niagara Movement. As she said, "The more the Afro-American yields and cringes and begs, the more he has to do so, the more he is insulted, outraged and lynched."

Wells-Barnett was always uncompromising. One of her friends wrote, "She has plenty of nerve, and is as sharp as a steel trap." Wells-Barnett helped make sure that black women had a place to come together to fight for their rights. At a time when African-American men had almost no power in the South, black women used clubs and associations as a way to fight in a quiet yet very determined way for justice.

Ida Wells-Barnett believed in racial justice and equality for women. She spoke out force-fully for the right to vote. And she struggled for justice within the suffrage movement as well. In 1913, when suffragists gathered from around the country for a parade in the nation's capital, they tried to segregate black women. Wells-Barnett would have none of that. With the help of friends, she slipped into the Illinois delegation at the very last moment. Regardless of what the leaders wanted, Ida Wells-Barnett made sure that the suffrage movement includ-ed all women—both white and black.

World War I brought great changes on the home front. Here, a member of the renowned Harlem "Hell-fighters" receives the thanks of a grateful citizen during the regiment's 1919 victory parade in New York City. Soon, such happiness would turn to great sorrow when blacks became the targets of vicious race riots. Below, a suffragist shouts at bystanders to support the right of women to vote. World War I made their victory possible.

AS THE STORY OF IDA B. WELLS-BARNETT shows, many of the women who fought for the right to vote were not believers in equality for all. White women in the North and South were willing to abandon their black sisters if doing so would win them the vote. Even with this compromise, suffragists were not making much headway anywhere in the country except the West. Before 1914, no state east of Kansas allowed women the right to vote. Campaigning state by state for the vote was proving to be ineffective.

With the start of World War I, suffragists began to work for a *national* constitutional amendment. They said they would show their patriotism by actively supporting the war. In return, they expected to be rewarded with the vote. At first, Wilson did not want to give women the right to vote, but he soon realized that his opposition only encouraged radical suffragists to chain themselves to fences and get arrested by the dozen. So in 1917 Wilson declared his support for woman's suffrage. Congress passed the 19th Amendment in 1919.

When Tennessee ratified the amendment the next year, providing the necessary three-quarters majority, women throughout the country gained the right to vote. However, Jim Crow laws kept southern black women from exercising this right.

Wilson did not handle the politics of peace as skillfully as he handled the suffrage issue. When World War I ended, Wilson traveled to Europe to help make sure that justice and democracy arose from the slaughter of millions. His "Fourteen Points" peace plan, which became part of the Treaty of Versailles that ended WWI, sought for all people "national self-determination"—the right to live in independent countries. The 14th point called for the creation of a League of Nations that would peacefully settle disputes among countries.

Many Americans who opposed Wilson's peace plan did so because they worried that the League of Nations would take control of American foreign policy decisions out of the hands of the United States. Wilson, who suffered a serious stroke while campaigning for the League, would not compromise on his peace plan, so Congress refused to ratify the Treaty of Versailles. The United States never signed the treaty that officially ended the war and didn't join the newly established League of Nations. Partly as a result of the U.S. refusing to join, the League of Nations proved far too weak to prevent the next great, and equally terrible, war.

Republican Warren G. Harding, who promised to bring a "return to normalcy," became President in 1921. After the strife-filled war years, most Americans very much wanted to settle down and

Radio appealed to all ages. Kids sent in cereal box tops to become members of Radio Orphan Annie's Secret Society.

enjoy the good life. Not all of them could, though. Many workers were unemployed, and farmers were in particularly bad shape after the war. In general, though, the decade of the 1920s was a time of economic prosperity which encouraged the growth of a real middle class.

Americans became consumers as never before. Electricity came into ordinary people's homes, giving them power to run new appliances such as washing machines and vacuum cleaners. Radios brought the world to millions of people in the form of instant news and entertainment. The whole family could sit around and listen to comedy shows as well as dramatic plays. They could hear advertisements, too, and the 1920s became a golden age for commercials. Americans also flocked to movie theaters. The first movie stars, celebrities like Mary Pickford and Douglas Fairbanks, Sr., became famous during these years.

Above all, people bought automobiles. The car changed the lives of Americans, giving many people the chance to go for long Sunday drives as well as the opportunity to commute from the suburbs to jobs in the city.

Literature and music saw important developments, too. None was more significant than the Harlem Renaissance, which brought to prominence African-American writers such as Langston Hughes and musicians such as Duke Ellington. Centered in Harlem, the movement extended throughout the country. Blacks were inspired to write highly political poetry, made jazz music a national treasure, and wrote novels that appealed to both blacks and whites.

Despite the overall prosperity and despite all

Americans at all economic levels bought automobiles during the 1920s, with one car for every six Americans. But few experienced the luxury of driving a 1929 Packard touring car (above).

Americans could never agree on the virtues of Prohibition. Many people evaded the law in innovative ways. Here a woman shows how easy it was to hide mini-kegs of bathtub gin under her coat.

the consumer goods, the 1920s had its problems. The decade began just after the passage of the 18th Amendment in 1919, banning all alcoholic beverages. This was known as Prohibition.

Prohibition was a cause fueled primarily by women. The largest women's political organization in the 1800s had been the Women's Christian Temperance Union. The WCTU not only had fought against alcohol but had pushed for programs to help mothers and children who suffered with alcoholic husbands and fathers. The Prohibition movement of the 20th century really only cared about getting rid of alcohol itself. It did not concern itself with helping families touched by alcoholism. Immigrants, with their alien cultures and strange ways, were often singled out for

blame. Prohibitionists believed that eliminating alcohol would clean up family life and politics, too.

Prohibition was a striking example of what sometimes happens when a government passes a law that a large proportion of its people do not want. It did not work. Many people did not like government interfering in their private lives. They felt government had gone too far by banning alcohol and making it unconstitutional to drink even in moderation. Organized crime, including operations run by Chicago's Al Capone, took over the business of providing liquor illegally, known as bootlegging. Nearly every town had a "speakeasy" where liquor was served illegally. And the federal government never provided the number of agents needed to enforce the ban on alcohol. Finally, in 1933, Congress repealed the 18th Amendment, and Prohibition ended.

Other movements were more successful in meeting their public goals, at least in the short term. The Ku Klux Klan was one of these. The KKK had begun as a terrorist organization in the South after the Civil War, but the Klan of the 1920s was different. The new Klan movement began in 1915 in Atlanta and soon spread to northern as well as southern cities. The Klan fought for "100 percent Americanism" and "White, Protestant Supremacy."

This KKK hated Catholics and Jews as much as it detested blacks. It boycotted their stores and

The 1920s were a decade of intolerance as well as an age of prosperity. The Ku Klux Klan, fighting against African Americans, Catholics, and Jews, was an active part of northern as well as southern society, as shown by this Fourth of July parade in New Jersey.

sought to keep them out of political office. By 1924, the Klan claimed more than three million members and even briefly controlled the governments of Indiana and Colorado. Women as well as men burned crosses on hillsides and attacked their enemies. Fortunately, laws passed to discourage Klan activities caused the organization to lose considerable power by the end of the decade.

Protestant fundamentalism also became a force in the 1920s. Fundamentalists, many of whom were southern Baptists, were upset that some other Protestant denominations preached salvation through good works rather than through the word of God as revealed in the Bible. Fundamentalists were suspicious of modern science, particularly evolution. Evolution taught that humans developed over millions of years from lower forms of life. In contrast, fundamentalists believed—and still do—that the biblical story of Genesis, in which God, on the sixth day of creation, made one man and one woman from whom all humanity is descended, is completely true.

Fundamentalists in the South had enough power to ban the teaching of evolution in many schools. In 1925, a 24-year-old biology teacher in Dayton, Tennessee, named John T. Scopes set out to break the law and get arrested so he could challenge the law in court. Supported by the American Civil Liberties Union, a prominent civil rights group, Scopes hired Clarence Darrow and other prominent lawyers to represent him. William Jennings Bryan led the prosecution.

The so-called monkey trial was a national sensation. The jury found Scopes guilty. Although many city folks believed the trial made the fundamentalists look silly, the result was the quiet removal of evolution from school textbooks until the 1960s. In fact, in areas where fundamentalism is strong, teaching evolution in the public schools is still a controversial issue.

Many fundamentalists, along with the Klan and other white Americans, had very strong anti-Jewish and, especially, anti-Catholic ideas. They believed that the pope was a dictator who controlled his millions of faithful, to the great harm of America. This feeling grew into a general intolerance of immigrants because most of the millions of foreigners who arrived between 1890 and 1920

These cartoons, although different in spirit, both reflect the growing concern during the 1920s that too many foreigners were being allowed into the U.S., and that if something weren't done, these undesirables would overrun American society and weaken the country.

were Catholics and Jews from southern and eastern Europe. In general, these people had darker skins than the British, Germans, Scandinavians, and other northern Europeans who had arrived before 1890. Many citizens began to fear that the white race—the so-called "true" America—was going to be overrun. The result was a 1924 law that drastically reduced immigration. The law struck particularly hard at immigrants from southern and eastern Europe. Immigrants from Mexico were not affected because they provided much needed labor for western farmers. Overall, immigration restriction was a dramatic departure from previous American policies that had welcomed newcomers from other countries. Some said that the Statue of Liberty wept upon the bill's passage.

The "Roaring Twenties" came to an abrupt end with the great stock market crash of 1929. The Great Depression that resulted would dramatically change the country's politics and economics.

During the 19th century, not many Americans had worried about stock markets. During the 20th century, however, millions of Americans, eager to own a piece of business, began buying stock—certificates that represented ownership of a share in a company. Stocks were traded (bought and sold) on Wall Street, home of the New York Stock Exchange. Corporations came to depend on the money earned from this trading to expand. They invested the money in new equipment and supplies in order to produce more goods.

During the twenties, investors bought and sold stock as if the economy would grow and grow forever. There was not much government regulation of the stock market at the time. People were allowed to buy stocks on credit, borrowing up to 90 percent of the stocks' worth. Investors thought that their stocks would continue to increase so much in value that when they sold them, they would have enough money to pay off their creditors and "make a killing" besides. With so many people playing the same game, the price of stocks

The economic problems of the 1930s led to violence and political rebellion. Farmers like this one (left) dumped containers of milk in the hope of creating a shortage that would drive prices up. The use of "scabs," nonunion workers hired by management to do the jobs of striking workers, led to violent labor conflicts. Here, striking factory workers seeking higher pay try to overturn a scab's car (right).

rose well above the actual worth of the companies they represented.

With such an artificial and unregulated economic situation, a crash had to come. And it did on Black Tuesday, October 29, 1929. Over the next few years, millions of Americans lost their jobs as companies were forced to close. At the height of the Depression, nearly one out of every four workers could not find a job. There was no government unemployment insurance then, and many became increasingly desperate and lost hope. One Houston woman told a welfare worker: "I've given up ever amounting to anything. It's no use." People lost their life savings when banks, which were uninsured, could no longer pay out the money that belonged to their customers.

Republican President Herbert Hoover, who took office just months before the stock market crash, relied on the growth of private business to get the country out of the Depression. That simply did not work, and Hoover overwhelmingly lost

the 1932 election to Franklin Delano Roosevelt, a Democrat and distant cousin of Theodore. FDR brought renewed confidence to the nation. In his first Inaugural Address, he declared, "The only thing we have to fear is fear itself." FDR was a hugely optimistic person. Struck with polio as an adult, he could not walk on his own. FDR overcame that obstacle to continue his political career.

Franklin Roosevelt came from an extremely wealthy and powerful New York family, yet he strove to speak for the common person. In turn, ordinary citizens responded to him with such trust that he was elected to four terms—the only President ever to have more than two terms in office. (The 22nd Amendment, ratified in 1951, now limits Presidents to two terms in office.)

When FDR accepted the Democratic nomination for President, he stated, "I pledge you, I pledge myself, to a new deal for the American people." Over the next five years, the New Deal became a set of programs larger and more ambi-

WORLD'S HIGHEST STANDARD OF LIVING

There's no way like the American Way

This advertisement boasting about the good life in America contrasts sharply with the reality of the hard times experienced by millions of Americans during the Depression and by these flood victims.

tious than anything the Progressives had ever dreamed possible. Together with Congress, FDR created government programs to help keep banks from folding; to put the unemployed to work building roads and dams and making improvements to national parks; to prop up agricultural prices; to get businesses to work together to control prices and production; to promote labor unions; to construct and operate electric power plants; and even to paint beautiful murals in thousands of post offices.

The New Deal was the most dramatic peacetime display of government power in American history. Yet FDR had many critics. Conservatives called the New Deal socialistic because they thought it transferred too much power from private businesses and individuals to the government. Socialists and communists—an important political and cultural force in the 1930s—thought that the New Deal had not gone nearly far enough to overcome the great poverty, despair, and inequality caused by the Depression. They worried that FDR's actions would only serve to repair and keep in place an economic system that kept most of the wealth in the hands of a few.

FDR's most powerful critic was oddly both "conservative" and "radical." His name was Huey P. Long, and his story tells us much about the state of American democracy during this period.

Huey P. Long

★ *Friend of the Common Man or Potential Dictator?* ★

HUEY P. LONG wanted to make American society more equal, but he didn't always use the democratic process to accomplish his goals. Indeed, many scholars of American history rank Long at the top of their list of potential dictators, and President Franklin Roosevelt called him one of the "most dangerous men in America."

Long was born in Winn Parish in 1893. The citizens of this part of the hill country of Louisiana had long been active participants in the Populist and socialist movements. Long built on that tradition in his career in state politics. Elected governor in 1928, Long used his office to attack the most powerful interests in Louisiana: the oil companies, the utilities, and New Orleans bankers. He passed a tax plan that made the rich pay more, and he provided much-improved schools and medical care for the poor.

But transforming Louisiana was not enough for Huey P. Long. To gain more power, he turned his attention to the national political scene. He was a prominent supporter of FDR in 1932 and was elected to the Senate that year himself. But within a year, he and the President had become enemies. Long believed that the New Deal gave the federal government too much power. He thought the states should have more power. He also believed the New Deal did not go far enough in taking money from the rich and making it available to the poor, so he developed an alternative, called the Share Our Wealth plan. Its purpose was "to break up the swollen fortunes of America and to spread the wealth among all the people" by taxing the super rich. "Every Man a King!" Long shouted.

Americans began to flock to his cause and even consider him for President.

But Long abused his power. As governor of Louisiana, he stripped almost all power from Louisiana's courts and local governments and required state government workers to turn over part of their incomes to fund his political machine. He used intimidation to make sure that his decisions went unchallenged. This abuse of power cost him his life. In 1935 he was assassinated while walking through the state capitol by the son of a man whose career he had destroyed.

Long had many important ideas. But in the end, his willingness to go to extremes to get what he wanted doomed the hopes of millions of ordinary Americans who believed that Long represented their best chance for equality.

FOR ALL HIS FAULTS, Huey Long was correct about one thing. The New Deal did not fully solve the country's economic problems. After an initial recovery, the economy remained in a slump with massive unemployment through the 1930s.

The ecological crisis called the Dust Bowl compounded the sense Americans had that recovery would never come. Starting in 1932, huge dust storms gripped the southern Great Plains, the result of too much get-rich-quick farming on fragile soil. Three hundred thousand poor farmers had no choice but to abandon the region and search for work elsewhere. Many headed for California.

FDR launched a Second New Deal in 1935 to try to solve the problems Americans continued to face. Many important policies resulted, including a Social Security Act that provided a government pension to the retired and disabled. But in 1938 the New Deal stalled. Conservative Republicans gained control of Congress. Franklin Roosevelt's political magic seemed to have run out.

Then came the fateful day that continues to "live in infamy."

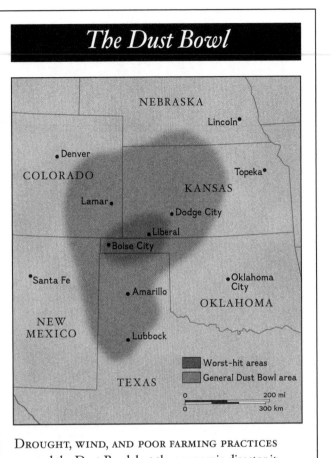

The Dust Bowl

DROUGHT, WIND, AND POOR FARMING PRACTICES created the Dust Bowl, but the economic disaster it caused led to much needed land-use reforms.

During the Dust Bowl, loose soil picked up by the wind created "black blizzards" that darkened the sky for miles. People had trouble breathing, and car engines became clogged and wouldn't start. The human costs of the Dust Bowl were enormous. Many families lost their farms. Some ended up homeless (right); others migrated from places like Oklahoma to California.

CHAPTER SEVEN

WAR, PROSPERITY, AND SOCIAL CHANGE

★ *1941-1968* ★

"Let both sides join in creating...a new world of law."

JOHN F. KENNEDY

1941

President Franklin D. Roosevelt in a radio broadcast announced America's entry into World War II after the Japanese attacked Pearl Harbor, Hawaii, on the morning of December 7, 1941.

1950s

The outbreak of the Korean War in 1950 made many Americans worry about the possibility of nuclear attack. Backyard bomb shelters like this one gained popularity in the early years of the Cold War.

1955

In April, after two years of testing, the government approved a polio vaccine developed by Dr. Jonas Salk (above, left) that helped bring this crippling disease under control.

1957

Following a court order, this girl and eight other African Americans bravely became the first black students to enroll in a previously all-white high school in Little Rock, Arkansas.

WHEN THE JAPANESE BOMBED PEARL HARBOR, Hawaii, in the early morning hours of December 7, 1941, the course of American history changed forever. The United States had been attacked on its own soil. Americans would never again feel that being separated from most of the rest of the world by two oceans would protect them from foreign wars.

The Pearl Harbor attack immediately led to the entrance of the United States into World War II and exposed it to all the horrors of the war. It also began a period of global leadership and economic prosperity for the country. Henry Luce, editor of *Time* magazine, named the postwar era "The American Century," because of the influence of American culture around the world.

1961

Shortly after his Inauguration, President John F. Kennedy created the Peace Corps, an organization of volunteers committed to helping people in less developed countries improve their lives.

1962

Astronaut John Glenn stands in front of the capsule in which he became the first American to orbit the Earth. His achievement was a major step toward the U.S. goal of beating the Russians to the moon.

1963

The Kennedy family, including Caroline and John Jr., led the nation in mourning the loss of its youngest elected President, John F. Kennedy, after his assassination in Dallas, Texas.

1965

Lyndon Johnson ordered the first U.S. ground troops into Vietnam. More than 58,000 Americans would lose their lives fighting communism in what became America's most unpopular war.

Historians disagree in their assessment of the postwar years. Some see them as a time of great progress toward a more democratic society, with significant progress in civil rights. Others describe these years as dangerous ones for American democracy. Tensions between the Soviet Union and the United States were so great that there was a real threat the world would come to an end in a nuclear war. According to these scholars, anticommunist hysteria and a focus on material wealth seemed to be all that most people cared about. Still other historians believe the conflicts of the 1960s brought about the downfall of American society. Immorality and selfishness triumphed, they say, with patriotism going out the window.

Whatever one's view of these years, this was surely one of the most interesting and varied periods in all of American history.

BY THE TIME OF THE ATTACK on Pearl Harbor, the conflicts that brought about World War II had been raging for several years. Italy had taken over Ethiopia in 1935, Japan had launched a full-scale invasion of China in 1937, and Germany had seized Austria and part of Czechoslovakia in 1938 and early 1939. All of these aggressor countries had profoundly undemocratic governments. The National Socialist (Nazi) Adolf Hitler in Germany and the Fascist Benito Mussolini in Italy made it clear that they cared only about power, not freedom. Mussolini proudly proclaimed: "We have buried the putrid corpse of liberty." The Germans and the Japanese dreamed of establishing empires that would lead to complete German control over Europe and Japanese control over Asia. These governments arrested, and often executed, political enemies. In Germany, groups such as Jews, Gypsies, homosexuals, the mentally ill, and the disabled were rounded up and eventually murdered by the Nazis.

Germany, Italy, and Japan formed a military alliance known as the Axis. Countries that opposed them, particularly Britain and, after 1941, the United States and the Soviet Union, were known as the Allies. Despite the clear threat to world peace and political liberty from Axis conquests of peaceful nations, Americans were not ready to rush into war in 1939. The great majority believed that World War I had accomplished nothing good. They felt it was better to stay out of European affairs. This isolationism was so strong that Congress passed three Neutrality Acts during the mid-1930s.

World War II would prove to be the most momentous event in the history of the 20th century, pitting defenders of democracy against dictators who wanted to rule as much of the world as possible. Adolf Hitler (above) became chancellor of Germany in 1933 and controlled most of the countries of Europe by the time the U.S. entered the war in December 1941. In 1945, U.S. Marines raised the flag on the Pacific island of Iwo Jima (left), site of one of the bloodiest battles in the war to stop Japan from creating an empire in Asia.

Franklin Delano Roosevelt (FDR) was elected for a third term in 1940. This was the first time in U.S. history that a President had served more than two consecutive terms in office. Roosevelt promised peace, but he was gravely concerned about the threat to democracy. Americans finally began to take the possibility of war seriously when Germany, in an act of pure aggression, invaded Poland on September 1, 1939. When Britain and France declared war on Germany two days later, World War II officially began. The Nazis quickly took over most of the rest of Europe, smashing the

In this cartoon, death marches with the Axis alliance. The leaders of Italy and Japan are chained to Germany's air force chief.

armies of Denmark, Norway, the Netherlands, Belgium, Luxembourg, and France by the middle of 1940. The year before, Germany had signed a non-aggression pact with its most powerful enemy in the East, the Soviet Union, allowing the Soviets to take over the Baltic States and eastern Poland. This made it possible for Hitler to devote his energy to attacking Britain, America's closest ally.

FDR feared the United States would be next in the Nazis' line of fire, so he promised "all aid to the Allies short of war." He asked Congress to pass the first-ever peacetime draft, which required young

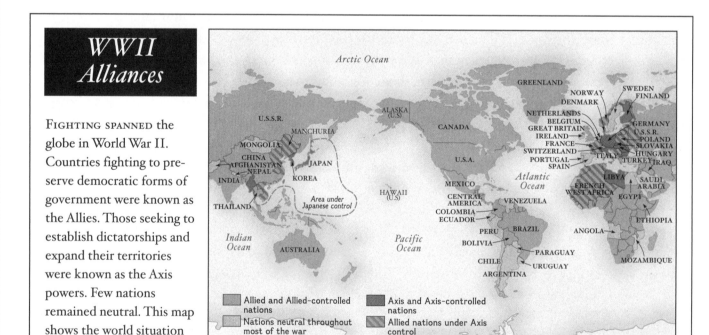

WWII Alliances

FIGHTING SPANNED the globe in World War II. Countries fighting to preserve democratic forms of government were known as the Allies. Those seeking to establish dictatorships and expand their territories were known as the Axis powers. Few nations remained neutral. This map shows the world situation in 1941.

Allied and Allied-controlled nations
Nations neutral throughout most of the war
Axis and Axis-controlled nations
Allied nations under Axis control

U.S. sailors brave a fiery sea to rescue a comrade fleeing the burning battleship U.S.S. West Virginia *after the Japanese bombed Pearl Harbor. Many American homes displayed banners (above) to show a family member was in the military.*

men to sign up for military service, and the United States began to lend weapons to the Allies. When Hitler launched a surprise invasion of the Soviet Union on June 22, 1941, it was clear that he wanted total world domination.

While Americans were focusing on the conflict in Europe, war came upon them from Asia. Tensions between Japan and the United States had mounted toward the end of the 1930s when Japan had gained control of parts of China. To get food for its army and to obtain tin, rubber, iron, and other crucial resources, Japan invaded Southeast Asia. In response, the United States cut off shipments of scrap iron, steel, and oil to Japan. Realizing that America stood in the way of its dreams of empire, Japan began planning an attack against American sea and air power at Pearl Harbor. The attack came as a complete surprise on December 7, 1941. In just two hours, Japan inflicted great damage to American battleships, destroyers, and planes. Nearly 2,400 Americans died. Hours later, Japanese pilots attacked other U.S. military installations in Guam, Wake Island, and the Philippines.

On December 8, FDR asked Congress to declare war on Japan, calling December 7 "a date that will live in infamy." There was one dissenting

vote (from Montana Congresswoman Jeannette Rankin who, as a pacifist, was opposed to any war). When Congress declared war on Japan, Japan's Axis allies, Germany and Italy, declared war on the United States. America would now be fighting its largest war ever, in Europe, Asia, and Africa and throughout the Atlantic and Pacific Oceans.

The war did not begin in a promising way for the Allies. Hitler had a tight grip on Europe, and Japan controlled much of China, Southeast Asia, and the Pacific. By the end of 1942, the tide had begun to turn on both fronts. In Europe, the Soviets took advantage of their brutal winter to launch a counterattack against the Nazis, who had conquered most of the western part of the country. The Germans were defeated at the Battle of Stalingrad, where nearly all of the 330,000 German soldiers died. By 1943, the Soviets had begun their long march westward, eventually reaching Berlin, Germany's capital. The cost would be high, though: By war's end, more than 20 million Soviets would be dead.

Meanwhile the Japanese had conquered almost all of Europe's colonies in Asia. They promised liberation from centuries of oppression, but they brought even harsher cruelties to these countries. As a result, the initial support that the Japanese received turned to opposition. Then, in June 1942, the Americans sank four of Japan's aircraft carriers in the Battle of Midway. This was the beginning of the end of Japanese control of the Pacific. No longer did Japan threaten Hawaii or the West Coast of the United States (which did receive some isolated Japanese bombing). The Americans could now begin their "island hopping" campaign, capturing bases where planes could refuel and resupply on their way to attacking the Japanese mainland.

World War II quickly became a war that almost all Americans proudly supported. World War II is still referred to as The Good War—the time when we fought for democracy and defeated some of the most monstrous governments the world has ever seen.

Democracy did not always win on the home front, though. The worst offense against people's liberties came in February 1942 when President Roosevelt formally took away the civil rights of people living in the United States who were from a country we were fighting, whether they were U.S. citizens or not. FDR specifically ordered the relocation of more than 100,000 Japanese Americans away from areas along the West Coast. Karl Yoneda wrote of his first reactions to his "camp" at Manzanar, California: "There were no lights, stoves, or window panes. My two cousins and I, together with seven others, were crowded into a 25 x 30 foot room....The next morning we discovered that there were no toilets or washrooms."

The President and the military charged that Japanese Americans were conspiring with Japan against the United States even though intelligence reports concluded that almost all Japanese Americans were loyal U.S. citizens. Indeed, many went on to fight heroically in Europe as part of the 442nd Regimental Combat Team, the most decorated unit in U. S. history. (They were not allowed

Most Americans were eager to make whatever sacrifices were needed to support the war effort. This giant cash register in New York City kept a tally of sales of war bonds.

to serve in the Pacific.) Still, the Supreme Court upheld the relocation program. Not until 1988 did the U.S. government apologize to Japanese Americans for this treatment.

Other groups suffered discrimination during the war. Mexican Americans wearing distinctive "zoot suits" were attacked by military personnel who believed the youths were avoiding the draft. This led to five days of rioting in Los Angeles.

Roosevelt signed an order banning racial discrimination in war industries, but this did not bring racial peace. Whites rioted against blacks throughout the war. The worst of these more than 200 conflicts came in 1943 in Detroit, where 34 people were killed. Despite their own enthusiasm for a war being fought against Nazi racism, black Americans were placed in segregated military units. In Salina, Kansas, a restaurant would serve

Americans fought in World War II primarily to preserve our democratic freedoms but also to combat Hitler's racism. But along the West Coast the United States took away the rights of thousands of American citizens of Japanese descent, along with Japanese citizens residing in the U.S., by sending them to internment camps, also known as relocation centers. The one above was in Wyoming.

German prisoners of war from local detention centers but not the town's black residents. Even the blood African Americans donated was segregated so as not to "contaminate" white soldiers. As African-American poet Langston Hughes asked: "Looky here America...You say you're fighting / For democracy. / Then why don't democracy / Include me?"

One segment of the population that gained more freedom during the war was women. Congress created women's corps in all branches of the military. They could not engage in combat, but they dug trenches, piloted airplanes in training missions, and, more commonly, served as nurses and administrators. As men went off to war, women took over jobs previously reserved for men. "Rosie the Riveter" posters celebrated women as highly paid welders, machinists, and shipyard workers.

The country was desperately short of raw materials to manufacture planes, guns, and bombs. These kids did their part to help by gathering scrap metal, paper, rubber, rags, and nylon stockings. Their fingers signal V for Victory.

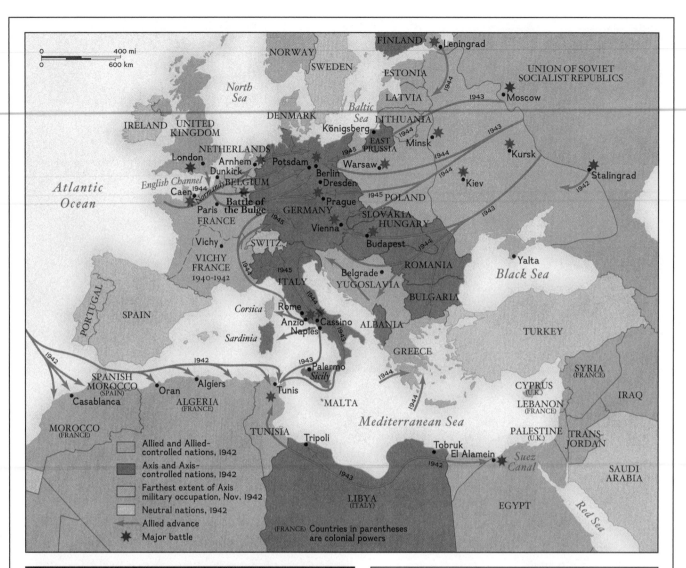

Map labels:

FINLAND • Leningrad
NORWAY
SWEDEN
ESTONIA
UNION OF SOVIET SOCIALIST REPUBLICS
North Sea
LATVIA
Baltic Sea
1943 • Moscow
DENMARK
LITHUANIA
IRELAND UNITED KINGDOM
Königsberg
EAST PRUSSIA
1944 • Minsk
1944
★ Kursk
NETHERLANDS
1945
Warsaw
1944
★ Stalingrad
London
Arnhem
Potsdam
• Berlin
★ Kiev
1942
Dunkirk
BELGIUM
• Dresden
1943
Atlantic Ocean
English Channel
Caen
1944
Normandy
Battle of the Bulge
• Prague
POLAND
1945
Paris
GERMANY
SLOVAKIA
1943
FRANCE
Vienna
HUNGARY
Vichy
SWITZ.
Budapest
1944
• Yalta
VICHY FRANCE 1940-1942
1944
1945
Belgrade •
ROMANIA
Black Sea
ITALY
YUGOSLAVIA
PORTUGAL
Corsica
Rome
BULGARIA
SPAIN
Anzio • Cassino
Naples
1944
ALBANIA
TURKEY
Sardinia
1943
Palermo
GREECE
SYRIA (FRANCE)
1942
1943
Sicily
1944
CYPRUS (U.K.)
SPANISH MOROCCO (SPAIN)
Oran • Algiers
Tunis
MALTA
1944
LEBANON (FRANCE)
IRAQ
Casablanca
ALGERIA (FRANCE)
Mediterranean Sea
PALESTINE (U.K.)
TRANS-JORDAN
MOROCCO (FRANCE)
TUNISIA
Tripoli
Tobruk
El Alamein
Suez Canal
SAUDI ARABIA
1943
1942
LIBYA (ITALY)
EGYPT
Red Sea

Legend:
- Allied and Allied-controlled nations, 1942
- Axis and Axis-controlled nations, 1942
- Farthest extent of Axis military occupation, Nov. 1942
- Neutral nations, 1942
- Allied advance
- ★ Major battle

(FRANCE) Countries in parentheses are colonial powers

Scale: 0–400 mi / 0–600 km

WWII in Europe and North Africa

IN THE FALL OF 1942, Hitler, having gained control of most of western Europe, ordered his troops to advance on Stalingrad, in the Soviet Union, and on the Suez Canal, in Egypt. They met defeat on both fronts. The Soviets headed west through Romania and Poland. British and American troops used Africa as a springboard to Sicily, then battled their way up the Italian peninsula. Allied invasions in southern France and at Normandy in the north opened new fronts in 1944, forcing the Nazis to retreat back toward German soil. They staged their last major offensive at the Battle of the Bulge in the Ardennes region of Belgium. Their defeat, plus news that the Soviets had taken Berlin, led Germany to surrender on May 8, 1945.

Supreme Allied Commander Dwight D. Eisenhower gives a pep talk to members of the 101st Airborne Division as they prepare for D-Day and the liberation of Europe.

Most women wanted to keep these jobs after the war, but many were removed by the combined forces of government, employers, and unions. Still, they had experienced the freedom that came from being able to support themselves and their families. From World War II on, more women began to hold jobs outside the home.

The war itself became much more terrible as time went on. By the middle of 1943, the Allies had taken control of northern Africa, which secured the Mediterranean and led to the liberation of Italy. Then the Allies tried to force the Axis to surrender by bombing civilians in a way never seen before. The worst raids were over Dresden, in Germany, and Tokyo, Japan's capital city. The biggest Allied invasion in Europe came on June 6, 1944. Known as Operation

The war gave women the unprecedented opportunity to work in high-paying factory jobs. This woman drives rivets into a bomber.

Overlord, or D-Day, it began when 175,000 troops came ashore on the beaches of Normandy, in northern France. Over the next few weeks almost a million more men landed to begin the liberation of Europe. In the following months, Germany lost its control of France, Belgium, the Netherlands, and Luxembourg. Hitler launched his last offensive in Belgium at the Battle of the Bulge in late 1944. Soon after the Allied victory there, the Soviets approached Berlin. The Nazi cause was now hopeless. Hitler committed suicide, and the Germans surrendered on May 8, 1945. V-E (Victory in Europe) Day brought huge celebrations throughout the United States.

That celebration was tempered by the news—and the pictures—of the grisly horrors of what

Under heavy German machine-gun fire, Allied troops wade ashore along 60 miles of beaches in northern France on D-Day, June 6, 1944. In spite of heavy casualties, the soldiers managed to secure the beach and clear the way for the largest amphibious landing in history. With the success of the D-Day invasion, Allied troops were able to begin the liberation of Europe from Nazi control.

President Roosevelt, looking worn and gaunt, sits between British Prime Minister Winston Churchill and Soviet leader Joseph Stalin at Yalta, on the Black Sea, in February 1945 (left) to discuss how to reshape Europe at war's end. Soon after, the whole world learned just how horrible Hitler's racism had been as the death camps for Jews, Gypsies, homosexuals, and the disabled were liberated (right).

came to be known as the Holocaust. American officials and Jewish leaders had long suspected the Nazis of ordering the mass murder of Jews and other "undesirable" populations. Once the atrocities of the death camps became public, Americans knew that they were witnessing the single worst horror of the century. As many as six million Jews were exterminated, along with several hundred thousand Gypsies and 60,000 homosexuals.

The world faced extinction as the age of nuclear weapons dawned after the U.S. dropped two atomic bombs on Japan near the end of World War II.

By the time the war ended in Europe, U.S. forces, with the aid of their allies, had liberated most of Southeast Asia from Japanese control and had successfully completed their island-hopping campaign in the Pacific. The capture of Iwo Jima and Okinawa brought American bombers close enough to Japan to launch intense bombing raids on Tokyo. The outcome of the war was now almost certain, but the Japanese refused to agree to the unconditional surrender demanded by the Americans and their allies. No one knew how much longer the Japanese would resist or how many more hundreds of thousands would die.

Franklin Roosevelt died on April 12, 1945, soon after starting his fourth term as President and about a month before victory in Europe. Vice President Harry S. Truman was sworn in immediately as President. His first job was to figure out how to end the war with Japan. His options became especially difficult when American scientists, with the help of Albert Einstein and others who had fled Europe, figured out how to create an atomic bomb. This was the most fearsome weapon ever created: a bomb that could use the mysterious power of the atomic chain reaction to destroy huge areas and unleash deadly radiation. Truman, believing the bomb would force Japan to surrender and save the lives of many American soldiers, finally gave the order to use the atomic weapon. On August 6, 1945, the B-29 *Enola Gay* dropped the first of these bombs on

WWII in Asia and the Pacific

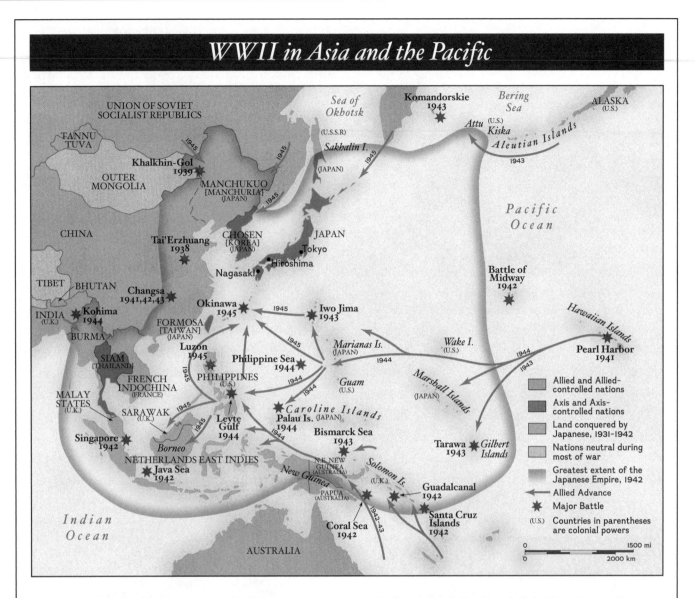

JAPAN'S RULE OVER THE PACIFIC reached some 4,500 miles from the mainland to the Solomon and Gilbert Islands in the east to the Netherlands East Indies in the west and the Aleutian Islands in the north. A much needed Allied victory over the Japanese fleet at Midway ended Japan's naval supremacy in the region. Fighting switched from sea to land as troops battled to take control of a string of islands including New Guinea, Borneo, the Philippines, Okinawa, and the Bonin Islands, which stretched northward toward the Japanese mainland. The goal was to gain bases from which to launch attacks on Japan. Only after the United States dropped two atomic bombs on Japanese cities did Japan surrender. The documents of surrender were signed on September 2, 1945.

Hiroshima, killing 70,000 people instantly and leading to the deaths—often through very painful radiation poisoning—of a total of 200,000. Three days later another B-29 bombed Nagasaki, killing another 35,000 people. Within a week the Japanese agreed to surrender.

At least 50 million people (including 400,000 Americans) had lost their lives in the "The Good War"—a war that was supposed to make the world safer. But people everywhere recognized that the explosion of the atomic bomb did not, in fact, make the world safer. Instead, people had to live

The Cold War started in Berlin in 1948 when the Soviet Union blocked ground access to West Berlin for 321 days. An Allied airlift brought in food and other supplies.

with the threat of a future war with weapons that could destroy the planet.

The uncertainty of the world's security became all too clear in the two years after the war ended. During that time the Soviet Union and the United States became bitter enemies. The two countries had very different political and economic systems. The Soviets claimed to believe in a form of communism that was based on the theories of Karl Marx, a 19th-century philosopher. While advocating economic equality for all workers around the world, in practice the Soviet Union was a brutal dictatorship. The longtime Soviet political leader Joseph Stalin ordered the killing of many more people than Adolf Hitler had.

The Soviets wanted to spread their form of communism throughout the world. They moved quickly to gain political control of countries along their border in eastern Europe. They installed Communist governments in some countries, such as Bulgaria and Hungary, and supported communist takeovers in others. Germany was divided between a Soviet-controlled eastern sector and a French-, British-, and American-controlled western area. The Soviet Union set up another "puppet" government in East Germany.

Truman realized that if western European countries were going to be able to stand up to the

Cold War Alliances

IN THE FOUR DECADES following World War II, the Cold War would spread around the globe. But Europe was the first and most intense battleground. The Soviet Union had fought with the Allies against Hitler. But now its armies occupied eastern Europe—countries such as Bulgaria, Poland, and Hungary—where it set up Communist governments. The stage was set for a bitter break-up between the former allies. In 1949, western European countries, Canada, and the United States formed the North Atlantic Treaty Organization, or NATO, to defend against Soviet aggression. Six years later, when West Germany joined NATO, the Soviets responded by forming the Warsaw Treaty Organization (also called the Warsaw Pact).

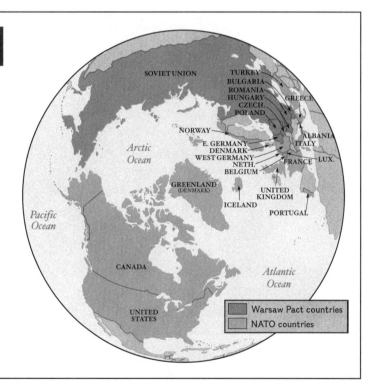

threat of Soviet expansion, they needed massive help to rebuild their cities, factories, and farms. This financial aid package was called the Marshall Plan, after Secretary of State George Marshall. The Soviets, who viewed the Marshall Plan as a sign of Western aggression, felt justified in using the countries of eastern Europe as a buffer against a takeover by the capitalist countries of the West. In 1946, Winston Churchill, the wartime prime minister of Great Britain, referred to this boundary between East and West as an iron curtain.

In 1949, the Soviets announced that they had set off their first atomic bomb. The arms race that followed led to the creation of two superpowers: the United States, with its democratic allies, on one side and the Soviet Union, with its communist comrades, on the other. Each side tried to outdo the other by developing a variety of nuclear weapons. Fear of the mass destruction that would result if either side used its nuclear weapons created a military standoff known as the Cold War.

President Truman, in what became known as the Truman Doctrine, declared that the United States had the right, even the obligation, to support anticommunist governments and movements throughout the world. Some critics saw this doctrine as a "strategic monstrosity" that would involve the United States in wars throughout the world. But within the government, the main debate was simply over whether to "contain" communism (keep the Soviets where they currently were) or to "roll back" the communists (push them out of eastern Europe and other areas).

Europe was not the only battleground of the Cold War. Communist rebellions sprouted in Latin America, Africa, and Asia, where many saw communism as a way to improve their lives. The most significant communist revolution was in China, where a civil war had raged before and after World War II. The Communist forces of Mao Zedong quickly proved to be more powerful than

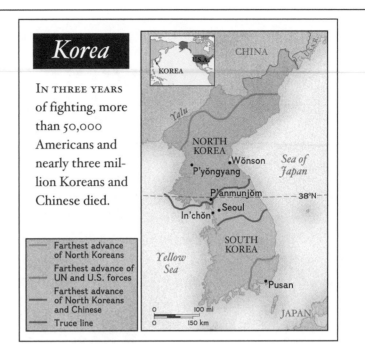

Korea

IN THREE YEARS of fighting, more than 50,000 Americans and nearly three million Koreans and Chinese died.

Farthest advance of North Koreans
Farthest advance of UN and U.S. forces
Farthest advance of North Koreans and Chinese
Truce line

the corrupt "Nationalists," the regime of Jiang Jieshi (known to Americans as Chiang Kai-shek). China fell to the Communists in 1949. Jiang Jieshi fled to the island of Taiwan, where he continued to claim control of all China.

Many Americans blamed Truman for "losing" the most populous country in the world. The following year, when the Communist government of North Korea invaded South Korea, Truman vowed not to let another country turn "red." With military support from the newly formed United Nations (the successor to the League of Nations except that the United States was a member), the United States went to war in support of South Korea. Initially, the North Koreans drove the UN troops to the southeast toward Pusan. American reinforcements landing at Inch'ŏn helped drive the North Koreans out of the south. When the United States advanced into North Korea, they were halted by Chinese troops south of the Yalu River and were eventually driven back beyond Seoul. After three years of fighting, the war ended in a stalemate. Korea was divided along the ceasefire line (roughly parallel 38°N) into Communist North Korea and pro-American South Korea.

Joseph McCarthy

★ Militant Anticommunist ★

THE COLD WAR was not just a conflict between the Soviet Union and the United States. It was a serious battle within the United States. The leader of the anticommunist movement of the 1950s was the Republican senator from Wisconsin, Joseph McCarthy.

McCarthy was catapulted to national fame when he gave a speech in 1950 in Wheeling, West Virginia. There "Tail Gunner Joe" (a nickname from his Army years) stated that he had the names of 205 communists in the State Department, the core of our government's foreign policy. For the next four years, McCarthy grabbed national headlines by exposing what was described as "a conspiracy so immense."

McCarthy shows Congress a map of supposed Communist Party activity in the United States.

He grilled witnesses from the government before his special subcommittee, almost always asking the question: "Are you now, or have you ever been, a Communist?" The people he accused were often assumed to be guilty. Many lost jobs though they had done nothing wrong.

The problem was, McCarthy had no names of communists in the State Department or anywhere else. Even worse, he used the label "communist" to attack anyone who disagreed with him or who expressed concern about the loss of civil liberties during the Cold War.

Eventually, he went too far. He accused the Democratic Party of being disloyal because of its "socialist" policies, which favored a larger role for government in the economy, and its supposedly pro-communist foreign policy. Then he accused the Army, and even President Eisenhower, of being sympathetic to the Reds—mainly because they would not agree to fire the people he told them to fire. Finally in 1954, after televised hearings, the Senate censured McCarthy for "conduct unbecoming a member." McCarthy was allowed to keep his Senate seat, but he no longer had any power. He died three years later.

In fact, there were communist spies in America and even within the government. Yet McCarthy's conspiracy didn't exist, and he knew it. We name the anticommunist crusade of this period McCarthyism, because Joe McCarthy was so powerful. The term is now used for any movement that makes irresponsible and politically motivated attacks on a particular group. Americans now generally agree that McCarthyism is dangerous to democratic political life because it destroys innocent lives and because it discourages the open discussion of different points of view necessary to make well-informed decisions.

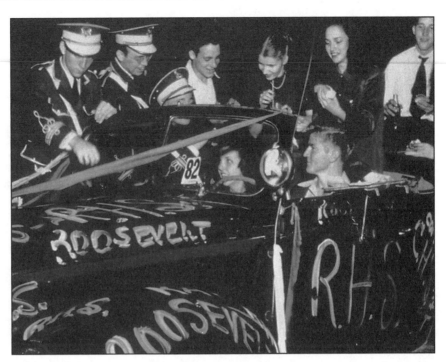

The 1950s was the decade when teenagers became recognized as a group with a culture all their own. Elvis Presley (above) was their rock-and-roll idol, and cars were their social meeting places (right). Prosperity made it possible for most American families to afford a new form of home entertainment: television. Popular kids' star Howdy Doody talks with his partner, Buffalo Bob Smith (below).

THE PRESIDENT WHO ENDED the Korean War and helped bring down Joe McCarthy was the man who had led the Allied command against Hitler: General Dwight D. Eisenhower. Elected in 1952 largely because he was a war hero, Eisenhower hoped to preside over a period of peace. Despite international tensions, "Ike" largely succeeded. Though he was a Republican, Eisenhower supported many of the liberal programs of Truman's Fair Deal, which had expanded the programs of FDR's New Deal. With Democrats and Republicans basically in agreement on domestic policies, the 1950s became a time of great prosperity for Americans. Millions of people took advantage of college loan and home mortgage programs to get a better education and move to the suburbs. With the aid of labor unions, which were more powerful than at any other time in American history, workers boosted their wages, moved up into the middle

class, and were able to afford more luxury items, especially televisions. This new invention spread rapidly into living rooms, bringing families together to watch programs such as *Leave It to Beaver* and *Father Knows Best* that emphasized traditional family values. Television also beamed in rock-and-roll stars such as Elvis Presley. Many parents were greatly concerned about this new music because they felt it encouraged teenage rebellion. Kids in the 13- to 19-year-old age bracket made up a large part of the population, and for the first time advertisers saw teens as big business. Indeed, the fifties could be called the golden age of the teenager.

Some groups, though, were left out of the general march to prosperity. African Americans continued to suffer constant discrimination, especially in the South, where they still could not vote, and their lives were in danger any time they protested their exclusion from schools, parks, or

The modern civil rights movement began with the 1954 Supreme Court case of Brown v. Board of Education. *Rosa Parks (below) refused to give up her seat to a white man and launched the Montgomery bus boycott. Over the next decade, African Americans campaigned against Jim Crow segregation, evident above in signs designating separate waiting rooms for whites and blacks.*

concert halls. Yet, the fifties saw the first organized stirrings of the Civil Rights Movement as blacks began to protest against segregation and Jim Crow laws. Although black people had been protesting their unequal treatment for centuries, they finally began to achieve substantial success in 1954. In that year, the Supreme Court ruled that school segregation was illegal. In a groundbreaking case, *Brown* v. *Board of Education,* Chief Justice Earl Warren and his colleagues declared unanimously that separate schools for blacks and whites were by their nature unequal, unjust, and unconstitutional. African Americans, led by chief NAACP lawyer and future Supreme Court Justice Thurgood Marshall, hailed the landmark decision as a second Emancipation Proclamation.

Change for African Americans, though, did not happen overnight. Laws upholding desegregation often were not enforced. Three years after the Court's historic decision, Americans would look on in horror as young black students in Little Rock, Arkansas, were cursed, pelted with rocks, and threatened with dogs as they tried to enter their previously all-white high school.

It became clear over the next decade that black people could not simply depend on the courts to defend their rights as American citizens. They would have to fight hard to get laws passed to protect their rights. The first major mass movement for African-American civil rights came in Alabama with the Montgomery bus boycott of 1955 and 1956. The boycott began when a black woman named Rosa Parks refused to give up her bus seat to a white man, even though she knew she was breaking a Jim Crow law. Parks was an NAACP organizer, and her arrest on December 1, 1955, put into motion a citywide bus boycott primarily organized by the Women's Political Council. These black women made sure that Montgomery's African Americans could get to work, even though most of them did not have cars. The boycott spurred the city's blacks to organize the Montgomery Improvement Association (MIA). The members of MIA elected a young minister named Martin Luther King, Jr., as its president. King used his speechmaking skills to keep up the spirits of the bus boycotters for more than a year. MIA sued the city to overturn the Jim Crow bus laws. The case went all the way to the Supreme Court, which ruled in MIA's favor. The boycott was a complete success for King, Parks, and the blacks of Montgomery, who now could sit

> "My feets is weary, but my soul is rested."
>
> MOTHER POLLARD, an elderly participant in the Montgomery bus boycott

anywhere they wanted on a bus. It would take a full decade, though, before the Civil Rights Act of 1964 made all Jim Crow laws in the United States illegal.

During that time the culture of America would change dramatically. The person who best symbolized the new spirit in the early 1960s was President John Fitzgerald Kennedy. JFK was the first Catholic ever elected President. During the campaign, he fought against the prejudice of Protestants who feared that as President he would take orders from the Pope. But once elected by a very slim margin over Richard Nixon in 1960, he put these fears to rest and became quite popular. Kennedy's youthful energy together with his wife's charm and his children's lively antics created a magical "Camelot" in the White House. (Camelot was the mythical kingdom of King Arthur.)

Television helped bring about the downfall of anticommunist Senator Joseph McCarthy, but it really came of age as a political tool in 1960 with the first televised presidential debate between Senator John F. Kennedy (left) and Vice President Richard M. Nixon (right). The handsome and youthful Kennedy won the debate—but by most accounts it was because of his appearance, not his arguments.

Members of the Birmingham, Alabama, Fire Department use super-high-powered water hoses to knock down civil rights demonstrators. Televised news reports showing the brutality in Birmingham, which included police dogs attacking young children, shocked the nation and persuaded President Kennedy to work for comprehensive civil rights legislation.

Like Martin Luther King, Jr., Kennedy had a gift for inspiring people to action with his speeches. In his Inaugural Address, he challenged all Americans to "ask not what your country can do for you—ask what you can do for your country."

JFK inspired the nation, but he did not accomplish much in his first two years in office. One exception was the creation of the Peace Corps, an organization that recruited young Americans to work with people in underdeveloped countries to help them improve their living conditions.

In 1963, Kennedy started to act more decisively. He had been scared by the Cuban missile crisis in October 1962, during which Soviet missiles aimed at the United States had been discovered in Cuba, a newly communist Caribbean country. The Soviet Union and the United States came closer to nuclear war then than they ever had before or since. Once the crisis was resolved, Kennedy moved to bring Cold War tensions under control with a treaty that banned certain types of nuclear-weapons testing.

He also began to support civil rights with much more vigor. Then, on November 22, 1963, Kennedy was shot in Dallas by Lee Harvey Oswald. To this day, many Americans do not believe that a lone gunman was responsible for this act, and it may never be known who else, if anyone, may have been involved in the killing.

In the years before Kennedy's death, the civil rights movement had become the leading issue in American life. African-American college students began the 1960s with "sit-ins" at white restaurants and stores in southern cities such as Greensboro, North Carolina. Those involved in the sit-ins would sit down at a lunch counter and refuse to leave until they had been served. In 1961, blacks and whites (mostly from the North) went on Freedom Rides through the South. Their goal was to desegregate buses as well as bus terminals. Several Freedom Ride buses were rocked by bombs, and gangs of whites severely beat many of the riders. The violent responses to these nonviolent protests were featured on the nightly news. Americans were forced to view civil rights as a national problem, not just a southern issue.

The years 1963 to 1965 were a time of terror. Firefighters turned their hoses on people in Birmingham, Alabama, and three men trying to register blacks to vote were kidnapped and killed in rural Mississippi. But it was a time of triumph, too. On August 28, 1963, during the hundredth anniversary of the Emancipation Proclamation, more than a quarter million people, whites and blacks, gathered to pledge their support for "jobs and freedom," and Martin Luther King, Jr., announced his glorious dream for America.

Martin Luther King

★ *Preaching Racial Equality* ★

"I HAVE A DREAM...that one day this nation will rise up and live out the true meaning of its creed: We hold these truths to be self-evident—that all men are created equal...."

These words were spoken by Martin Luther King, Jr., during the 1963 March on Washington. They speak to the dreams of equality and justice shared by all Americans. But there is much more to King's life than his "I have a dream" speech.

Martin Luther King, Jr., was born in Atlanta, Georgia. His grandfather and father were pastors of Ebenezer Baptist Church, one of the most important churches in Atlanta's black community. From his family, Martin learned the value of mixing religion and politics. He came to believe that it was just as important for ministers to protest against unequal salaries for black teachers as it was to preach in church on Sunday.

King, who went on to become a minister himself, believed in a personal, living God who gave people the strength to fight injustice. He blended his religious convictions with the ideas of pacifist Mahatma Gandhi. In fighting injustice, Gandhi, and now King, argued that people should never become unjust.

By the March on Washington, King was the most prominent leader of the Civil Rights Movement. In 1964, he received the Nobel Peace Prize for advocating nonviolence as a way to bring about social change. Yet many people intensely disliked him. FBI director J. Edgar Hoover believed, without any evidence, that King was a communist who was determined to destroy America. Hoover did what he could to damage King's reputation.

King came to believe not only in the harm of racial discrimination, but in the need to combat economic inequality. In the last years of his life, Martin Luther King, Jr., began to act on these economic beliefs. He traveled to the North to fight for the rights of the poor and of black people. In early spring 1968, he went to Memphis to help striking sanitation workers. While relaxing on the balcony of his room at the Lorraine Motel on April 4, 1968, King was assassinated by a white racist named James Earl Ray. The night before, he had told a crowd: "I just want to do God's will. He's allowed me to go up to the mountain. And I've looked over. And I've seen the Promised Land. I may not get there with you. But I want you to know tonight that we as a people will get to the Promised Land."

The 1963 March on Washington for Jobs and Freedom brought together hundreds of thousands of blacks (along with many whites) to demand voting rights and an end to discrimination. King's nonviolent approach to achieving black equality was increasingly challenged during the middle and late 1960s by advocates of Black Power, such as Malcolm X (below), who were frustrated by what they considered slow progress in achieving change. Rioting in African-American ghettos in Newark, New Jersey (above), and other cities broke out in 1967 and again in 1968 after King's assassination.

MARTIN LUTHER KING, JR., accomplished a great deal in his lifetime. With his leadership at the forefront of the Civil Rights Movement that he had helped to create, the United States took great political strides. Congress passed the Civil Rights Act of 1964, ending Jim Crow forever. The following year, the Voting Rights Act ensured that blacks everywhere in the country could go to the ballot box in safety.

With African Americans now able to vote in great numbers, the country saw a political revolution, with the number of African-American mayors, county supervisors, and congressional representatives increasing rapidly.

King's leadership within the Civil Rights Movement, however, never went unchallenged. In 1960, a group of young, primarily African-American college students formed SNCC, the Student Nonviolent Coordinating Committee. SNCC members did much of the nitty gritty work of the civil rights struggle, such as going door to door in isolated, poor rural areas. SNCC activists were far less in the public spotlight

The assassination of President John Kennedy on November 22, 1963, stunned the nation. Kennedy's widow, Jacqueline Kennedy (right), stood next to Lyndon Johnson when he took the presidential oath of office aboard Air Force One on the way back to Washington, D.C., from Dallas, Texas. Many Americans became obsessed with trying to figure out who really killed JFK. The Warren Report officially laid the blame on Lee Harvey Oswald.

than King and his supporters, and they were far more likely to get beaten up and even killed for their efforts.

In the North, Malcolm X offered a powerful alternative to King's policy of nonviolence. Malcolm, originally a member of the all-black Nation of Islam, believed that blacks should take control of their lives and emphasized the need to use "any means necessary" to fight white oppression. (Later in his life he left the Nation of Islam and became an orthodox, nonracist Muslim.)

By the end of the decade, SNCC and other groups, such as the Black Panthers, began speaking of "Black Power." Black Power supporters generally attacked what they saw as "white" values, "white" thinking, and "white" lifestyles, whereas King and his allies had emphasized their hope for integrating the best of all races and cultures for the greater good.

The movement for racial justice in the 1960s was much more than a struggle between blacks and whites. Mexican Americans and Puerto Ricans vigorously protested their unequal treatment in schools, in housing, and at the hands of police. Native Americans began to overcome tribal divisions to fight for their rights.

In 1965, this new spirit of equality led to the repeal of the discriminatory immigration laws of the 1920s. Massive migration from all parts of the world, especially Asia, resulted. Asian Americans, arriving over the next three decades from China, India, the Philippines, Vietnam, Cambodia, Laos, Korea, and many other countries, would demand equality as well.

The Great Debate

★ *The Rise of Feminism and the New Fight for Women's Rights* ★

THE 1960S WERE FULL of open strife and conflict. Thousands demonstrated in the streets, and TV networks covered news of the great public events of the era. But many of the period's most important changes happened in private. They occurred in kitchens, in station wagons, and at parks, as women tried to figure out how they—like other protesters in the age of struggle for civil rights—might achieve genuine equality.

Women had won the right to vote in 1920, but they continued to encounter a number of obstacles. In many states, women still could not serve on juries. Men often would not hire women to fill jobs they were qualified to do. When women did get hired, they usually received lower pay than men who did the same job. Married women often could not obtain insurance or credit cards in their own names. These could only be issued in their husbands' names.

Women were often viewed as the only people qualified to raise children and look after the household. Many married women felt trapped in their role of wife and mother, and an increasing number sought escape through divorce.

Betty Friedan was the first person who publically expressed the frustration women—especially housewives—felt. Friedan had been a liberal political activist and journalist before quitting her job to raise a family in the suburbs. Her 1963 book *The Feminine Mystique* has been one of the most influential books in American history. Friedan argued that women were discriminated against, not just legally but culturally. Psychologists and educators were just as guilty as lawmakers for their role in making women feel inferior. Women, Friedan argued, needed to stop living life solely for their husbands and children. She believed that women and men should work and live together as equals.

Friedan and many of her allies began the present-day feminist movement when they founded NOW (the National Organization for Women). Its goal was "to bring women into full participation in the mainstream of American society." NOW campaigned to end every kind of inequality and injustice. Above all, NOW pushed to have an Equal Rights Amendment added to the Constitution, formally banning legal and political discrimination against women.

This kind of feminism led to huge arguments. Friedan and her allies were attacked from two sides. On the one hand, many younger feminists in the late 1960s and early 1970s believed that

> "The feminine mystique...kept us passive and apart, and kept us from seeing our real problems and possibilities."
>
> BETTY FRIEDAN

Friedan and NOW were only addressing the most minor abuses of women's rights. These "radical feminists" thought that the power that men exercised in society, and especially within families and other personal relationships, needed to be totally uprooted. "Women's liberation," their new phrase, depended on the complete transformation, even the elimination, of traditional family life. These radical feminists staged sit-ins at offices and legislative halls in order to achieve their goals. Along with NOW activists, they founded rape crisis centers that offered medical and legal advice to victims, as well as shelters for battered women, where women could find protection from abusive husbands, boyfriends, and fathers. They fought especially hard for the right of women to have abortions. In 1973, the U.S. Supreme Court granted this right in the landmark case of *Roe v. Wade*.

Many women (not just men) opposed the feminism of Betty Friedan and the women's liberationists. They were led by experienced political figures, especially Phyllis Schlafly, who had long been involved in anticommunist political affairs. These conservative women believed in the need to uphold traditional values. According to Schlafly and her followers, a family, consisting of a husband and a wife, was sacred. Women and men each had their own special roles to play within the family and within society. Certainly, women should be treated fairly, but equality in all realms of life was not what God intended.

Polls showed that most women supported at least a moderate kind of feminism, but anti-feminists remained politically powerful. During the 1970s, they helped ensure the defeat of the Equal Rights Amendment. Despite that defeat, feminism has had a dramatic effect on the way American society views women and men. It has changed the way women are treated in the workplace, how much fathers and husbands are involved in raising children and in sharing household duties, and even the way women dress. So, the great debate continues, as Americans try to figure out the most effective ways to negotiate the often conflicting values of equality and traditional family values.

The sign, held by a member of the class of 1921 of all-female Smith College, tells it all. In the 50 years since these women graduated, there had been astounding changes in the lives of American women. The younger women, who are members of the Class of 1971 at Smith, and others like them, would serve as the main supporters of a renewed feminist movement represented by organizations like NOW.

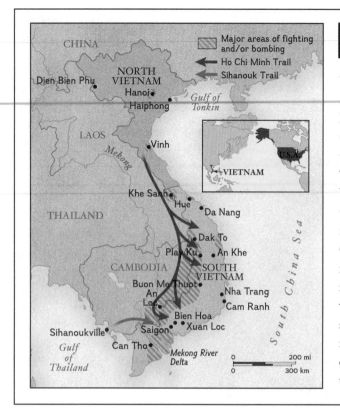

CHINA
NORTH VIETNAM
Dien Bien Phu
Hanoi
Haiphong
Gulf of Tonkin
LAOS
Vinh
Mekong
Khe Sanh
Hue
Da Nang
Dak To
Pla Ku
An Khe
CAMBODIA
SOUTH VIETNAM
Buon Me Thuot
An Loc
Nha Trang
Cam Ranh
Bien Hoa
Sihanoukville
Saigon
Xuan Loc
Can Tho
Mekong River Delta
Gulf of Thailand
THAILAND
South China Sea

Major areas of fighting and/or bombing
Ho Chi Minh Trail
Sihanouk Trail

U.S.A.
VIETNAM

0   200 mi
0   300 km

Vietnam War

UNITED STATES INVOLVEMENT IN VIETNAM in the 1950s and early 1960s consisted of sending military advisers to help the South Vietnamese in their struggle against Communists in the North. But when it was reported that North Vietnam had fired on U.S. ships in the Gulf of Tonkin, President Johnson responded by bombing North Vietnam and sending in ground troops in 1965. Within three years, more than a half million Americans were fighting in the jungles and cities of Southeast Asia. Communist supplies and troops were carried along two major trails *(see map)*. Fighting was heaviest in the west, in the delta of the Mekong River, and along the border with Cambodia. Years of fighting failed to bring any signs that the Communists could be defeated. Pressure from antiwar protests led President Nixon to begin withdrawing U.S. troops in 1969. In 1975 South Vietnam fell to the Communists.

THE PRESIDENT WHO PRESIDED OVER this great opening of American society was John Kennedy's Vice President and successor, Lyndon Baines Johnson. Vowing to honor Kennedy's legacy, Johnson went even further than JFK in his support for liberal social programs. LBJ provided crucial support for the 1964 Civil Rights Act and 1965 Voting Rights Act. He believed it was shameful that a rich country like America had so many poor people. Johnson declared that we could have a "Great Society," where the government would launch a range of programs to end poverty and benefit all Americans. At his urging, Congress enacted programs such as Head Start, a preschool program for disadvantaged youths, and Medicare, which helped pay health costs for the elderly. Johnson hoped that such government policies would help stop the rioting that became more and more frequent after 1965, when black ghetto residents became increasingly frustrated about their slow progress toward racial and economic equality.

Unfortunately the Vietnam War kept LBJ from achieving his Great Society. Vietnam was the country where the Cold War became hot—very hot—for the United States. Since 1954, when rebels took control of the country from France, Vietnam had been involved in a civil war between Ho Chi Minh's Communist government in the North and the anticommunist regime in the South. In an effort to stop communist aggression, Presidents Eisenhower and Kennedy had sent advisers and weapons to South Vietnam.

LBJ went well beyond this indirect involvement by sending hundreds of thousands of U.S. ground troops into Vietnam. He was convinced that with American help, South Vietnam could win the war. But in time it became clear that no amount of troops or money was going to achieve victory. Money that was supposed to go to the War on Poverty at home was eaten up by the huge costs of the Vietnam war. As the war dragged on it became more and more unpopular and gave rise to

As the Vietnam War went on, ultimately becoming the longest war in U.S. history, Americans increasingly questioned why so many soldiers were being killed or wounded (above). Anti-war demonstrations ranged from peaceful expressions, such as sticking flowers in the rifles of soldiers (below) to violent confrontations. The increasing unpopularity of the war finally convinced LBJ not to run for reelection.

a strong antiwar movement at home. By 1967 anti-war rallies, made up largely of college students, were drawing as many as 300,000 people. Protesters argued that a democratic country such as the United States should not be forcing its form of government and way of life on other countries.

By 1968, Robert F. Kennedy, the former President's brother, had joined the antiwar cause. He believed the war was immoral and victimized not only the Vietnamese but also poor and nonwhite Americans. When LBJ decided not to seek reelection in 1968, Kennedy became a candidate. He was gaining considerable popularity when he was shot and killed in California. RFK's assassination just months after that of Martin Luther King, Jr., caused many Americans to lose faith in the political system's ability to allow free and open discussion.

As police and protesters engaged in violent battles, the Democrats met in Chicago to nominate Hubert Humphrey as their presidential candidate. The Republicans chose Richard Nixon. George Wallace, the governor of Alabama, joined the race as an independent. The election of 1968 was one of the most tension-filled elections in U.S. history. The winner was Richard Nixon, who would dominate the national political scene for the next six years.

CHAPTER EIGHT

THE AGE OF CONSERVATISM

★ *1969 TO THE PRESENT* ★

"The era of big government is over."
BILL CLINTON

1969

On July 20, American astronaut Neil Armstrong became the first man to set foot on the moon. In 1971, astronaut James Irwin (above) was a member of the first mission to use a lunar rover to explore the moon's surface.

1973

The Supreme Court issued one of its most important decisions of the century in Roe v. Wade. This ruling, which ensured a woman's right to an abortion, was a major victory for feminists.

1974

On August 9, Richard Nixon became the first person ever to resign as President of the United States. Had he remained in office, he would have faced almost certain removal by Congress for his abuses of power.

1979

Nuclear power was one of the hottest issues of the 1970s. The issue became even hotter in March 1979 when one of the reactors at the Three Mile Island plant in Pennsylvania developed a leak.

THE LAST THREE DECADES have been turbulent ones for America. At times, Americans have seemed to be on top of the world, as when the United States became the first country to put men on the moon in 1969 or when the country celebrated the end of the Cold War in 1989. At other times, these decades have brought great tragedy, as represented by the Vietnam War, Watergate, and the attacks on the World Trade Center and the Pentagon.

It is difficult to evaluate history that is so close to the present. Events are still unfolding and will continue to play out for years, perhaps decades. Historians need time to gain a perspective on events. But this task is not just for historians. Everyone can, and should, take part in the conversation.

1989

The Cold War ended when one by one Communist governments in Eastern Europe fell from power. In Berlin, Germans celebrated the dismantling of the wall (above) that had divided the city since 1961.

1991

The United States led a coalition of nations in a successful war to free Kuwait from Iraqi control. The war helped demonstrate U.S. determination to shape a new world order.

1998

Workers show their frustration at the news that General Motors was closing yet another plant. A rise in foreign-car purchases forced U.S. manufacturers to cut costs by closing factories.

2001

The worst terrorist attack ever on American soil occurred on September 11, when terrorists crashed planes into the World Trade Center and the Pentagon. In response, President Bush launched a war on terrorism.

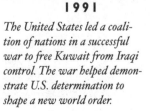

There is one thing on which most historians agree: People can change history even when events seem beyond their control. The decade of the 1960s was an era of radical politics when young people tried, often successfully, to transform the world.

Few people at the time would have dreamed that in just a few years, the country would enter a period of profound political conservatism, when leaders would seek to preserve rather than change the country's political and economic structure. The new era's defining figures would be four Presidents: Richard Nixon, Ronald Reagan, and two Presidents named Bush.

During the same period, the United States has become in many ways a "rainbow nation," in which people of all races and ethnic groups join together fully, if not always equally, in shaping the nation's politics, culture, and society. All these changes happened because millions of people decided that it was time for them to happen.

Perhaps the greatest lesson of our history is that our democratic system offers us the opportunity to shape history itself. This is an awesome responsibility and a truly wonderful opportunity. It is important to read newspapers, write to elected officials, talk with family, friends, teachers, and others, and, above all, get involved in debate. This is the "stuff of history."

THE LATE 1960S were one of America's most stressful times. The country endured riots, assassinations, and tumultuous antiwar demonstrations. Many people hoped that such events would eventually lead to a more peaceful world, with greater racial and economic equality. Others feared that the violence of the time would deteriorate into chaos, and they concluded that what was needed was law and order. This group, sometimes called the "silent majority," believed Richard M. Nixon, Dwight Eisenhower's Vice President, was the person who could save the United States.

Nixon was a controversial political figure. Many people felt that he had won his first seat in Congress in 1946 by spreading lies about his opponent. His dishonest campaign practices were in part responsible for earning him the nickname "Tricky Dick." Still, in the late 1960s millions of people were attracted to him because he vigorously supported the police, the military, and the flag. He appealed specifically to white voters, especially those in the South who were upset about the rapid pace of the civil rights movement. Although he held fairly liberal views on many social and economic issues, overall Nixon was the first truly conservative President of the modern era.

American pride ran high with the launching of the first space shuttle (left) in 1981. On September 11, 2001, the worst terrorist attack in U.S. history united Americans in grief (above) and in their determination to preserve their freedom by launching a war on terrorism.

The use of busing to force the integration of schools was one of the most controversial issues of the 1970s, especially in the North. Here an anti-busing student at a white high school in Boston uses an American flag to threaten an African-American attorney.

Busing students to achieve racial integration of schools was one of the most important issues of the 1970s, and Nixon was strongly opposed to it. Before the *Brown* v. *Board of Education* decision of 1954, most schools in America were segregated by race. In the South, this was mostly due to Jim Crow laws; in the North, it was due primarily to the fact that blacks and whites lived in separate neighborhoods. Schools in these neighborhoods were predominantly black or white. In the late 1960s, judges began to order black children to be bused to white schools and white students to be bused to black schools. At the time, busing seemed to be the only way to bring children of different races together to learn.

Opponents of busing argued that children should be allowed to go to schools in their own

Hippies, with their long hair and free-wheeling lifestyle, challenged tradition in the 1960s. Here a group of hippies celebrates on their psychedelic bus.

neighborhoods. Some ethnic groups, especially people of Italian, Irish, and Jewish ancestry living in northern cities, often said that it was not their fault that whites lived in white areas and blacks lived in black areas. Whites had not discriminated against blacks on purpose, they argued, so their children should not have to endure a 45-minute bus ride to and from an "inferior" school each morning and afternoon. Supporters of busing, including most veterans of the Civil Rights Movement, responded by declaring that whites had encouraged segregation by preventing blacks from buying houses in white areas. The conservative viewpoint eventually won out. By the late 1970s busing was no longer commonly used as a way of integrating schools.

Although Nixon sided with those who wished

Protests against the Vietnam War reached new levels of violence at Kent State University (left) when Ohio National Guardsmen killed four students. A veteran (right) mourns the lives of 58,000 Americans whose names are etched into a memorial wall in Washington, D.C.

to slow the progress of racial equality, his policies in other areas were more liberal. Like other Republicans before 1980, Nixon favored expanding the welfare system so that fewer families would have to live in poverty. He also supported the establishment of the Environmental Protection Agency to safeguard our natural resources.

Two events defined Nixon's Presidency: the Vietnam War and Watergate. Both would greatly damage the country and his reputation, and both offer important lessons about the abuse of power.

In his campaign for the Presidency in 1967, Nixon promised that he had a secret plan to end the war. Yet it took four years after Nixon entered office for the United States to withdraw from a war that took the lives of more than 58,000 Americans and more than a million Vietnamese. In fact, Nixon expanded the war into neighboring Cambodia and Laos in the spring of 1970. He did not have permission from Congress to do this, and it was one of the most controversial presidential decisions of the century. University campuses

erupted in revolt against the war. The most dramatic events occurred at Kent State University in Ohio. There, 28 National Guardsmen fired into an unarmed crowd of several thousand students, killing four of them. Ten days later, two students were shot to death by Mississippi state troopers during a demonstration at Jackson State University.

With the war coming home to American soil in such a deadly way, Nixon renewed secret peace talks, begun during the Johnson Administration, with the North Vietnamese. Finally, in January 1973, the two governments reached an agreement for the withdrawal of American troops.

Two years after the peace agreement, North Vietnam defeated the South and reunited the country under a Communist government. Thousands of Vietnamese fled the brutality of the new government. Those who came to the United States established vibrant communities that became one of the most visible legacies of the war.

Although Nixon is credited with bringing American troops home, his overall Vietnam policy

In 1972, Richard Nixon toured the Great Wall of China (left) during his visit to reestablish relations with Communist China. At home, Nixon engaged in illegal and unconstitutional activities. In his second term, the public turned against him (right).

was a failure. He had greater diplomatic success with other countries, most notably China. Seeking to expand trade and gain an ally against the Soviet Union, Nixon re-established relations with the world's most populous country. This was possible in large part because differences of opinion about the best way to achieve a Communist society had made China and the Soviet Union enemies.

Nixon had success with the Soviet Union, too. Although most Americans did not trust the Soviet Union, they believed that the buildup of nuclear weapons was expensive and dangerous. They welcomed the agreement, signed by Nixon and the Soviets, to limit the production of these weapons.

Instead of building on these foreign policy successes, Nixon destroyed himself. He was probably our most secretive leader. He had few friends, and he believed that most people were out to get him. Nixon combined these personal fears with a willingness to use illegal means to punish his political enemies both at home and abroad. For example, he supported the violent overthrow of socialist Salvador Allende in Chile, even though Allende had been elected by the people, because he worried Allende would turn against the United States.

Above all, Nixon hated to have government secrets "leaked" to the press. When Daniel Ellsberg, a former Defense Department worker, gave the *New York Times* classified documents showing how much the government had lied about the Vietnam War, Nixon ordered aides to break into Ellsberg's psychiatrist's office and collect information that would discredit Ellsberg.

The Ellsberg break-in was the first of Nixon's many illegal uses of the government to spy on and silence his political opponents. Nixon's whole spy system began to unravel when members of his reelection committee were caught stealing information from the Democratic Party's headquarters in the Watergate building, in Washington, D.C., on June 17, 1972. Over the next two years, it became clear that Nixon knew about the break-in and also that he was involved in a massive effort to hide these activities from the American people. Finally, rather than face impeachment, Nixon resigned—the first and only President to do so.

"Our long national nightmare is over," the new President, Gerald Ford, told Americans. Before becoming Nixon's Vice President, Ford had been a longtime congressman from Michigan. His brief

The 1970s were a time of major new concern for the environment, as seen in the first Earth Day (left). But American dependence on foreign oil, caused in part by the country's use of much more energy than the rest of the world, led to a major gasoline crisis in 1973.

Presidency is not especially memorable, but he did face some very difficult problems.

Ford inherited a tremendously tricky economic situation. Unemployment and inflation (a rise in prices and wages) had begun to spiral out of control. Increased government spending for welfare and the war had greatly added to the budget deficit, which meant the government was spending more than it collected in taxes. Then came the oil crisis.

By the early 1970s, the United States was importing most of its fuel oil from Arab countries in the Middle East. These countries stopped exporting oil to the U.S. when America supported Israel in the Yom Kippur War in 1973. Americans had to get used to waiting in long lines at the gas pump.

The great economic boom of the post–World War II period was over. The 1970s and early 1980s would be lean years. Despite these difficulties, many Americans continued to engage in new kinds of liberal activism. Building on the triumphs of feminism and the Civil Rights Movement, homosexuals began to fight for their right to live free from violence and discrimination. Environmentalism

AIM activist Oscar Running Bear stands guard at Wounded Knee.

became a household word. People showed their concern for the quality of Earth's air, water, land, and animal life by celebrating the first Earth Day on April 22, 1970. Consumer groups, led by Ralph Nader, increased their protests against the high prices and poorly produced products of many corporations. Native American groups also renewed their political activities. Among these groups was the American Indian Movement (AIM), formed by young, urban Native Americans. In 1973, armed AIM members took over the village of Wounded Knee, on the Lakota Pine Ridge Reservation. By holding their protest at the site of the Wounded Knee massacre of 1890, they hoped to draw attention to the poor treatment of Indians and the government's betrayal of treaty rights. Not all members of the Lakota and other tribes supported the action, which resulted in the wounding of a federal marshal and the deaths of two Indians when the FBI stormed Wounded Knee.

Latinos—Spanish-speaking people of Mexican, Central American, South American, or Caribbean heritage—are another group that has gained considerable power during the last 40 years.

César Chávez

★ *Speaking Out for Migrant Workers* ★

CÉSAR CHÁVEZ TOOK AS HIS MISSION organizing the most exploited group of Latinos: migrant farmworkers.

Chávez was born in Arizona in 1927 to parents who had fled their harsh life in Mexico during the 1880s. During the Great Depression of the 1930s, his parents lost their grocery store. Like many other people at that time, they survived by becoming migrant workers. They traveled from region to region, harvesting whatever crops were ready, living from month to month. Migrant farming was backbreaking work, done for low pay and with little protection from the abuses of dishonest and greedy employers.

After serving in World War II, Chávez rejoined his wife and eight children on the farm labor circuit in California. But he did not spend all of his time picking apricots or almonds. Instead, in 1952 he began working with the Community Service Organization, a group dedicated to fighting discrimination against Mexican Americans in schools, jobs, housing, and voting rights. Chávez realized that Mexican Americans should fight for their economic as well as their political rights, so he organized California farmworkers into a union. Although California is the country's richest agricultural state, at the time its migrant workers were paid some of the lowest wages and worked some of the longest hours under some of the worst conditions in the nation. Chávez and the union he helped form, the United Farm Workers (UFW), targeted large farmers. They asked citizens to boycott grapes, lettuce, and wine from California until migrant workers there received more pay and better treatment.

Chávez and the UFW scored tremendous victories in California, especially after they allied themselves with Governor Jerry Brown. Passage of the 1975 Agricultural Labor Relations Act gave agricultural workers the right to negotiate contracts with their employers. The UFW also won basic improvements in working conditions, such as access to toilets and drinking water in the fields and protection from the pesticides used on crops.

Millions of people around the world watched Chávez's funeral Mass on television in 1993. To honor his achievements, President Clinton awarded him the National Medal of Freedom a year after his death.

In 1978, President Jimmy Carter (center) brought together the leaders of Egypt (Anwar Sadat, left) and Israel (Menachem Begin, right) at the presidential retreat at Camp David. The result was the first peace agreement between an Arab nation and the Jewish state. In spite of this historic treaty, peace in the Middle East continued to prove elusive in the decades to come.

NOT ALL THE POLITICAL MOVEMENTS of the 1970s were as liberal as the one led by César Chávez. In fact, the most powerful trends were conservative. Taxpayers began to protest against high taxes and government spending. Issues like affirmative action, which gave preference in hiring and college admissions to women and minorities, suffered major setbacks in the courts and Congress. And most forcefully, a new religious right gained more visibility by the end of the seventies. Led by Christian ministers, these conservative groups, such as Jerry Falwell's Moral Majority, fought what they saw as anti-Christian immorality within American society.

The electronics and information industries revolutionized the economy of post-World War II America. The Apple I computer (above) had only a circuit board when it debuted in 1976. The owner of this one added his own keyboard and case.

The new conservatism in American politics soon made its way to the White House. During his 1976 campaign against Gerald Ford, Democrat Jimmy Carter promised to bring morality back into the political process. Once elected, he turned out to be, in the words of one critic, "a Democrat who often talks and thinks like a Republican." For example, Carter refused to expand welfare programs, even with thousands of families being thrown into poverty by the faltering economy.

Initially, Carter based his foreign policy on the effort to expand peace and human rights. This led to a major triumph when he brought the leaders of Egypt and Israel together to sign the first peace

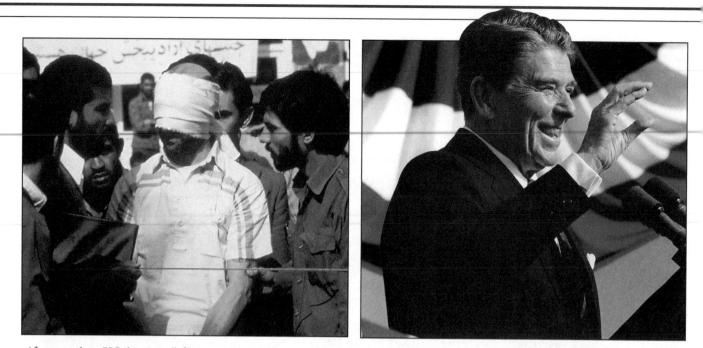

After 444 days, U.S. hostages (left) were released from captivity in Iran. Ronald Reagan, who was known as the Great Communicator, (right), promised to bring a sense of glory and triumph back to America. After the tragedies and humiliations of Vietnam and Watergate, many Americans were open to Reagan's optimistic message that called for renewed global power for the United States.

treaty ever between an Arab country and the Jewish state. But after the Soviet Union's brutal invasion of Afghanistan in 1979, Carter became much more interested in military solutions to America's foreign problems. Carter and his Republican successor, Ronald Reagan, both supported Islamic opposition to the Soviets in that central Asian country. But Carter angered Islamic revolutionaries in Iran by supporting the Shah, Iran's dictatorial but anticommunist ruler. After the rebels succeeded in replacing the Shah with one of their religious leaders, they humiliated the United States by holding 52 employees of the American Embassy in Tehran hostage for 444 days.

These hostages were not released until Ronald Reagan was sworn in as President on January 20, 1981. Reagan soon became the most powerful conservative political figure in American history, as well as the most influential 20th-century President after Franklin Roosevelt.

Reagan grew up as a Democrat in a relatively poor family in Illinois. As a young man he became a movie actor. His political career began when, as

president of the Screen Actor's Guild, he helped the government uncover Communist influence in the Hollywood film industry during the McCarthy era. In 1966, he successfully ran for governor of California as a Republican. There Reagan established a reputation for opposing high taxes and being tough with student radicals. In 1980, he defeated Jimmy Carter and Independent candidate John Anderson in the presidential race.

Ronald Reagan came into office as a crusader against big government. He helped push a massive tax cut through Congress. The immediate result was a sharp downturn in the economy that led to even more unemployment and caused many people to criticize "Reaganomics." But by the time of his reelection campaign in 1984, the economy had rebounded enough to allow Reagan to win a second term easily. Throughout his eight years in office, Reagan relaxed regulations designed to protect the environment and workers' safety in order to help businesses cut their expenses. Along with cutting welfare, this was all part of the "Reagan Revolution."

Sandra Day O'Connor

★ *First Woman on the Supreme Court* ★

ONE OF RONALD REAGAN'S more popular political decisions was his appointment of Sandra Day O'Connor as the first woman ever to serve on the Supreme Court. Since that time, she has become, according to many, the most influential woman in American politics.

Sandra Day was born in El Paso, Texas, in 1930. She grew up on her family's 200,000-acre ranch in Arizona before moving back to El Paso to live with her grandmother Mamie. As a child, Sandra showed that she had unusual talents. By the time she was eight, she knew how to shoot a rifle, ride a horse, and drive a truck. She graduated with honors from Stanford Law School in 1952 but could only get a job as a law clerk at a private law firm—even though all the men in her class, including her husband, John, were hired as lawyers.

The O'Connors settled in Phoenix, Arizona, where they raised three boys. When their youngest child was three, Sandra Day O'Connor took a part-time job with the Arizona attorney general's office. Her rise to political prominence within the state was rapid after that. In 1969, only four years after she took her first job, she became a state senator. Within another four years she became the majority leader of the Arizona Senate. A year later she became a judge. Then, in 1981, Ronald Reagan, seeking to name a conservative, a woman, and someone from the West to the Supreme Court, appointed Sandra Day O'Connor to the highest court in the land.

During her first seven years on the Supreme Court, O'Connor voted with the other conservatives. She sought to limit affirmative action for women and especially for racial minorities, and she supported the death penalty. Though she upheld a woman's right to an abortion, she thought state governments should be able to place limitations on that practice. During the 1990s, however, she was much more likely to vote for the liberal position than when she was first appointed. Since the Court was bitterly divided after 1988, O'Connor was often the crucial "swing vote" that resulted in either a liberal or a conservative decision.

Since 1993 there has been another woman on the Court. Ruth Bader Ginsburg is a liberal and a feminist, and so she and O'Connor vote differently as often as they vote alike. According to O'Connor, to understand a female judge, you have to know much more than the obvious fact that she is a woman.

The Reagan and Bush presidencies were times of great conflict as well as celebration. Oliver North (left) testified before Congress in the worst political scandal of the 1980s, the Iran-Contra arms for hostages affair. On the domestic side, when the white policemen who had been videotaped beating African-American motorist Rodney King were found not guilty, deadly rioting broke out (right).

THE REAGAN REVOLUTION extended to foreign affairs. Above all, Reagan was a staunch anticommunist who believed that the Soviet Union was an "evil empire." Declaring that he stood for "peace through strength," Reagan succeeded in getting Congress to approve huge increases in military spending. In 1983, Reagan ordered the invasion of the tiny Caribbean island of Grenada after communists overthrew the government there.

In what was to be the worst scandal of Reagan's presidency, he supported the Contras in Nicaragua, a revolutionary group fighting against the communist Sandinista government. High-ranking officials in the Reagan Administration secretly and illegally sold weapons to the same radical government in Iran that had held Americans hostage. Then money from the sale was channeled to the Contras. Although Reagan denied knowledge of the scandal, congressional investigations revealed that some of his aides had falsified documents and lied to Congress. On a more positive note, Reagan

> "Those who say that we are in a time when there are no heroes just don't know where to look."
>
> President Ronald Reagan

negotiated treaties with the Soviets to control nuclear weapons after Soviet President Mikhail Gorbachev initiated *glasnost* (political openness) and *perestroika* (economic freedoms)—policies that would soon lead to the breakup of the Soviet Union and the end of the Cold War.

The Reagan presidency was, for many Americans, a glorious time. The 1984 Los Angeles Olympics were a particularly proud moment for Americans, with lots of flag waving and cheering for American athletes. There was a sense that the country had recovered from the humiliation of Vietnam and the Iran hostage ordeal. But there were still deeply troubling problems in the country during the 1980s and into the 1990s. The economy grew stronger, but the distribution of wealth became more and more unequal. Workers found it increasingly difficult to buy a house or pay for their children's college education—two important symbols of middle-class America. The Northeast and Midwest were especially hard hit, as huge

The new electronic age had its own icons. Teenagers rocked to MTV (left), and Americans of all ages entered a new age of word processors, e-mail, the Internet, and the computerized office, in large part thanks to Microsoft's Bill Gates, shown here (right) with the next generation of personal computers.

steel and automobile factories shut down because they could not compete with lower-priced goods made overseas—particularly in Europe and Japan. This trend was known as "deindustrialization."

The economic slowdown contributed to worsening racial and ethnic tensions. Whites in certain areas, particularly the Northeast and parts of the rural West, resented the financial success of Native Americans who were taking advantage of exclusive treaty rights to own and operate highly successful gambling casinos. Increased immigration from Central America and Southeast Asia dramatically changed the cultural makeup of communities across the country. Many citizens worried once again that our borders were too open and our immigration laws were too lenient. These people feared that immigrants were taking away jobs from American workers and driving up welfare costs. In response, many employers argued that they needed cheap labor to be able to make a profit and compete with foreign prices.

The most deadly incidents resulting from tensions created by this increasingly multicultural society occurred in Los Angeles in 1992. There, four white policemen beat up Rodney King, a black motorist they had pulled over for speeding. A witness videotaped the incident. Soon what looked like a clear case of police brutality was televised throughout the world. But an all-white jury declared the officers not guilty on all but one charge. Los Angeles erupted with anger as news of the verdict spread. More than 50 people were killed and 1,500 buildings were damaged or destroyed in three full days of rioting. Stores in poor neighborhoods were looted and burned. In the end, almost 10,000 people were arrested.

But this was a complex riot. For example, more Latinos than blacks were arrested. Both groups were upset about economic discrimination and police abuse. In turn, many rioters targeted Korean business owners who had recently moved into the community. What at first looked like a classic black versus white riot turned out to be something much more reflective of the changing cultural makeup of the nation.

Throughout the country, illegal drug use

became a major issue. Especially in urban ghettos, "crack," a cheap and extremely addictive kind of cocaine, led to an increase in violent crimes as addicts used any means necessary to get more drugs.

In addition, by the end of the 1980s, auto-immune deficiency syndrome (AIDS) had become an epidemic in the United States. Spread among drug addicts through dirty, or shared, needles and in the general population through sex with an infected person, AIDS is an illness that destroys the body's immune system.

Drugs, AIDS, and rising poverty together were largely responsible for a sharp increase in the number of homeless people living on the streets of major cities during this period.

The country also was affected by dramatic events taking place in Europe in the late 1980s and early 1990s. The Cold War officially came to an end in a way that almost no one could have imagined five years earlier. Soviet President Gorbachev's emphasis on openness led people in the Soviet Union and Eastern Europe to criticize the repressive Communist governments that controlled their lives. The Communist Party lost its grip on these countries one by one, beginning with Poland, as the first free elections in decades were held. Nothing symbolized this amazing event better than the tearing down of the Berlin Wall, which had for so long

In October 1988, activists blanketed the Mall in Washington, D.C., with the AIDS memorial quilt. Each of the 8,288 patches represented a victim of the deadly disease.

kept East Germans from fleeing tyranny. In 1991, the Soviet Union—America's enemy for more than 40 years—simply dissolved as each of its republics broke away to form an independent nation. The Cold War officially ended.

While these events were playing out in Europe, George Herbert Walker Bush, Reagan's Vice President, was elected President in 1988. Bush continued many of Reagan's conservative policies. The most important issue Bush had to deal with was the Persian Gulf War. During the summer of 1990, Iraq, ruled by the dictator Saddam Hussein, invaded Kuwait, its tiny neighbor on the Persian Gulf, to gain control of that country's huge oil fields. The United States vowed to win Kuwait's freedom, protect neighboring Saudi Arabia and other Persian Gulf states from Iraqi aggression, and ensure its own access to Middle East oil. Congress only narrowly voted to authorize Bush to use military force to get Hussein out of Kuwait. By January 1991, more than a half million American soldiers and UN forces were in the region. Opponents of war believed that economic sanctions, such as cutting off Iraq's supplies of industrial goods and even food, should have been attempted before resorting to military action.

On January 16, Bush began Operation Desert Storm, an unprecedented alliance with a number of European and Middle Eastern countries. Desert Storm started in the air, with American pilots dropping 88,000 tons of bombs on Iraq and Kuwait. This action, plus a five-day ground war, finally forced Hussein to leave Kuwait. One hundred and eighty-four American soldiers died in combat, compared with estimates of 100,000 Iraqi deaths. One Iraqi who survived was Saddam Hussein. Bush later received strong criticism for not overthrowing his government, though neither Congress nor America's Gulf War allies had authorized killing Hussein or removing him from power. Even so, the United States had shown that it could act decisively as the world's only superpower.

George Bush enjoyed enormous popularity during and immediately after the Gulf War. But his failure to deal with the country's economic problems led to his defeat by William "Bill" Jefferson Clinton in 1992. (Independent Ross Perot, by focusing on government corruption and

The Gulf War caused massive environmental devastation. Before retreating from Kuwait, Iraqi President Saddam Hussein filled the skies with smoke by ordering hundreds of oil wells set on fire. Almost six million barrels of oil were dumped into the Persian Gulf, killing thousands of marine creatures. After the war, specialists were sent in to survey the damage and suggest measures that would help repair the environment.

Gulf War

THE GULF WAR was the first test of American power after the end of the Cold War. President George H. W. Bush crafted an alliance of Arab and European nations in order to remove Iraq from Kuwait. The war ended in a great victory for Bush's "new world order," although critics felt that the United States and its allies should have overthrown Iraqi President Saddam Hussein.

Later, in the wake of the September 11, 2001, terrorist attacks, Bush's son, President George W. Bush, included Hussein on his list of terrorist leaders potentially dangerous to America.

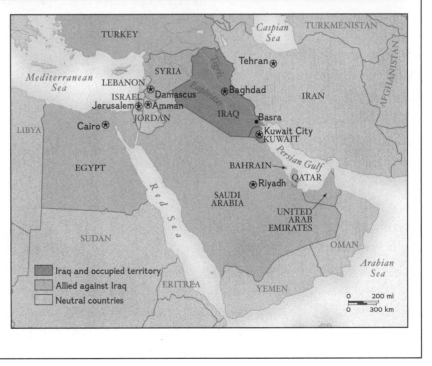

In October 1996 President Clinton (left, center), hosted talks between (clockwise, left to right) Palestinian leader Yasir Arafat, Jordan's King Hussein, and Israeli Prime Minister Benjamin Netanyahu. While peace seemed to blossom in the Middle East, domestic terrorism shocked the nation when a federal office building in Oklahoma City was bombed by antigovernment militants (right).

financial irresponsibility, received 19 percent of the vote, more than any third-party candidate since Theodore Roosevelt in 1912.)

Clinton called himself a "New Democrat." Unlike liberal Democrats, he did not believe that government should get bigger and bigger. Still, in his first two years he advocated a number of new welfare programs, the most ambitious of which was a national health care system. But this proposal, like many others, was defeated by Republicans who continued to control the Senate after the 1992 elections. These conservatives disliked Clinton and rallied to defeat the programs he proposed. They were even more successful after the 1994 Congressional elections, when Republicans won a majority of seats in the House of Representatives as well as in the Senate. Arch-conservative Newt Gingrich became Speaker of the House, promising in his "Contract with America" to dramatically reduce the size of the government, increase military spending, and work toward term limits—limiting the number of terms an official could serve in a particular office.

> "In crucial things, unity; in important things, diversity; in all things, generosity."
>
> GEORGE H. W. BUSH

Yet Clinton did win a few victories early in his presidency. One of the most significant was the North American Free Trade Agreement (NAFTA). The purpose of the treaty was to remove barriers to business between the U.S., Canada, and Mexico. But many in Clinton's own Democratic Party worried that the agreement would cause American jobs to flow to Mexico, where nonunion workers earned far less than union workers in the U. S.

Clinton also sent military assistance to countries, such as Somalia, Haiti, and Bosnia, where civil wars were being fought. He was extremely cautious about using American troops in these places. He feared the United States would be dragged into unwinnable conflicts that would produce casualties that the American people would not tolerate.

The 1990s were punctuated by news of seemingly pointless violence. Many citizens thought that anti-government ideas had gone too far when two right-wing, racist militia members blew up the Alfred P. Murrah Federal Building in Oklahoma City on April 19, 1995, in order to attack what they

President Clinton appointed United Nations ambassador Madeleine Albright (left) the first female secretary of state in 1996. She faced a number of diplomatic challenges, especially in the the former Yugoslavia, where fighting broke out between rival ethnic groups. American soldiers, like these in Bosnia (right), were part of peacekeeping troops sent into the region to help restore order.

saw as a tyrannical government. This bombing killed 168 people, including children in day care. The horror continued with a series of school shootings, including those at Columbine High School, in Colorado. There, two students killed 12 classmates and a teacher before committing suicide. Americans began to worry that a culture of violence was infecting our society.

Clinton was reelected in 1996. But shortly afterward, he was impeached by the House of Representatives. He was accused of lying under oath in a court proceeding about his relationship with a young White House intern, Monica Lewinsky. Most Republicans argued that Clinton needed to be removed from office for breaking the law. Most Democrats believed that what he had done was not serious enough to cause Congress to remove him

Despite controversies about exactly when the new millennium started— at the start of 2000 or 2001—people throughout the world celebrated Y2K on January 1, 2000. Although the media warned of major computer crashes that would cripple airlines, banks, and other commercial enterprises, none occurred.

from office. In February 1999, the Senate agreed and refused to convict Clinton. By then, Gingrich, realizing the unpopularity of his positions, had resigned from Congress.

Most Americans believed that the historic impeachment proceedings against Bill Clinton would be the most dramatic domestic political event for years to come. Little did they know that in less than two years, the country would be rocked by an event that would challenge our electoral process and the very foundation of our system of government: the 2000 presidential election.

The 2000 campaign was waged between two evenly matched candidates with similar programs. Democrat Al Gore was Clinton's Vice President and a former U.S. senator from Tennessee. He was proud of his record on the environment as well as of the efficiency he had brought to government operations while Vice President. Gore promised to fight for greater economic prosperity for working-class families.

George W. Bush was the governor of Texas, a former businessman, and the son of former President George H. W. Bush. Bush promised to lower taxes and use the presidency to bring about a more "compassionate conservatism." Ralph Nader, candidate of the environmentalist Green Party, charged that Gore and Bush were too supportive of corporations and were not doing enough for working- and middle-class Americans.

Polls showed Gore and Bush running neck and neck, with Nader being popular enough to affect the outcome of the race. Finally, when the votes were counted, all eyes were on Florida. The popular vote there was so close that the major television networks at first declared Gore the winner, then

Bush. Then they reported that the vote was too close to call. One thing was certain. Whoever won in Florida would be President. The election remained in doubt for five weeks while voting machine ballots were recounted and officials argued over what to do about ballots that had to be counted by hand or that had been improperly counted the first time. Meanwhile, Bush supporters claimed that Gore did not recognize the legitimacy of the Constitution. Gore supporters charged that Bush was trying to steal the election.

Ultimately, the Supreme Court, for the first time ever, was called on to make a ruling that would decide who would be President of the United States. In a 5 to 4 decision (with Justice Sandra Day O'Connor voting with the majority), the Court ruled that the recount in Florida must stop. This decision gave Florida's electoral college votes to Bush. Some hailed this decision as the Court's worst

Election 2000

THE PRESIDENTIAL ELECTION of 2000 was one of the most dramatic and controversial in the entire history of the nation. Democratic Vice President Al Gore garnered the highest number of popular votes, but his Republican opponent, George W. Bush, won the highest number of votes in the electoral college and became President on January 20, 2001. Florida became the center of attention after election day, as battles over who won this crucial swing state's 25 electoral college votes were fought for 38 days before being settled by the U.S. Supreme Court. This map shows how Bush's chief support came from the South and interior West, whereas Gore swept the Pacific Coast, the upper Midwest, and most of the Northeast.

*1 elector from Washington, D.C. abstained

| Presidential Election, 2000 | | | |
Candidate	Electoral Vote	Popular Vote	Political Party
Bush	271	50,456,002	Republican
Gore	266	50,999,897	Democrat

Firefighters raise a flag amid the ruins of the World Trade Center (left). Such images provided Americans comfort amid the horrors of the worst terrorist attack in the country's history. Immediately after the September 11 attacks, George W. Bush (sitting between Vice President Richard Cheney, left, and Secretary of State Colin Powell) met with advisers to plan a strategy to combat terrorism.

since *Dred Scott* in 1857. Others felt it was the only fair way to solve the problem.

So although Al Gore was the winner of the overall popular vote, George Bush won the most votes in the electoral college, the institution created by the Constitution to do the actual electing of a President. Because of the electoral crisis, George W. Bush took office as a greatly weakened President. Less than a year later, however, he had reached great heights of popularity. A horrible tragedy brought about this dramatic change.

On September 11, 2001, Islamic terrorists staged a devastating attack on America. As the nation watched and listened in horror, hijackers crashed two fully fueled jumbo jets into the twin towers of the World Trade Center in New York City and another into the side of the Pentagon, the national defense building outside Washington, D.C. Rather than creating chaos, though, the terrorists united Americans in a way not seen since Japan attacked Pearl Harbor in 1941.

President Bush and his advisers immediately announced an all-out global war on terrorism and went to work to find out who was to blame for the attack. Osama bin Laden, a wealthy businessman from Saudi Arabia, was named the chief suspect in organizing the attacks. Bin Laden, who had long engaged in terrorism to advance his fanatical brand of Islam, was hiding in Afghanistan under the protection of the Taliban, the radical Islamic group who controlled that country. When the Taliban refused to hand over bin Laden and members of his al Qaeda terrorist network, President Bush ordered an extensive bombing campaign of suspected al Qaeda hideouts in Afghanistan. His goal was to overthrow the Taliban and capture or kill bin Laden. To fight this war, the United States enlisted the help of allies such as Great Britain and anti-Taliban forces within Afghanistan. Meanwhile Bush continued to warn the world that any country that did not help in the global effort against terrorism was America's enemy.

The Great Debate

★ *How Should America Combat the War on Terrorism at Home?* ★

ALL WARS IN AMERICAN HISTORY have raised important questions on the home front as well as on the battlefield: Should the new American nation take away the property of Loyalists fighting for the British in the American Revolution? Should basic constitutional liberties apply to those jailed for supporting the South during the Civil War? Should the government crack down on immigrants and free speech in order to fight a war to make the world safe for democracy during World War I? Should the government jail conscientious objectors, censor news, launch an active propaganda campaign, and, most seriously, remove thousands of American citizens of Japanese descent from their homes and force them to live in relocation camps during World War II?

The war against Osama bin Laden, mastermind of the September 11 attacks, and his al Qaeda network of global terrorism is no different. The great debate is about how best to preserve personal freedom while at the same time increasing national security to prevent other acts of terrorism. There are great differences of opinion about how to accomplish these two goals.

On one side is President Bush and his administration, particularly Attorney General John Ashcroft. Their top priority is the complex task of defending the country against further terrorism. Terrorists in the 21st century use both extremely sophisticated methods and everyday technology to kill thousands of people. They use e-mail, fake identification, and illegal credit card transactions in order to plan their deadly activities. And terrorists operate throughout the world, sometimes in alliance with governments that hide them, making it even more difficult to track them down.

On October 26, 2001, Congress passed the PATRIOT Act to help strengthen America. (PATRIOT stands for Providing Appropriate Tools Required to Intercept and Obstruct Terrorism.) This act increases the ability of the government to use electronic devices such as wiretaps to listen in on phone conversations, to monitor e-mail and a person's use of the Internet, and to listen in on conversations between jailed suspects and their lawyers—conversations that have traditionally been kept private to ensure a fair trial.

Most controversially, perhaps, the administration wants to prosecute Taliban fighters and al Qaeda members in military rather than civilian courts. Military courts have different rules for prosecuting a defendant. Evidence that would be illegal in a civilian court (for example, evidence

gained by using force) can be used in a military tribunal. And only three-quarters of a jury, rather than the whole jury, is needed to determine whether a defendant is guilty or innocent. The administration wants the arrest and trials of suspected terrorists to be secret, so that it will be more difficult for al Qaeda and its supporters to spread information about their activities.

Critics of the government's plans are known as civil libertarians because they emphasize to Americans the importance of protecting their basic liberties. They warn that far too often when the country is threatened by external danger, citizens lose their freedoms to an overly aggressive government. Civil libertarians are concerned that many of the new measures being put in place to combat terrorism could be used against U.S. citizens, even though they are meant to apply to foreign terrorists and illegal immigrants. Once the government receives expanded powers to monitor

e-mail in order to prevent terrorism, what will prevent it from checking the e-mail of people who simply have unpopular—but not dangerous—political views? There is also concern about "racial profiling"—singling out certain groups, such as people of Arab ancestry, for observation. There are those who say even terrorists deserve open, public trials where basic constitutional liberties are preserved. They agree with Benjamin Franklin, who said, "They that give up essential liberty to obtain a little temporary safety deserve neither liberty nor safety."

It is too soon to tell who will win this debate. We don't know if the war on terrorism will be short-lived or if it will be fought for as long as the Cold War, with the same kinds of profound effects on American society. Two things are certain, though: that the great issue of security versus freedom will continue for the foreseeable future, and that the debate itself is an example of democracy in action.

Osama bin Laden (left) is the leader of the al Qaeda terrorist network that was responsible for the September 11 bombings. Hazardous materials experts (above) closed the Hart Building of the U.S. Senate during their investigation of mail laced with anthrax spores.

IT HAS OFTEN BEEN OBSERVED that Americans have been removed from the horrors of European and Asian wars by two oceans. But the world is becoming more and more "globalized." Businesses reach out to all parts of the world, American fast food and music is sold in the poorest countries of Asia and Africa, and the Internet makes it possible to connect instantly with people everywhere. There is great promise in bringing the world's people together in this way. Globalization might usher in an age of peace and understanding, in which the world's different cultures and peoples finally have the chance to meet and get to know one another. Unfortunately, at the time of this writing, peace and understanding do not seem to be winning. There have been further incidents of terrorism, including letters laced with deadly anthrax spores that made many Americans afraid to open their mail. Will the hatred and conflict created by the differences among peoples ultimately win out?

The events of history can't predict the future. History shows us that the past, for far too long, has been terribly bloody. But history can also help us see that the best human impulses—compassion, concern, and justice—have triumphed even in the most difficult times. We can only hope that compassion, concern, and justice will win again.

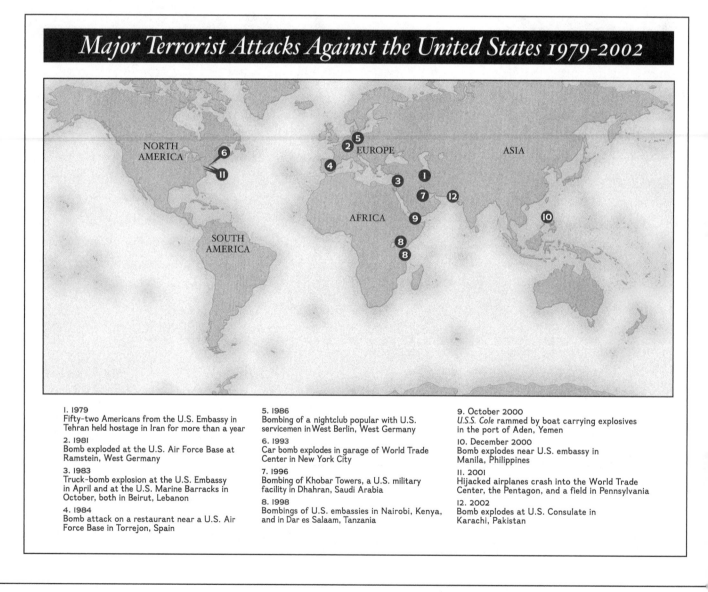

Major Terrorist Attacks Against the United States 1979-2002

1. 1979
Fifty-two Americans from the U.S. Embassy in Tehran held hostage in Iran for more than a year

2. 1981
Bomb exploded at the U.S. Air Force Base at Ramstein, West Germany

3. 1983
Truck-bomb explosion at the U.S. Embassy in April and at the U.S. Marine Barracks in October, both in Beirut, Lebanon

4. 1984
Bomb attack on a restaurant near a U.S. Air Force Base in Torrejon, Spain

5. 1986
Bombing of a nightclub popular with U.S. servicemen in West Berlin, West Germany

6. 1993
Car bomb explodes in garage of World Trade Center in New York City

7. 1996
Bombing of Khobar Towers, a U.S. military facility in Dhahran, Saudi Arabia

8. 1998
Bombings of U.S. embassies in Nairobi, Kenya, and in Dar es Salaam, Tanzania

9. October 2000
U.S.S. Cole rammed by boat carrying explosives in the port of Aden, Yemen

10. December 2000
Bomb explodes near U.S. embassy in Manila, Philippines

11. 2001
Hijacked airplanes crash into the World Trade Center, the Pentagon, and a field in Pennsylvania

12. 2002
Bomb explodes at U.S. Consulate in Karachi, Pakistan

Beams from 88 high-powered searchlights (left) form twin towers of light where the two buildings of the World Trade Center once stood.
This memorial in light marked the six-month anniversary of the terrorist attack that destroyed the buildings.

★ Historical Documents ★

THERE ARE MANY DOCUMENTS that are important in our history, but the ones that have been selected—The Declaration of Independence, The Constitution and The Bill of Rights, The Gettysburg Address, The Pledge of Allegiance, and "The Star-Spangled Banner"—define our nation and who we are as a people. You will find a host of other interesting documents by exploring the Web sites listed on page 219.

The Declaration of Independence
The Unanimous Declaration of the Thirteen United States of America

WHEN IN THE COURSE OF HUMAN EVENTS, it becomes necessary for one People to dissolve the Political Bands which have connected them with another, and to assume among the Powers of the Earth, the separate and equal Station to which the Laws of Nature and of Nature's God entitle them, a decent Respect to the Opinions of Mankind requires that they should declare the causes which impel them to the Separation.

We hold these Truths to be self-evident, that all Men are created equal, that they are endowed by their Creator with certain unalienable Rights, that among these are Life, Liberty, and the Pursuit of Happiness—That to secure these Rights, Governments are instituted among Men, deriving their just Powers from the Consent of the Governed, That whenever any Form of Government becomes

The painting at left shows Thomas Jefferson handing the Declaration of Independence to John Hancock in the Continental Congress in 1776. The relief above is one of a series illustrating the Preamble to the Constitution that decorate the exterior of the community center in Greenbelt, Maryland.

destructive of these Ends, it is the Right of the People to alter or to abolish it, and to institute new Government, laying its Foundation on such Principles and organizing its Powers in such Form, as to them shall seem most likely to effect their Safety and Happiness. Prudence, indeed, will dictate that Governments long established should not be changed for light and transient Causes; and accordingly all Experience hath shewn, that Mankind are more disposed to suffer, while Evils are sufferable, than to right themselves by abolishing the Forms to which they are accustomed. But when a long Train of Abuses and Usurpations, pursuing invariably the same Object, evinces a Design to reduce them under absolute Despotism, it is their Right, it is their Duty, to throw off such Government, and to provide new Guards for their future Security. Such has been the patient Sufferance of these Colonies; and such is now the Necessity which constrains them to alter their former Systems of Government. The History of the present King of Great Britain is a History of repeated Injuries and Usurpations, all having in direct Object the Establishment of an absolute Tyranny over these States. To prove this, let Facts be submitted to a candid World.

He has refused his Assent to Laws, the most wholesome and necessary for the public good.

He has forbidden his Governors to pass Laws of immediate and pressing Importance, unless suspended in their Operation till his Assent should be obtained; and when so suspended, he has utterly neglected to attend to them.

He has refused to pass other Laws for the Accommodation of large Districts of People, unless those People would relinquish the Right of Representation in the Legislature, a Right inestimable to them and formidable to Tyrants only.

He has called together Legislative Bodies at Places unusual, uncomfortable, and distant from the Depository of their Public Records, for the sole Purpose of fatiguing them into Compliance with his Measures.

He has dissolved Representative Houses repeatedly, for opposing with manly Firmness his Invasions on the Rights of the People.

He has refused for a long Time, after such Dissolutions, to cause others to be elected; whereby the Legislative Powers, incapable of Annihilation, have returned to the People at large for their exercise; the State remaining in the mean time exposed to all the Dangers of Invasion from without, and Convulsions within.

He has endeavoured to prevent the Population of these States; for that Purpose obstructing the Laws for Naturalization of Foreigners; refusing to pass others to encourage their Migrations hither, and raising the Conditions of new Appropriations of Lands.

He has obstructed the Administration of Justice, by refusing his Assent to Laws for establishing Judiciary Powers.

He has made Judges dependent on his Will alone, for the Tenure of their Offices, and the Amount and payment of their Salaries.

He has erected a Multitude of New Offices, and sent hither Swarms of Officers to harrass our People, and eat out their Substance.

He has kept among us, in Times of Peace, Standing Armies, without the consent of our Legislatures.

He has affected to render the Military independent of and superior to the Civil Power.

He has combined with others to subject us to a Jurisdiction foreign to our Constitution, and unacknowledged by our Laws; giving his Assent to their Acts of pretended Legislation: For quartering large Bodies of Armed Troops among us:

For protecting them, by a mock Trial, from Punishment for any Murders which they should commit on the Inhabitants of these States:

For cutting off our Trade with all parts of the World:

For imposing Taxes on us without our Consent:

For depriving us, in many Cases, of the Benefits of Trial by Jury:

For transporting us beyond Seas to be tried for pretended Offences:

For abolishing the free System of English Laws in a neighbouring Province, establishing therein an Arbitrary government, and enlarging its Boundaries, so as to render it at once an Example and fit Instrument for introducing the same absolute Rule into these Colonies:

For taking away our Charters, abolishing our most valuable Laws, and altering fundamentally the Forms of our Governments:

For suspending our own Legislatures, and declaring themselves invested with Power to legislate for us in all Cases whatsoever.

He has abdicated Government here, by declaring us out of his Protection and waging War against us.

He has plundered our Seas, ravaged our Coasts, burnt our towns, and destroyed the Lives of our People.

He is at this Time, transporting large Armies of foreign Mercenaries to compleat the works of Death, Desolation, and Tyranny, already begun with circumstances of Cruelty & Perfidy scarcely paralleled in the most barbarous Ages, and totally unworthy the Head of a civilized Nation.

He has constrained our fellow Citizens taken Captive on the high Seas to bear Arms against their Country, to become the Executioners of their Friends and Brethren, or to fall themselves by their Hands.

He has excited domestic Insurrections amongst us, and has endeavoured to bring on the Inhabitants of our Frontiers, the merciless Indian Savages, whose known Rule of Warfare, is an undistinguished Destruction, of all Ages, Sexes and Conditions.

In every stage of these Oppressions we have Petitioned for Redress in the most humble Terms: Our repeated Petitions have been answered only by repeated Injury. A Prince, whose Character is thus marked by every act which may define a Tyrant, is unfit to be the Ruler of a free People.

Nor have we been wanting in Attentions to our British Brethren. We have warned them from Time to Time of Attempts by their Legislature to extend an unwarrantable Jurisdiction over us. We have reminded them of the circumstances of our Emigration and Settlement here. We have appealed to their native Justice and Magnanimity, and we have conjured them by the Ties of our common Kindred to disavow these Usurpations, which, would inevitably interrupt our connections and correspondence. They too have been deaf to the voice of Justice and of Consanguinity. We must, therefore, acquiesce in the Necessity, which denounces our Separation, and hold them, as we hold the rest of Mankind, Enemies in War, in Peace, Friends.

We, therefore, the Representatives of the UNITED STATES OF AMERICA, in General Congress, Assembled, appealing to the Supreme Judge of the world for the Rectitude of our Intentions, do, in the Name, and by Authority of the good People of these Colonies, solemnly Publish and Declare, That these United Colonies are, and of Right ought to be, Free and Independent States; that they are absolved from all Allegiance to the British Crown, and that all political Connection between them and the State of Great Britain, is and ought to be totally dissolved; and that as Free and Independent States, they have full Power to levy War, conclude Peace, contract Alliances, establish Commerce, and to do all other Acts and Things which Independent States may of right do. And for the support of this declaration, with a firm Reliance on the Protection of Divine Providence, we mutually pledge to each other our lives, our Fortunes, and our sacred Honor.

The Constitution of the United States

PREAMBLE: WE, THE PEOPLE OF THE UNITED STATES, in Order to form a more perfect Union, establish Justice, insure domestic Tranquility, provide for the common defense, promote the general Welfare, and secure the Blessings of Liberty to ourselves and our Posterity, do ordain and establish this Constitution for the United States of America.

ARTICLE I

Section 1. All legislative Powers herein granted shall be vested in a Congress of the United States, which shall consist of a Senate and House of Representatives.

Section 2. The House of Representatives shall be composed of Members chosen every second Year by the People of the several States, and the Electors in each State shall have the Qualifications requisite for Electors of the most numerous Branch of the State Legislature.

No person shall be a Representative who shall not have attained to the Age of twenty-five Years, and been seven Years a Citizen of the United States, and who shall not, when elected, be an Inhabitant of that State in which he shall be chosen.

(Representatives and direct taxes shall be apportioned among the several States which may be included within this Union, according to their respective Numbers, which shall be determined by adding to the whole Number of free Persons, including those bound to Service for a Term of Years, and excluding Indians not taxed, three-fifths of all other persons.)* The actual Enumeration shall be made within three Years after the first Meeting of the Congress of the United States, and within every subsequent Term of ten Years, in such Manner as they shall by Law direct. The Number of Representatives shall not exceed one for every thirty Thousand, but each State shall have at Least one Representative; and until such enumeration shall be made, the State of New Hampshire shall be entitled to chuse three, Massachusetts eight, Rhode-Island and Providence Plantations one, Connecticut five, New-York six, New Jersey four, Pennsylvania eight, Delaware one, Maryland six, Virginia ten, North Carolina five, South Carolina five, and Georgia three.

When vacancies happen in the Representation from any State, the Executive Authority thereof shall issue Writs of Election to fill such Vacancies.

The House of Representatives shall chuse their Speaker and other Officers; and shall have the sole Power of Impeachment.

Section 3. The Senate of the United States shall be composed of two Senators from each State, (chosen by the Legislature thereof) for six Years; and each Senator shall have one Vote.

Immediately after they shall be assembled in Consequence of the first Election, they shall be divided as equally as may be into three Classes. The Seats of the Senators of the first Class shall be vacated at the Expiration of the second Year, of the second Class at the Expiration of the fourth Year, and of the third Class at the Expiration of the sixth Year, so that one third may be chosen every second Year; (and if vacancies happen by Resignation, or otherwise, during the Recess of the Legislature of any State, the Executive thereof may make temporary Appointments until the next Meeting of the Legislature, which shall then fill such Vacancies.)

No person shall be a Senator who shall not have attained to the Age of thirty Years, and been nine Years a Citizen of the United States, and who

Text in parentheses has been superceded or modified by an Amendment and is identified by a note at the beginning of appropriate Amendments.

shall not, when elected, be an Inhabitant of that State for which he shall be chosen.

The Vice President of the United States shall be President of the Senate, but shall have no Vote, unless they be equally divided.

The Senate shall chuse their other Officers, and also a President pro tempore, in the absence of the Vice President, or when he shall exercise the Office of President of the United States.

The Senate shall have the sole Power to try all Impeachments. When sitting for that Purpose, they shall be on Oath or Affirmation. When the President of the United States is tried, the Chief Justice shall preside: And no Person shall be convicted without the Concurrence of two thirds of the Members present.

Judgment in Cases of Impeachment shall not extend further than to removal from Office, and disqualification to hold and enjoy any Office of honor, Trust or Profit under the United States: but the Party convicted shall nevertheless be liable and subject to Indictment, Trial, Judgment and Punishment, according to Law.

Section 4. The Times, Places and Manner of holding Elections for Senators and Representatives, shall be prescribed in each State by the Legislature thereof; but the Congress may at any time by Law make or alter such Regulations, except as to the Place of Chusing Senators.

The Congress shall assemble at least once in every Year, and such Meeting shall (be on the first Monday in December,) unless they shall by Law appoint a different Day.

Section 5. Each House shall be the Judge of the Elections, Returns and Qualifications of its own Members, and a Majority of each shall constitute a Quorum to do Business; but a smaller number may adjourn from day to day, and may be authorized to compel the Attendance of absent Members, in such manner, and under such Penalties as each House may provide.

Each House may determine the Rules of its Proceedings, punish its members for disorderly Behavior, and, with the Concurrence of two thirds, expel a Member.

Each House shall keep a Journal of its Proceedings, and from time to time publish the same, excepting such Parts as may in their Judgment require Secrecy; and the Yeas and Nays of the Members of either House on any question shall, at the Desire of one fifth of those Present, be entered on the Journal.

Neither House, during the Session of Congress, shall, without the Consent of the other, adjourn for more than three days, nor to any other Place than that in which the two Houses shall be sitting.

Section 6. The Senators and Representatives shall receive a Compensation for their Services, to be ascertained by Law, and paid out of the Treasury of the United States. They shall in all Cases, except Treason, Felony and Breach of the Peace, be privileged from Arrest during their Attendance at the Session of their respective Houses, and in going to and returning from the same; and for any Speech or Debate in either House, they shall not be questioned in any other Place.

No Senator or Representative shall, during the Time for which he was elected, be appointed to any civil Office under the Authority of the United States, which shall have been created, or the Emoluments whereof shall have been increased during such time; and no Person holding any Office under the United States, shall be a Member of either House during his Continuance in office.

Section 7. All bills for raising Revenue shall originate in the House of Representatives; but the Senate may propose or concur with Amendments as on other Bills.

Every Bill which shall have passed the House of Representatives and the Senate, shall, before it become a Law, be presented to the President of the United States; If he approve he shall sign it, but if not he shall return it, with his Objections to that House in which it shall have originated, who shall enter the Objections at large on their Journal, and proceed to reconsider it. If after such Reconsideration two thirds of that House shall agree to pass the Bill, it shall be sent, together with the Objections, to the other House, by which it shall likewise be reconsidered, and if approved by two thirds of that House, it shall become a Law. But in all such Cases the Votes of both Houses shall be determined by Yeas and Nays, and the names of the Persons voting for and against the Bill shall be entered on the Journal of each House respectively. If any Bill shall not be returned by the President within ten days (Sundays excepted) after it shall have been presented to him, the Same shall be a Law, in like manner as if he had signed it, unless the Congress by their Adjournment prevent its Return, in which Case it shall not be a Law.

Every order, Resolution, or Vote to which the Concurrence of the Senate and House of Representatives may be necessary (except on a question of Adjournment) shall be presented to the President of the United States; and before the Same shall take Effect, shall be approved by him, or being disapproved by him, shall be repassed by two thirds of the Senate and House of Representatives, according to the Rules and Limitations prescribed in the Case of a Bill.

Section 8. The Congress shall have Power To lay and collect Taxes, Duties, Imposts and Excises, to pay the Debts and provide for the common Defense and general Welfare of the United States; but all Duties, Imposts and Excises shall be uniform throughout the United States;

To borrow money on the credit of the United States;

To regulate Commerce with foreign Nations, and among the several States, and with the Indian Tribes;

To establish a uniform Rule of Naturalization, and uniform Laws on the subject of Bankruptcies throughout the United States;

To coin Money, regulate the Value thereof, and of foreign Coin, and fix the Standard of Weights and Measures;

To provide for the Punishment of counterfeiting the Securities and current Coin of the United States;

To establish Post Offices and post Roads;

To promote the Progress of Science and useful Arts, by securing for limited Times to Authors and Inventors the exclusive Right to their respective Writings and Discoveries;

To constitute Tribunals inferior to the Supreme Court;

To define and punish Piracies and Felonies committed on the high seas, and Offenses against the Law of Nations;

To declare War, grant Letters of Marque and Reprisal, and make Rules concerning Captures on Land and Water;

To raise and support Armies, but no Appropriation of Money to that Use shall be for a longer Term than two Years;

To provide and maintain a Navy;

To make Rules for the Government and Regulation of the land and naval Forces;

To provide for calling forth the Militia to execute the Laws of the Union, suppress Insurrections and repel Invasions;

To provide for organizing, arming, and disciplining the militia, and for governing such Part of them as may be employed in the Service of the United States, reserving to the States respectively, the Appointment of the Officers, and the Authority of training the Militia according to the discipline prescribed by Congress;

To exercise exclusive Legislation in all Cases

whatsoever, over such District (not exceeding ten Miles square) as may, by Cession of particular States, and the acceptance of Congress, become the Seat of the Government of the United States, and to exercise like Authority over all Places purchased by the Consent of the Legislature of the State in which the Same shall be, for the Erection of Forts, Magazines, Arsenals, dock Yards, and other needful buildings;—And

To make all Laws which shall be necessary and proper for carrying into Execution the foregoing Powers, and all other Powers vested by this Constitution in the Government of the United States, or in any Department or Officer thereof.

Section 9. The migration or Importation of such Persons as any of the States now existing shall think proper to admit, shall not be prohibited by the Congress prior to the Year one thousand eight hundred and eight, but a tax or duty may be imposed on such Importation, not exceeding ten dollars for each Person.

The privilege of the Writ of Habeas Corpus shall not be suspended, unless when in Cases of Rebellion or Invasion the public Safety may require it.

No Bill of Attainder or ex post facto Law shall be passed.

No capitation, or other direct, Tax shall be laid, unless in Proportion to the Census or Enumeration herein before directed to be taken.

No Tax or Duty shall be laid on Articles exported from any State.

No Preference shall be given by any Regulation of Commerce or Revenue to the Ports of one State over those of another: nor shall Vessels bound to, or from, one State, be obliged to enter, clear, or pay Duties in another.

No Money shall be drawn from the Treasury, but in Consequence of Appropriations made by Law; and a regular Statement and Account of the Receipts and Expenditures of all public Money shall be published from time to time.

No Title of nobility shall be granted by the United States: and no Person holding any Office of Profit or Trust under them, shall, without the Consent of the Congress, accept of any present, Emolument, Office, or Title, of any kind whatever, from any King, Prince, or foreign State.

Section 10. No State shall enter into any Treaty, Alliance, or Confederation; grant Letters of Marque and Reprisal; coin Money; emit Bills of Credit; make Anything but gold and silver Coin a Tender in Payment of Debts; pass any Bill of Attainder, ex post facto Law, or Law impairing the Obligation of Contracts, or grant any Title of Nobility.

No State shall, without the Consent of the Congress, lay any Imposts or Duties on Imports or Exports, except what may be absolutely necessary for executing its inspection Laws: and the net Produce of all Duties and Imposts, laid by any State on Imports or Exports, shall be for the Use of the Treasury of the United States; and all such Laws shall be subject to the Revision and Control of the Congress.

No State shall, without the Consent of Congress, lay any duty of Tonnage, keep Troops, or Ships of War in time of Peace, enter into any Agreement or Compact with another State, or with a foreign Power, or engage in War, unless actually invaded, or in such imminent Danger as will not admit of delay.

ARTICLE II

Section 1. The executive Power shall be vested in a President of the United States of America. He shall hold his Office during the Term of four Years, and, together with the Vice President, chosen for the same Term, be elected, as follows.

Each State shall appoint, in such Manner as the Legislature thereof may direct, a Number of

Electors, equal to the whole Number of Senators and Representatives to which the State may be entitled in the Congress: but no Senator or Representative, or Person holding an Office of Trust or Profit under the United States, shall be appointed an Elector.

(The Electors shall meet in their respective States, and vote by Ballot for two persons, of whom one at least shall not be an Inhabitant of the same State with themselves. And they shall make a List of all the Persons voted for, and of the Number of Votes for each; which List they shall sign and certify, and transmit sealed to the Seat of the Government of the United States, directed to the President of the Senate. The President of the Senate shall, in the Presence of the Senate and House of Representatives, open all the Certificates, and the Votes shall then be counted. The Person having the greatest Number of Votes shall be the President, if such Number be a Majority of the whole Number of Electors appointed; and if there be more than one who have such Majority, and have an equal Number of Votes, then the House of Representatives shall immediately chuse by Ballot one of them for President; and if no Person have a Majority, then from the five highest on the List the said House shall in like Manner chuse the President. But in chusing the President, the Votes shall be taken by States, the representation from each State having one Vote; A quorum for this Purpose shall consist of a Member or Members from two thirds of the States, and a Majority of all the States shall be necessary to a Choice. In every Case, after the Choice of the President, the Person having the greatest Number of Votes of the Electors shall be the Vice President. But if there should remain two or more who have equal Votes, the Senate shall chuse from them by Ballot the Vice-President.)

The Congress may determine the Time of chusing the Electors, and the Day on which they shall give their Votes; which Day shall be the same throughout the United States.

No person except a natural born Citizen, or a Citizen of the United States, at the time of the Adoption of this Constitution, shall be eligible to the Office of President; neither shall any Person be eligible to that Office who shall not have attained to the Age of thirty five Years, and been fourteen Years a Resident within the United States.

In Case of the Removal of the President from Office, or of his Death, Resignation, or Inability to discharge the Powers and Duties of the said Office, the same shall devolve on the Vice President, and the Congress may by Law provide for the Case of Removal, Death, Resignation or Inability, both of the President and Vice President, declaring what Officer shall then act as President, and such Officer shall act accordingly, until the Disability be removed, or a President shall be elected.

The President shall, at stated Times, receive for his Services, a Compensation, which shall neither be encreased nor diminished during the Period for which he shall have been elected, and he shall not receive within that Period any other Emolument from the United States, or any of them.

Before he enter on the Execution of his Office, he shall take the following Oath or Affirmation:— "I do solemnly swear (or affirm) that I will faithfully execute the Office of President of the United States, and will to the best of my Ability, preserve, protect and defend the Constitution of the United States."

Section 2. The President shall be Commander in Chief of the Army and Navy of the United States, and of the Militia of the several States, when called into the actual Service of the United States; he may require the Opinion, in writing, of the principal Officer in each of the executive

Departments, upon any subject relating to the Duties of their respective Offices, and he shall have Power to Grant Reprieves and Pardons for Offenses against the United States, except in Cases of Impeachment.

He shall have Power, by and with the Advice and Consent of the Senate, to make Treaties, provided two thirds of the Senators present concur; and he shall nominate, and by and with the Advice and Consent of the Senate, shall appoint Ambassadors, other public Ministers and Consuls, judges of the Supreme Court, and all other Officers of the United States, whose Appointments are not herein otherwise provided for, and which shall be established by Law: but the Congress may by Law vest the Appointment of such inferior Officers, as they think proper, in the President alone, in the Courts of Law, or in the Heads of Departments.

The President shall have Power to fill up all Vacancies that may happen during the Recess of the Senate, by granting Commissions which shall expire at the End of their next Session.

Section 3. He shall from time to time give to the Congress Information of the State of the Union, and recommend to their Consideration such Measures as he shall judge necessary and expedient; he may, on extraordinary Occasions, convene both Houses, or either of them, and in Case of Disagreement between them, with Respect to the Time of Adjournment, he may adjourn them to such Time as he shall think proper; he shall receive Ambassadors and other public Ministers; he shall take Care that the Laws be faithfully executed, and shall Commission all the Officers of the United States.

Section 4. The President, Vice President and all civil Officers of the United States, shall be removed from Office on Impeachment for, and Conviction of, Treason, Bribery, or other high Crimes and Misdemeanors.

ARTICLE III

Section 1. The judicial Power of the United States, shall be vested in one supreme Court, and in such inferior Courts as the Congress may from time to time ordain and establish. The Judges, both of the supreme and inferior Courts, shall hold their Offices during good Behaviour, and shall, at stated Times, receive for their Services, a Compensation, which shall not be diminished during their Continuance in office.

Section 2. The judicial Power shall extend to all Cases, in Law and Equity, arising under this Constitution, the Laws of the United States, and Treaties made, or which shall be made, under their Authority;—to all Cases affecting Ambassadors, other public Ministers and Consuls;—to all Cases of admiralty and maritime Jurisdiction;—to Controversies to which the United States shall be a Party;—to Controversies between two or more States;—between a State and Citizens of another State;—between Citizens of different States;—between Citizens of the same State claiming Lands under Grants of different States, and between a State, or the Citizens thereof, and foreign States, Citizens or Subjects.

In all Cases affecting Ambassadors, other public Ministers and Consuls, and those in which a State shall be Party, the supreme Court shall have original Jurisdiction. In all the other Cases before mentioned, the supreme Court shall have appellate Jurisdiction, both as to Law and Fact, with such Exceptions, and under such Regulations as the Congress shall make.

The trial of all Crimes, except in Cases of Impeachment, shall be by Jury; and such trial shall be held in the State where the said Crimes shall have been committed; but when not committed within any State, the Trial shall be at such Place or Places as the Congress may by Law have directed.

Section 3. Treason against the United States, shall consist only in levying War against them, or in adhering to their Enemies, giving them Aid and Comfort. No Person shall be convicted of Treason unless on the Testimony of two Witnesses to the same overt Act, or on Confession in open Court.

The Congress shall have Power to declare the Punishment of Treason, but no Attainder of Treason shall work Corruption of Blood, or Forfeiture except during the Life of the Person attainted.

ARTICLE IV

Section 1. Full Faith and Credit shall be given in each State to the public Acts, Records, and judicial Proceedings of every other State. And the Congress may by general Laws prescribe the Manner in which such Acts, Records, and Proceedings shall be proved, and the Effect thereof.

Section 2. The Citizens of each State shall be entitled to all Privileges and Immunities of Citizens in the several States.

A Person charged in any State with Treason, Felony, or other Crime, who shall flee from Justice, and be found in another State, shall on demand of the executive Authority of the State from which he fled, be delivered up, to be removed to the State having Jurisdiction of the Crime.

(No Person held to Service or Labor in one State, under the Laws thereof, escaping into another, shall, in Consequence of any Law or Regulation therein, be discharged from such Service or Labor, but shall be delivered up on Claim of the Party to whom such Service or Labor may be Due.)

Section 3. New States may be admitted by the Congress into this Union; but no new States shall be formed or erected within the Jurisdiction of any other State; nor any State be formed by the Junction of two or more States, or parts of States, without the Consent of the Legislatures of the States concerned as well as of the Congress.

The Congress shall have Power to dispose of and make all needful Rules and Regulations respecting the Territory or other Property belonging to the United States; and nothing in this Constitution shall be so construed as to Prejudice any Claims of the United States, or of any particular State.

Section 4. The United States shall guarantee to every State in this Union a Republican Form of Government, and shall protect each of them against Invasion; and on Application of the Legislature, or of the Executive (when the Legislature cannot be convened) against domestic Violence.

ARTICLE V

The Congress, whenever two thirds of both Houses shall deem it necessary, shall propose Amendments to this Constitution, or, on the Application of the Legislatures of two thirds of the several States, shall call a Convention for proposing Amendments, which, in either Case, shall be valid to all Intents and Purposes, as part of this Constitution, when ratified by the Legislatures of three fourths of the several States, or by Conventions in three fourths thereof, as the one or the other Mode of Ratification may be proposed by the Congress: Provided that no Amendment which may be made prior to the Year One thousand eight hundred and eight shall in any Manner affect the first and fourth Clauses in the Ninth Section of the first Article; and that no State, without its Consent, shall be deprived of its equal Suffrage in the Senate.

ARTICLE VI

All Debts contracted and Engagements entered into, before the Adoption of this Constitution, shall be as valid against the United States under this Constitution, as under the Confederation.

This Constitution, and the Laws of the United States which shall be made in Pursuance thereof; and all Treaties made, or which shall be made, under the Authority of the United States, shall be the supreme Law of the Land; and the Judges in every State shall be bound thereby, Anything in the Constitution or Laws of any State to the Contrary notwithstanding.

The Senators and Representatives before mentioned, and the Members of the several State Legislatures, and all executive and judicial Officers, both of the United States and of the several States, shall be bound by Oath or Affirmation, to support this Constitution; but no religious Test shall ever be required as a Qualification to any Office or public Trust under the United States.

ARTICLE VII

The Ratification of the Conventions of nine States, shall be sufficient for the Establishment of this Constitution between the States so ratifying the Same.

Done in Convention by the unanimous Consent of the States present the Seventeenth Day of September in the Year of our Lord one thousand seven hundred and Eighty seven and of the Independence of the United States of America the Twelfth.

In witness whereof We have hereunto subscribed our Names.

Amendments 1–10: The Bill of Rights
Ratified December 15, 1791

AMENDMENT I

Congress shall make no law respecting an establishment of religion, or prohibiting the free exercise thereof; or abridging the freedom of speech, or of the press; or the right of the people peaceably to assemble, and to petition the Government for a redress of grievances.

AMENDMENT II

A well regulated Militia, being necessary to the security of a free State, the right of the people to keep and bear Arms, shall not be infringed.

AMENDMENT III

No Soldier shall, in time of peace be quartered in any house, without the consent of the Owner, nor in time of war, but in a manner to be prescribed by law.

AMENDMENT IV

The right of the people to be secure in their persons, houses, papers, and effects, against unreasonable searches and seizures, shall not be violated, and no Warrants shall issue, but upon probable cause, supported by Oath or affirmation, and particularly describing the place to be searched, and the persons or things to be seized.

AMENDMENT V

No person shall be held to answer for a capital, or otherwise infamous crime, unless on a presentment or indictment of a Grand Jury, except in cases arising in the land or naval forces, or in the Militia, when in actual service in time of War or public danger; nor shall any person be subject for the same offence to be twice put in jeopardy of life or limb; nor shall be compelled in any criminal case to be a witness against himself, nor be deprived of life, liberty, or property, without due process of law; nor shall private property be taken for public use,without just compensation.

AMENDMENT VI

In all criminal prosecutions, the accused shall enjoy the right to a speedy and public trial, by an impartial jury of the State and district wherein the crime shall have been committed, which district shall have been previously ascertained by law, and to be informed of the nature and cause of the accusation; to be confronted with the witnesses against him; to have compulsory process for obtaining witnesses in his favor, and to have the Assistance of Counsel for his defence.

AMENDMENT VII

In suits at common law, where the value in controversy shall exceed twenty dollars, the right of trial by jury shall be preserved, and no fact tried by a jury, shall be otherwise reexamined in any Court of the United States, than according to the rules of the common law.

AMENDMENT VIII

Excessive bail shall not be required, nor excessive fines imposed, nor cruel and unusual punishments inflicted.

AMENDMENT IX

The enumeration in the Constitution, of certain rights, shall not be construed to deny or disparage others retained by the people.

AMENDMENT X

The powers not delegated to the United States by the Constitution, nor prohibited by it to the States, are reserved to the States respectively, or to the people.

Amendments 11–27

AMENDMENT XI
Proposed by Congress March 4, 1794;
Ratified February 7, 1795.

Note: Article III, section 2, of the Constitution was modified by Amendment II.

The Judicial power of the United States shall not be construed to extend to any suit in law or equity, commenced or prosecuted against one of the United States by Citizens of another State, or by Citizens or Subjects of any Foreign State.

AMENDMENT XII
Proposed by Congress December 9, 1803;
Ratified June 15, 1804.

Note: A portion of Article II, section 1 of the Constitution was superseded by Amendment XII.

The Electors shall meet in their respective states and vote by ballot for President and Vice-President, one of whom, at least, shall not be an inhabitant of the same state with themselves; they shall name in their ballots the person voted for as President, and in distinct ballots the person voted for as Vice-President, and they shall make distinct lists of all persons voted for as President, and of all persons voted for as Vice-President, and of the number of votes for each, which lists they shall sign and certify, and transmit sealed to the seat of the government of the United States, directed to the President of the Senate;—the President of the Senate shall, in presence of the Senate and House of Representatives, open all the certificates and the votes shall then be counted;—The person having the greatest number of votes for President, shall be the President, if such number be a majority of the whole number of Electors appointed; and if no person have such majority, then from the persons having the highest numbers not exceeding three on the list of those voted for as President, the House of Representatives shall choose immediately, by ballot, the President. But in choosing the President, the votes shall be taken by states, the representation from each state having one vote; a quorum for this purpose shall consist of a member or members from two-thirds of the states, and a majority of all the states shall be necessary to a choice. (And if the House of Representatives shall not choose a President whenever the right of choice shall devolve upon them, before the fourth day of March next following, then the Vice-President shall act as President, as in case of the death or other constitutional disability of the President.) *The person having the greatest number of votes as Vice-President, shall be the Vice-President, if such number be a majority of the whole number of Electors appointed, and if no person have a majority, then from the two highest numbers on the list, the Senate shall choose the Vice-President; a quorum for the purpose shall consist of two-thirds of the whole number of Senators, and a majority of the whole number shall be necessary to a choice. But no person constitutionally ineligible to the office of President shall be eligible to that of Vice-President of the United States.

*Superseded by section 3 of the 20th amendment.

Amendment XIII

Proposed by Congress January 31, 1865;
Ratified December 6, 1865.

Note: A portion of Article IV, section 2, of the Constitution was superseded by Amendment XIII.

Section 1. Neither slavery nor involuntary servitude, except as a punishment for crime whereof the party shall have been duly convicted, shall exist within the United States, or any place subject to their jurisdiction.

Section 2. Congress shall have power to enforce this article by appropriate legislation.

Amendment XIV

Proposed by Congress June 13, 1866;
Ratified July 9, 1868.

Note: Article I, section 2, of the Constitution was modified by section 2 of Amendment XIV.

Section 1. All persons born or naturalized in the United States, and subject to the jurisdiction thereof, are citizens of the United States and of the State wherein they reside. No State shall make or enforce any law which shall abridge the privileges or immunities of citizens of the United States; nor shall any State deprive any person of life, liberty, or property, without due process of law; nor deny to any person within its jurisdiction the equal protection of the laws.

Section 2. Representatives shall be apportioned among the several States according to their respective numbers, counting the whole number of persons in each State, excluding Indians not taxed. But when the right to vote at any election for the choice of electors for President and Vice-President of the United States, Representatives in Congress, the Executive and Judicial officers of a State, or the members of the Legislature thereof, is denied to any of the male inhabitants of such State, (being twenty-one years of age,) and citizens of the United States, or in any way abridged, except for participation in rebellion, or other crime, the basis of representation therein shall be reduced in the proportion which the number of such male citizens shall bear to the whole number of male citizens twenty-one years of age in such State.

Section 3. No person shall be a Senator or Representative in Congress, or elector of President and Vice-President, or hold any office, civil or military, under the United States, or under any State, who, having previously taken an oath, as a member of Congress, or as an officer of the United States, or as a member of any State legislature, or as an executive or judicial officer of any State, to support the Constitution of the United States, shall have engaged in insurrection or rebellion against the same, or given aid or comfort to the enemies thereof. But Congress may by a vote of two-thirds of each House, remove such disability.

Section 4. The validity of the public debt of the United States, authorized by law, including debts incurred for payment of pensions and bounties for services in suppressing insurrection or rebellion, shall not be questioned. But neither the United States nor any State shall assume or pay any debt or obligation incurred in aid of insurrection or rebellion against the United States, or any claim for the loss or emancipation of any slave; but all such debts, obligations and claims shall be held illegal and void.

Section 5. The Congress shall have power to enforce, by appropriate legislation, the provisions of this article.

AMENDMENT XV

Proposed by Congress February 26, 1869;
Ratified February 3, 1870.

Section 1. The right of citizens of the United States to vote shall not be denied or abridged by the United States or by any State on account of race, color, or previous condition of servitude—

Section 2. The Congress shall have power to enforce this article by appropriate legislation.

AMENDMENT XVI

Proposed by Congress July 12, 1909;
Ratified February 3, 1913.

Note: Article I, section 9, of the Constitution was modified by Amendment XVI.

The Congress shall have power to lay and collect taxes on incomes, from whatever source derived, without apportionment among the several States, and without regard to any census or enumeration.

AMENDMENT XVII

Proposed by Congress May 13, 1912;
Ratified April 8, 1913.

Note: Article I, section 3, of the Constitution was modified by the Amendment XVII.

The Senate of the United States shall be composed of two Senators from each State, elected by the people thereof, for six years; and each Senator shall have one vote. The electors in each State shall have the qualifications requisite for electors of the most numerous branch of the State legislatures.

When vacancies happen in the representation of any State in the Senate, the executive authority of such State shall issue writs of election to fill such vacancies: Provided, That the legislature of any State may empower the executive thereof to make temporary appointments until the people fill the vacancies by election as the legislature may direct.

This amendment shall not be so construed as to affect the election or term of any Senator chosen before it becomes valid as part of the Constitution.

AMENDMENT XVIII

Proposed by Congress December 18, 1917; Ratified January 16, 1919: Repealed by Amendment XXI.

Section 1. After one year from the ratification of this article the manufacture, sale, or transportation of intoxicating liquors within, the importation thereof into, or the exportation thereof from the United States and all territory subject to the jurisdiction thereof for beverage purposes is hereby prohibited.

Section 2. The Congress and the several States shall have concurrent power to enforce this article by appropriate legislation.

Section 3. This article shall be inoperative unless it shall have been ratified as an amendment to the Constitution by the legislatures of the several States as provided in the Constitution, within seven years from the date of the submission hereof to the States by the Congress.

AMENDMENT XIX

Proposed by Congress June 4, 1919;
Ratified August 18, 1920.

The right of citizens of the United States to vote shall not be denied or abridged by the United States or by any State on account of sex.

Congress shall have power to enforce this Article by appropriate legislation.

AMENDMENT XX

Proposed by Congress March 2, 1932;
Ratified January 23, 1933.

Note: Article I, section 4, of the Constitution

was modified by section 2 of this amendment. In addition, a portion of the Amendment XII was superseded by section 3.

Section 1. The terms of the President and Vice President shall end at noon on the 20th day of January, and the terms of Senators and Representatives at noon on the 3d day of January, of the years in which such terms would have ended if this article had not been ratified; and the terms of their successors shall then begin.

Section 2. The Congress shall assemble at least once in every year, and such meeting shall begin at noon on the 3d day of January, unless they shall by law appoint a different day.

Section 3. If, at the time fixed for the beginning of the term of the President, the President elect shall have died, the Vice President elect shall become President. If a President shall not have been chosen before the time fixed for the beginning of his term, or if the President elect shall have failed to qualify, then the Vice President elect shall act as President until a President shall have qualified; and the Congress may by law provide for the case wherein neither a President elect nor a Vice President shall have qualified, declaring who shall then act as President, or the manner in which one who is to act shall be selected, and such person shall act accordingly until a President or Vice President shall have qualified.

Section 4. The Congress may by law provide for the case of the death of any of the persons from whom the House of Representatives may choose a President whenever the right of choice shall have devolved upon them, and for the case of the death of any of the persons from whom the Senate may choose a Vice President whenever the right of choice shall have devolved upon them.

Section 5. Sections 1 and 2 shall take effect on the 15th day of October following the ratification of this article.

Section 6. This article shall be inoperative unless it shall have been ratified as an amendment to the Constitution by the legislatures of three-fourths of the several States within seven years from the date of its submission.

AMENDMENT XXI
Proposed by Congress February 20, 1933;
Ratified December 5, 1933.

Section 1. The eighteenth article of amendment to the Constitution of the United States is hereby repealed.

Section 2. The transportation or importation into any State, Territory, or possession of the United States for delivery or use therein of intoxicating liquors, in violation of the laws thereof, is hereby prohibited.

Section 3. This article shall be inoperative unless it shall have been ratified as an amendment to the Constitution by conventions in the several States, as provided in the Constitution, within seven years from the date of the submission hereof to the States by the Congress.

AMENDMENT XXII
Proposed by Congress March 24, 1947;
Ratified February 27, 1951.

Section 1. No person shall be elected to the office of the President more than twice, and no person who has held the office of President, or acted as President, for more than two years of a term to which some other person was elected President shall be elected to the office of President more than once. But this Article shall not apply to any person holding the office of President when this Article was proposed by the Congress, and shall not prevent any person who may be holding the office of President, or acting as President, during the term within which this Article becomes operative from holding the office of President or acting as President during the remainder of such term.

Section 2. This article shall be inoperative

unless it shall have been ratified as an amendment to the Constitution by the legislatures of three-fourths of the several States within seven years from the date of its submission to the States by the Congress.

Amendment XXIII

Proposed by Congress June 16, 1960;
Ratified March 29, 1961.

Section 1. The District constituting the seat of Government of the United States shall appoint in such manner as the Congress may direct:

A number of electors of President and Vice President equal to the whole number of Senators and Representatives in Congress to which the District would be entitled if it were a State, but in no event more than the least populous State; they shall be in addition to those appointed by the States, but they shall be considered, for the purposes of the election of President and Vice President, to be electors appointed by a State; and they shall meet in the District and perform such duties as provided by the twelfth article of amendment.

Section 2. The Congress shall have power to enforce this article by appropriate legislation.

Amendment XXIV

Proposed by Congress August 27, 1962;
Ratified January 23, 1964.

The right of citizens of the United States to vote in any primary or other election for President or Vice President, for electors for President or Vice President, or for Senator or Representative in Congress, shall not be denied or abridged by the United States or any State by reason of failure to pay any poll tax or other tax.

Section 2. The Congress shall have power to enforce this article by appropriate legislation.

Amendment XXV

Proposed by Congress July 6, 1965;
Ratified February 10, 1967.

Note: Article II, section 1, of the Constitution was affected by the Amendment XXV.

Section 1. In case of the removal of the President from office or of his death or resignation, the Vice President shall become President.

Section 2. Whenever there is a vacancy in the office of the Vice President, the President shall nominate a Vice President who shall take office upon confirmation by a majority vote of both houses of Congress.

Section 3. Whenever the President transmits to the President pro tempore of the Senate and the Speaker of the House of Representatives his written declaration that he is unable to discharge the powers and duties of his office, and until he transmits to them a written declaration to the contrary, such powers and duties shall be discharged by the Vice President as Acting President.

Section 4. Whenever the Vice President and a majority of either the principal officers of the executive departments or of such other body as Congress may by law provide, transmit to the President pro tempore of the Senate and the Speaker of the House of Representatives their written declaration that the President is unable to discharge the powers and duties of his office, the Vice President shall immediately assume the powers and duties of the office as Acting President.

Thereafter, when the President transmits to the President pro tempore of the Senate and the Speaker of the House of Representatives his written declaration that no inability exists, he shall resume the powers and duties of his office unless the Vice President and a majority of either the principal officers of the executive department or of such other body as Congress may by law provide, transmit within four days to the President pro tempore of the Senate and the Speaker of the House of Representatives their written declaration that the President is unable to discharge the pow-

shall decide the issue, assembling within forty-eight hours for that purpose if not in session. If the Congress, within twenty-one days after receipt of the latter written declaration, or, if Congress is not in session, within twenty-one days after Congress is required to assemble, determines by two-thirds vote of both Houses that the President is unable to discharge the powers and duties of his office, the Vice President shall continue to discharge the same as Acting President; otherwise, the President shall resume the powers and duties of his office.

AMENDMENT XXVI
Proposed by Congress March 23, 1971;
Ratified July 1, 1971.
Note: Amendment XIV, section 2, of the Constitution was modified by section 1 of the Amendment XXVI.

Section 1. The right of citizens of the United States, who are eighteen years of age or older, to vote shall not be denied or abridged by the United States or by any State on account of age.

Section 2. The Congress shall have the power to enforce this article by appropriate legislation.

AMENDMENT XXVII
Proposed by Congress Sept. 25, 1789;
Ratified May 7, 1992.

No law, varying the compensation for the services of the Senators and Representatives, shall take effect, until an election of representatives shall have intervened.

The Gettysburg Address
November 19, 1863
BY ABRAHAM LINCOLN

FOURSCORE AND SEVEN YEARS AGO our fathers brought forth on this continent a new nation, conceived in liberty and dedicated to the proposition that all men are created equal.

Now we are engaged in a great civil war, testing whether that nation or any nation so conceived and so dedicated can long endure. We are met on a great battle field of that war. We have come to dedicate a portion of that field, as a final resting-place for those who here gave their lives that that nation might live. It is altogether fitting and proper that we should do this.

But, in a larger sense, we cannot dedicate—we cannot consecrate—we cannot hallow—this ground. The brave men, living and dead, who struggled here, have consecrated it, far above our poor power to add or detract. The world will little note, nor long remember, what we say here, but it can never forget what they did here. It is for us the living rather to be dedicated here to the unfinished work which they who fought here have thus far so nobly advanced. It is rather for us to be here dedicated to the great task remaining before us—that from these honored dead we take increased devotion to that cause for which they gave the last full measure of devotion—that we here highly resolve that these dead shall not have died in vain—that this nation, under God, shall have a new birth of freedom—and that government of the people, by the people, for the people, shall not perish from the earth.

Pledge of Allegiance

I pledge allegiance to the flag
of the United States of America,
and to the republic for which it stands,
one nation under God, indivisible, with liberty
and justice for all.

"The Star-Spangled Banner"

(The Defense of Fort McHenry, September 20, 1814)

BY FRANCIS SCOTT KEY

Oh, say can you see by the dawn's early light
What so proudly we hailed at the
twilight's last gleaming?
Whose broad stripes and bright stars
thru the perilous fight,
O'er the ramparts we watched were so
gallantly streaming?
And the rocket's red glare, the
bombs bursting in air,
Gave proof through the night that our flag
was still there.
Oh, say does that star-spangled banner yet wave
O'er the land of the free and the
home of the brave?

On the shore, dimly seen through the
mists of the deep,
Where the foe's haughty host in
dread silence reposes,
What is that which the breeze,
o'er the towering steep,
As it fitfully blows, half conceals, half discloses?
Now it catches the gleam of the
morning's first beam,
In full glory reflected now shines in the stream:
'Tis the star-spangled banner! Oh long may it wave
O'er the land of the free and the home of the brave!

And where is that band who so vauntingly swore
That the havoc of war and the battle's confusion,
A home and a country should leave us no more!
Their blood has washed out their
foul footsteps' pollution.
No refuge could save the hireling and slave
From the terror of flight, or the gloom of the grave:
And the star-spangled banner in triumph doth wave
O'er the land of the free and the home of the brave.

Oh! thus be it ever, when freemen shall stand
Between their loved home and the
war's desolation!
Blest with victory and peace, may the
heav'n rescued land
Praise the Power that hath made and
preserved us a nation.
Then conquer we must, for our cause it is just,
And this be our motto: "In God is our trust."
And the star-spangled banner
in triumph shall wave
O'er the land of the free and the
home of the brave!

★ More Information ★

HISTORY IS ALL AROUND US. Wherever we go, others likely have been before. Where we live, history has been made. This section will give you ideas for further investigating American history. I have selected a few Web sites you might enjoy exploring and a sampling of history museums, battlefields, and other historic places to visit. There's some basic information about our states and Presidents. And there's a long bibliography of the books that I used while writing this one. Enjoy!

American History Web Sites to Explore

There are many Web sites that focus on American history. Here are a few that my son Sandy and I find most helpful:

History Matters: http://historymatters.gmu.edu/browse/wwwhistory/ The best overall Web site, with links to other history Web sites, from George Mason University.

Library of Congress: http://memory.loc.gov/ammem/ and *Gilder Lehrman Institute of American History:* http://www.gliah.uh.edu/index.cfm—The two most impressive Web sites for those interested in documents, information, and just plain fun in American history.

For Today in History: http://memory.loc.gov/ammem/today/—Check it out each morning when you wake up.

Ask the HyperHistorian: http://www.gliah.uh.edu/ask_historian.cfm—Here you can ask a professional historian any question you might have about American history.

Not Just for Kids at the National Museum of American History: http://americanhistory.si.edu/notkid/index.htm—This site gives you the chance to "Be a Historian."

For African-American history: http://www.loc.gov/exhibits/african/intro.html

For Latino history: http://www.si.edu/resource/faq/nmah/latino.htm

University of California at Berkeley Oral history project: http://www.itp.berkeley.edu/-asam150/—Learn about the past through Asian-American oral histories, and then go interview your grandparents!

Women and Social Movements in the United States, 1775–2000: http://womhist.binghamton.edu—Prize-winning historians supervise the site.

University of North Carolina: http://docsouth.unc.edu/—A great collection of sources on the American South.

Valley of the Shadow: http://jefferson.village.virginia.edu/vcdh/—This site allows readers to look at the Civil War through the experiences of residents living across from each other on the Confederate/Union border in Augusta County, Virginia, and Franklin County, Pennsylvania.

New Deal: http://newdeal.feri.org—A wonderful collection of photos, documents, music, etc., on the New Deal.

John F. Kennedy Presidential Library: http://www.cs.umb.edu/jfklibrary/history_day_2000_resources.html—Speeches, documents, and information on events such as the Cuban missile crisis and the 1960s debate between JFK and Richard Nixon.

History News Network: http://www.historynewsnetwork.org/—Here are challenging essays from diverse perspectives that link the past and the present. Find out about gun control through the history of the Second Amendment, about previous attempts in U.S. history to control terrorism, and much, much more.

University of Kansas: www.cc.ukans.edu/carrie/docs/amdocs_index.html. The best collection that I have found on the Web for political and military history.

Historical Places to Visit

★ ALABAMA ★

Fort Morgan NHL, Gulf Shores. Completed in 1834, this star-shaped stronghold on the Gulf of Mexico is the nation's third largest fort and was used extensively during the Civil War. www.preserveala.org/sites/sites-morgan.html

Tuskegee Institute NHS, Tuskegee. One of the first colleges for African Americans, Tuskegee was founded in 1881. Booker T. Washington was its first president, and George Washington Carver taught there. The museum has exhibits on Carver's scientific experiments. www.nps.gov/tuin/

U.S.S. Alabama Battleship Memorial, Mobile. This ship earned nine battle stars during World War II. Visitors tour decks, quarters, and wheelhouse and sit behind 40-mm anti-aircraft guns. You can also go aboard the submarine U.S.S. *Drum* docked alongside. www.USSalabama.com

★ ALASKA ★

Klondike Gold Rush NHP, Skagway. Visitors relive the days of the last great gold rush. www.nps.gov/klgo

Sitka NHP, Sitka. Here the Tlingit Indians made their last stand against Russian fur traders. The park has an excellent collection of totem poles. www.nps.gov/sitk/

★ ARIZONA ★

Coronado NMem, Hereford. The spot on the U.S.-Mexican border where Francisco Vasquez de Coronado entered the present United States in 1540 looking for the legendary Seven Golden Cities of Cibola. www.USparks.about.com

Pioneer Arizona, Phoenix. A 90-acre museum-village that recreates a late 19th-century settlement of the Southwest. Exhibits include houses, craft shops, a saloon, a miner's camp, a bank, a schoolhouse, a stagecoach stop, and an 1860 ranch with livestock. www.pioneer-arizona.com

★ ARKANSAS ★

Arkansas Territorial Restoration, Little Rock. Thirteen buildings on their original sites re-create the Little Rock of the 1820s. www.ohwy.com/ar/a/arterelr.htm

Old Washington Historic SP, Washington. Reconstructed tavern, courthouse, several homes, and the blacksmith shop where the first Bowie knife is supposed to have been made. www.yournet.com/washington.html

★ CALIFORNIA ★

Columbia SHP, Columbia. Tour a gold mine, ride a stage-coach, see fire-fighting equipment at one of the country's richest mining areas. www.sierra.parks.state.ca.us/coconten.htm

Marshall Gold Discovery SHP, Coloma. See a replica of the sawmill where James Marshall spotted the first flecks of California gold in 1848.

San Francisco Maritime NHP, San Francisco. This floating museum recalls California's seafaring past with a double-end paddle wheel ferryboat, a 1891 flat-bottomed schooner, a sleek, three-masted lumber schooner designed in 1895, and more. www.maritime.org

★ COLORADO ★

Bent's Old Fort NHS, La Junta. This fortress was a fur-trading post, a meeting place for trappers and Indians, a way station on the Santa Fe Trail, and a military base for the American conquest of New Mexico. www.nps.gov/beol

★ CONNECTICUT ★

Mystic Seaport, Mystic. This popular maritime museum re-creates a typical 19th-century seafaring village with all the excitement of the age of sail. www.mystic.org

Old New-Gate Prison, East Granby. Colonial America's first copper mine (1707) was turned into a prison for Tories and others during the Revolutionary War. View the underground dungeons, the restored guardhouse, and the ruins of prison buildings. www.ohwy.com/ct/o/ongprcom.htm

★ DELAWARE ★

Fort Christina NHL, Wilmington. Commemorates the site of the first permanent European settlement in Delaware by Swedes in 1638. A typical long cabin introduced to America by Swedish settlers stands in the park.

★ DISTRICT OF COLUMBIA ★
WASHINGTON, D.C.)

Washington, D.C., is full of history, with numerous monuments and museums. See the ***Washington Monument,*** the ***Lincoln Memorial,*** the ***Holocaust Museum,*** and the ***Smithsonian Museum of American History,*** among many, many others.

KEY TO ABBREVIATIONS

HD=Historic District	NHS=National Historic Site	SHP=State Historical Park
HP=Historic Park	NM=National Monument	SHS=State Historic Site
NBP=National Battlefield Park	NMem=National Memorial	SM=State Memorial
NHL=National Historic Landmark	NMP=National Military Park	SP=State Park
NHP=National Historical Park	SHM=State Historic Monument	

★ FLORIDA ★

John F. Kennedy Space Center, Merritt Island, near Titusville. Take a tour of this NASA facility, which launched Apollo missions and Skylab and now launches the space shuttle.

Fort Matanzas NM, St. Augustine. Take a ferry to this limestone fort built by the Spanish in the 1740s. www.nps.gov/foma

★ GEORGIA ★

Andersonville NHS, Andersonville. Largest and most infamous of Civil War prison camps. Still visible within the stockade are holes dug by prisoners searching for fresh water or trying to tunnel to freedom.

New Echota SHS, Calhoun. The short-lived capital of the Cherokee Nation. Thirteen years after its founding in 1825, the Cherokees were herded away to Oklahoma. www.stepintohistory.com/States/GA/New_Echota.htm

Westville Village, Lumpkin. A rural village of the 1850s, including farmhouse and mansion, shops, church, and general store. Watch blacksmiths, weavers, quilters, potters, and brickmakers at work. www.ohwy.com/ga/w/westville.htm

★ HAWAII ★

Pu'uhonua o Honaunau NHP, Honaunau. Visit a reconstructed temple-mausoleum and relics of this 15th-century refuge on a six-acre lava shelf facing the Pacific. Guides in native costume demonstrate carving, weaving, and other crafts, and visitors can ride an outrigger canoe in a sparkling coral lagoon. www.nps.gov/puho

U.S.S. Arizona NMem, Honolulu. This battleship took a direct hit during the Japanese attack on Pearl Harbor in 1941. The bodies of most of the 1,177 crewmen are still entombed in the sunken hull, which you can view from a memorial walkway. www.nps.gov/usar/index/htm

★ IDAHO ★

Old Fort Hall Replica. Several log dwellings, a blacksmith shop, and a museum surrounded by a stout stockade dating from 1834.

★ ILLINOIS ★

Nauvoo. Restored buildings recall the seven years when Nauvoo flourished as the principal settlement of the Mormons before their trek west in 1846. www.goto avvoo.com

Springfield. In the heart of Lincoln country stand his home, law offices, tomb, and the Old State Capitol. www.nps.gov/liho

★ INDIANA ★

Levi Coffin House NHL, Fountain City. The home of Levi and Catharine Coffin, who between 1826 and 1846 helped some 2,000 runaway slaves escape to freedom in Canada.

Lincoln Boyhood NMem, near Gentryville. A living histori-cal farm that portrays farm life as Lincoln knew it from 1816 to 1830. www.nps.gov/libo/pphtml/basics/html

★ IOWA ★

Fort Dodge Historical Museum and Fort, Fort Dodge. A replica of the fort built to protect settlers from hostile Sioux Indians during the 1862 uprising. www.fortmuseum.com/index.html

Pella Historical Village, Pella. Twenty restored buildings commemorate the Dutch who settled here in 1847. www.pellatuliptime.com/news.htm

★ KANSAS ★

Dodge City. Wild West make-believe recalls the heritage of a town that reigned as the world's largest cattle market in the 1800s. www.americanwest.com/pages/dodges.htm

Fort Leavenworth. Established in 1827 to protect wagon trains, the post now includes a cemetery and a museum displaying horse-drawn vehicles including a 1790 Conestoga wagon. http://leav-www.army.mil/cac/history.htm

★ KENTUCKY ★

Cumberland Gap NHP, Middlesboro. The path over the Allegheny Mountains that Daniel Boone used when opening Kentucky for settlement. www.nps.gov/cuga/

Fort Boonesborough SP, Richmond. Reconstruction of the first frontier outpost built in 1775 by Daniel Boone. www.state.ky.us/agencies/parks/ftboones.htm

★ LOUISIANA ★

Chalmette Battlefield and National Cemetery, Chalmette. Andrew Jackson led his troop to victory over British forces here in 1815 at the Battle of New Orleans. www.nps.gov/jela/chalmette%20Battlefield.htm

Plantation houses along the Mississippi River and in its bayous from New Orleans to St. Francisville recall the days when cotton and sugarcane reigned.

★ MAINE ★

Maine Maritime Museum, Bath. The maritime history of Maine since 1607, emphasizing the 19th-century sailing ship era, is traced here. www.bathmaine.com

Old York Gaol, York. Visitors tour the gloomy dungeon and jailer's living quarters in one of the oldest public buildings in English-settled America, built in 1719. www.oldyork.org

★ MARYLAND ★

Chesapeake and Ohio Canal NHP. Begun in 1828, this canal transported goods between Cumberland and Washington, D.C. Hike or bike along the towpath past locks, lockhouses, and aqueducts or take a ride in a mule-drawn barge. www.nps.gov/choc/co_geo.htm

Fort Washington Park, Fort Washington. The first fort here was destroyed during the War of 1812. Tour the present fortress, rebuilt in 1824.

★ MASSACHUSETTS ★

Minute Man NHP, along the route between Lexington and Concord. Costumed citizens each year observe the anniversary of the April 19, 1775, battle at Old North Bridge.

Plimoth Plantation, Plymouth. Reconstructed buildings and costumed interpreters give visitors a sense of what life was like for the settlers who had come on the *Mayflower.* www.plimoth.org/Museum/museum.htm

Salem. First town in Massachusetts Bay Colony, Salem became famous for witchcraft trials and worldwide maritime trade.

★ MICHIGAN ★

Fayette SP, Garden. Restoration has breathed new life into this ghost town, re-creating its iron-smelting heyday of the late 19th century. www.exploringthenorth.com/fayette/park.html

Greenfield Village and Henry Ford Museum, Dearborn. Homes and workshops of inventors such as Thomas Edison, Henry Ford, and the Wright brothers have been assembled here. www.hfmgv.org

★ MINNESOTA ★

Soudan Iron Mine, Tower-Soudan HP, Soudan. Explore the state's oldest and deepest iron mine, which operated from 1884 to 1962. Ex-miner guides take you on a tour that includes a 2,400-foot plunge in a mine elevator and an electric train ride through a 3,000-foot tunnel. www.dnr.state.mn.us/state_parks/soudan_underground_mine/index.htm

★ MISSISSIPPI ★

Natchez. Established by the French in 1716, Natchez has many pre–Civil War mansions.

Vicksburg NMP. Site of a decisive battle of the Civil War. Visitors follow a 16-mile tour road to battle sites, forts, trenches, and the burial ground of 17,000 Union soldiers. www.nps.gov/vick/index.htm

★ MISSOURI ★

Jefferson National Expansion Memorial, St. Louis. A memorial to commemorate President Jefferson's acquisition of the Louisiana Purchase in 1803, this is the home of the Gateway Arch, a 630-foot structure. Visitors ride small cars inside the arch to an observatory on top. Also in the park are the *Museum of Western Expansion,* and the *Old Courthouse,* the site of the Dred Scott trial. www.nps.gov/jeff

Pony Express Museum, St. Joseph. This brick building served as the eastern staring point for the Pony Express. www.ponyexpress.org

★ MONTANA ★

Indian Memorial at Little Bighorn Battlefield NM, Crow Agency. Commemorating the Battle of the Little Bighorn, this monument includes the ridge where Custer made his "last stand."

Grant Kohrs Ranch NHS, Deer Lodge. A restored 19th-century ranch, including the main house, bunkhouses, stables, barns, blacksmith shop, etc. www.nps.gov/grko

★ NEBRASKA ★

Stuhr Museum of the Prairie Pioneer, Grand Island. Fifty-five buildings form a typical prairie town. A vintage steam train makes scheduled runs over tracks that lead to an old depot.

★ NEVADA ★

Virginia City HD. Nevada's largest mining town has been restored to its 1870s appearance. www.desertusa.com/cities/nv/nv_virginiacity.html

★ NEW HAMPSHIRE ★

Canterbury Shaker Village, Canterbury. Founded in 1792, this village has been restored to showcase Shaker life. www.shakers.org

★ NEW JERSEY ★

Edison NHS, West Orange. Thomas Alva Edison developed many of his inventions and scientific ideas at this laboratory, which he built in 1887. See his library, chemical lab, machine shop, and inventions. www.nps.gov/edis

Historic Towne of Smithville, Smithville. The re-creation of an early 1800s crossroads community, including a stagecoach stop, a sweet shop, a general store, and a wood carving factory. www.smithvillenj.com

★ NEW MEXICO ★

Lincoln County Courthouse SHM, Lincoln. This adobe building held the jail from which the notorious outlaw Billy the Kid escaped in 1881 after killing two guards. Exhibits depict frontier history. www.nmculture.org/cgibin/showInst.pl

Taos Pueblo NHL, Taos. Here more than 500 Indian families live in two five-story communal dwellings little different from those the Spanish saw in 1450. www.cr.nps.gov/world heritage/taos.htm

★ NEW YORK ★

Farmer's Museum, Cooperstown. A printshop, pharmacy, doctor's and lawyer's offices, and other relocated buildings form a rural village that represents life in early America. www.farmersmuseum.org

New York City is full of historical landmarks, including the *Statue of Liberty, Ellis Island, Theodore Roosevelt Birthplace NHS,* and *Castle Clinton NM* in Battery Park. One of the most fun places to visit is *South Street Seaport,* a seven-block restoration of New York's first shipping center along the East River. Climb aboard ships, visit restored shops, and explore the neighborhood.

Saratoga NHP, Stillwater. A tour of this important Revolutionary War battlefield includes the American and British headquarters and a log cabin similar to those used by British and colonial troops. www.nps.gov/sara

★ NORTH CAROLINA ★

Oconaluftee Indian Village, Cherokee. Located on the Cherokee reservation, this village re-creates Indian life as it was over 200 years ago. www.westernncattractions.com/village/htm

Wright Brothers NMem, Kill Devil Hills. Full-scale reproductions of the Wright brothers' planes are displayed along with a reconstruction of their work sheds. www.nps.gov/wrbr

★ NORTH DAKOTA ★

Fort Totten SHS, southwest of Devils Lake. One of the best-preserved relics from the era of the Plains Indian wars, this fort contains 16 of its original brick buildings plus a pioneer museum, general store, and wildlife center. www.ohwy.com/nd/f/fttosths.htm

Frontier Village, Jamestown. A re-creation of pioneer life on the Dakota prairies. www.ohwy.com/nd/f/fronvill.htm

★ OHIO ★

Campus Martius SM Museum, Marietta. A pioneer museum on the site of the oldest pioneer community in Ohio, dating from 1788. www.mariettaohio.info/history/museum/index.php

Hale Farm and Western Reserve Village, Bath. A museum village centered around an 1826 farmhouse. Artisans demonstrate pioneer crafts. www.wrhs.org/sites/hale.htm

Zoar Village SM, Zoar. Restored homes, gardens, and shops depict life in Zoar, established in 1817 as a communal society by members of a German pietist sect.

★ OKLAHOMA ★

National Cowboy and Western Heritage Museum, Oklahoma City. This center commemorates the men and women who contributed to the development of the West. www.cowboyhalloffame.og/index2.html

★ OREGON ★

Aurora Colony Historical Society Buildings, Aurora. Visitors tour the restored buildings of the Aurora Colony, which was established in the 1850s. www.robinwill.com/aur.html

Fort Clatsop NMem, Astoria. A historical reconstruction of Lewis and Clark's 1805-06 winter headquarters, including costumed demonstrations and interpretive displays. www.lewisandclarktrail.com/section4/orcities/astoria/fortclatsop/index.htm

★ PENNSYLVANIA ★

Gettysburg NMP, Gettysburg. Here, in the bloodiest battle of the Civil War, the Union defeated the Confederacy.

Philadelphia is full of history. Many of early America's most significant events took place there, including meetings of the Continental Congress, adoption of the Declaration of Independence, the ringing of the Liberty Bell, and the writing of the Constitution. Visit *Independence NHP,* including the *Liberty Bell, Independence Hall,* and *Franklin Court.* www.nps.gov/inde

Valley Forge NHP. See where the Revolutionary Army wintered in 1777-78, including the fortifications, reconstructed soldiers' huts, and General Washington's headquarters.www.nps.gov/vafo

★ RHODE ISLAND ★

Slater Mill NHS, Pawtucket. This restored cotton mill commemorates the beginnings of America's cotton industry. www.ohwy.com/ri/s/slmihisti.htm

★ SOUTH CAROLINA ★

Fort Sumter NM, Sullivan's Island. The Civil War's first battle took place at this site. www.nps.gov/fosu/pphtml/feespermits.html

Georgetown HD. At the Rice Museum, exhibits recount the development of rice planting in the Unites States. www.georgetown-sc.com/history/district.htm

★ SOUTH DAKOTA ★

1880 Train, Hill City. Vintage steam locomotives haul open and closed coaches on a trip between two old mining camps, following the historical prospector's route and climbing the nation's steepest railroad grade. www.1880train.com

Mount Rushmore NMem, Keystone. Massive 60- to 70-foot-high heads of George Washington, Thomas Jefferson, Theodore Roosevelt, and Abraham Lincoln were sculpted here between 1927 and 1941. www.nps.gov/moru/pphtml/feespermits.html

★ TENNESSEE ★

Marble Springs Historic Farm NHL, Knoxville. A trading post and refuge for early settlers, Marble Springs features a two-story log house, a barn, a loom house, a kitchen, and a smokehouse. www.vic.com/~andretti/knoxville-poi.html#Homes

The Woodruff-Fontaine House, Victorian Village HD, Memphis. This brick home's exhibits include a dollhouse, a carriage house, and a gingerbread playhouse. www.ohwy.com/tn/w/woofonho.htm

★ TEXAS ★

Fort Davis NHS, Fort Davis. Twenty-four buildings, including officers' quarters and troop barracks, are preserved in this fort built in 1854. www.nps.gov/foda

The Alamo, San Antonio. The Alamo commemorates the 189 colonists, including Davey Crockett, who died here in 1836 resisting a 13-day siege by Mexican General Santa Anna's troops. www.thealamo.org

★ UTAH ★

Golden Spike NHS, Brigham City. This site commemorates the completion of the first American transcontinental railroad. www.nps.gov/gosp

★ VERMONT ★

Shelburne Museum, Shelburne. This 45-acre outdoor museum records three centuries of American life.

★ VIRGINIA ★

Colonial NHP, Yorktown. A 23-mile parkway connects ***Jamestown***, the first permanent English settlement; ***Yorktown***, site of the last major battle of the American Revolution, and ***Williamsburg***, colonial capital of Virginia, which includes restorations of more than a hundred buildings. www.nps.gov/colo

Manassas NBP, Manassas. Exhibits and programs describe the Civil War battles fought here. Visit battle sites, monuments, and original buildings, including a tavern used by the Union as a field hospital. www.nps.gov/mana

Mount Vernon. George Washington lived on this Potomac River estate. Tour his house and outbuildings, including stables, kitchen, and slave quarters. www.mountvernon.org

★ WASHINGTON ★

Fort Walla Walla Museum, Walla Walla. The past of this 1856 fort lives on in original and rebuilt structures—including an early homestead, a schoolhouse, and the West's largest collection of horse-drawn farm equipment. www.fortwallawallamuseum.org

Point Defiance Park, Tacoma. The park includes several historic attractions, including Camp 6, a replica turn-of-the-century steam logging camp—including donkey engines, old tracks and trestles, railroad-car camps, and an operating steam locomotive. www.tacomaparks.com/parks&gardens/point_defiance.htm

★ WEST VIRGINIA ★

Harpers Ferry NHP, Harpers Ferry. This restored 19th-century town was the scene of abolitionist John Brown's raid on a federal arsenal. www.nps.gov/hafe

★ WISCONSIN ★

Historylands Logging Camp, Hayward. This reconstructed logging camp features lumbering operations of the past, a log bunkhouse, and a paddle wheel steamboat. www.historylands.com

Stonefield, Nelson Dewey SP, Cassville. On this 2,000-acre farm stands a 19th-century frontier village. www.nationalregisterofhistoricplaces.com/wi/grant/state.html

★ WYOMING ★

Fort Bridger SHS, Fort Bridger. Partially restored, this 1843 fort includes a guard house, Pony Express stables, and exhibits of Wyoming's fur-trapping days. www.spacr.state.wy.us/sphs/bridger.htm

Independence Rock SHS, southwest of Casper. Known as "the great registry of the desert," this 193-foot rock promontory, a landmark on the Oregon Trail, bears messages and inscriptions from westward-bound pioneers.

The Great Seal of the United States of America

FRONT

BACK

On the day that the United States declared its independence, the Founding Fathers realized that the country would need an official seal. In Charles Thomson's design, which was adopted on June 20, 1782, the motto E Pluribus Unum on the front means "one out of many." The pyramid on the reverse side stands for strength, and the motto Novus Ordo Seclorum announces the dawn of a New Order of the Ages. Both sides of the seal appear on the back of the one dollar bill.

Dates States Entered the Union

	STATE	DATE ENTERED UNION		STATE	DATE ENTERED UNION
1	Delaware	December 7, 1787	27	Florida	March 3, 1845
2	Pennsylvania	December 12, 1787	28	Texas	December 29, 1845
3	New Jersey	December 18, 1787	29	Iowa	December 28, 1846
4	Georgia	January 2, 1788	30	Wisconsin	May 29, 1848
5	Connecticut	January 9, 1788	31	California	September 9, 1850
6	Massachusetts	February 6, 1788	32	Minnesota	May 11, 1858
7	Maryland	April 28, 1788	33	Oregon	February 14, 1859
8	South Carolina	May 23, 1788	34	Kansas	January 29, 1861
9	New Hampshire	June 21, 1788	35	West Virginia	June 20, 1863
10	Virginia	June 25, 1788	36	Nevada	October 31, 1864
11	New York	July 26, 1788	37	Nebraska	March 1, 1867
12	North Carolina	November 21, 1789	38	Colorado	August 1, 1876
13	Rhode Island	May 29, 1790	39	North Dakota	November 2, 1889
14	Vermont	March 4, 1791	40	South Dakota	November 2, 1889
15	Kentucky	June 1, 1792	41	Montana	November 8, 1889
16	Tennessee	June 1, 1796	42	Washington	November 11, 1889
17	Ohio	March 1, 1803	43	Idaho	July 3, 1890
18	Louisiana	April 30, 1812	44	Wyoming	July 10, 1890
19	Indiana	December 11, 1816	45	Utah	January 4, 1896
20	Mississippi	December 10, 1817	46	Oklahoma	November 16, 1907
21	Illinois	December 3, 1818	47	New Mexico	January 6, 1912
22	Alabama	December 14, 1819	48	Arizona	February 14, 1912
23	Maine	March 15, 1820	49	Alaska	January 3, 1959
24	Missouri	August 10, 1821	50	Hawaii	August 21, 1959
25	Arkansas	June 15, 1836		Washington, D.C.	February 21, 1871
26	Michigan	January 26, 1837			

U.S. Presidents and Their Terms of Office

1. George Washington, 1789–1797
2. John Adams, 1797–1801
3. Thomas Jefferson, 1801–1809
4. James Madison, 1809–1817
5. James Monroe, 1817–1825
6. John Quincy Adams, 1825–1829
7. Andrew Jackson, 1829–1837
8. Martin Van Buren, 1837–1841
9. William Henry Harrison, 1841*
10. John Tyler, 1841–1845
11. James Knox Polk, 1845–1849
12. Zachary Taylor, 1849–1850*
13. Millard Fillmore, 1850–1853
14. Franklin Pierce, 1853–1857
15. James Buchanan, 1857–1861
16. Abraham Lincoln, 1861–1865*
17. Andrew Johnson, 1865–1869
18. Ulysses Simpson Grant, 1869–1877
19. Rutherford Birchard Hayes, 1877–1881
20. James Abram Garfield, 1881*
21. Chester Alan Arthur, 1881–1885
22. Grover Cleveland, 1885–1889
23. Benjamin Harrison, 1889–1893
24. Grover Cleveland, 1893–1897
25. William McKinley, 1897–1901*
26. Theodore Roosevelt, 1901–1909
27. William Howard Taft, 1909–1913
28. Woodrow Wilson, 1913–1921
29. Warren Gamaliel Harding, 1921–1923
30. Calvin Coolidge, 1923–1929
31. Herbert Clark Hoover, 1929–1933
32. Franklin Delano Roosevelt, 1933–1945*
33. Harry S. Truman, 1945–1953
34. Dwight David Eisenhower 1953–1961
35. John Fitzgerald Kennedy, 1961–1963*
36. Lyndon Baines Johnson, 1963–1969
37. Richard Milhous Nixon, 1969–1974**
38. Gerald Rudolph Ford, 1974–1977
39. James Earl Carter, Jr., 1977–1981
40. Ronald Wilson Reagan, 1981–1989
41. George Herbert Walker Bush, 1989–1993
42. William Jefferson Clinton, 1993–2001
43. George Walker Bush, 2001–Present

*Died in office; ** Resigned*

Bibliography

A general history of this kind relies on the work of literally thousands of scholars, archivists, librarians, and citizens dedicated to preserving and transmitting history. In this bibliography, I list just some of the many scholarly books that serve as the foundation for *The Making of America*. I list general histories of the United States first and then sources that proved useful for each chapter.

GENERAL

The first category of general histories is textbooks that offer coverage of the entire span of the country's past.

The one I have found most useful is:

John Mack Faragher, et al., *Out of Many: A History of the American People* (4th ed., Prentice Hall, Upper Saddle River, N.J.: 2002).

Other excellent texts include:

Edward L. Ayers, et al., *American Passages: A History of the United States* (Vol. 1, Wadsworth Publishing Co., Belmont, Calif.: 1999);

Nelson Lichtenstein, Susan Strasser, and Roy Rosenzweig, *Who Built America? Working People and the Nation's Economy, Politics, Culture, and Society,* Vol. 2, Since 1877 (Worth Publishers, New York, 2000);

John Murrin, et al., *Liberty, Equality, Power: A History of the American People* (Vol. 2, 3rd ed., Wadsworth, Belmont, Calif: 2001);

Gary B. Nash, Julie Roy Jeffrey, et al., *The American People: Creating a Nation and a Society* (2 vols., 5th ed., Addison-Wesley, Reading, Mass.: 2000); and

Mary Beth Norton, et al., *A People and a Nation: A History of the United States* (6th ed., Houghton Mifflin, Boston: 2000).

Joy Hakim, *History of Us* (11 vols.: 2nd rev. ed., Oxford University Press Children's Books, New York: 1999) is written for children.

Second, various reference books offer important information about a variety of topics. The best include:

Paul S. Boyer, et al., eds., *The Oxford Companion to United States History* (Oxford University Press, New York: 2001);

John Mack Faragher, *The American Heritage Encyclopedia of American History* (Henry Holt, New York: 1998);

Eric Foner and John A. Garraty, eds., *The Reader's Companion to American History* (Houghton Mifflin, Boston: 1991); and

Richard B. and Jeffrey B. Morris, eds., *Encyclopedia of American History* (7th rev. ed., HarperCollins, New York: 1996).

Third, historians have written many important works about a host of themes and groups. Among those I recommend the following:

Rodolfo Acuña, *Occupied America: A History of Chicanos* (4th ed., Addison Wesley, Reading, Mass: 1999);

Jon Butler, Grant Wacker, and Randall Balmer, *A Short History of Religion in America* (Oxford University Press, New York: 2002);

Nancy F. Cott, *No Small Courage: A History of Women in the United States* (Oxford University Press, New York: 2000);

Sara M. Evans, *Born For Liberty: A History of Women in America* (Free Press, New York: 1989);

Robert V. Hine and John Mack Faragher, *The American West: A New Interpretive History* (Yale University Press, New Haven, Conn.: 2000);

James Oliver Horton and Lois Horton, *Hard Road to Freedom: The Story of African America* (Rutgers University Press, New Brunswick, N.J.: 2001);

Ronald Takaki, *From Different Shores: Perspectives on Race and Ethnicity in America* (2nd ed., Oxford University Press, New York: 1994) and *A Different Mirror: A History of Multicultural America* (Little, Brown, Boston: 1993);

Stephan Thernstrom, et al., eds., *Harvard Encyclopedia of American Ethnic Groups* (Belknap Press, Cambridge, Mass.: 1980);

Nancy Woloch, *Women and the American Experience, A Concise History* (2nd ed., McGraw-Hill, New York: 2001).

Finally, there are creative interpretive works that cover the entire sweep of American history. These often have a strongly political nature that makes them quite intellectually challenging. Some of the most interesting are:

Eric Foner, *The Story of American Freedom* (W.W. Norton, New York: 1998);

Paul Johnson, *A History of the American People* (HarperCollins, New York: 1999); and

Howard Zinn, *A People's History of the United States: 1492 to the Present* (Harper Perennial, New York, rev. ed.: 2001). (Johnson writes from a conservative point of view, while Foner and Zinn write from a radical perspective.)

★ CHAPTER ONE ★
A New World from Many Old Worlds

Fred Anderson, *A People's Army: Massachusetts Soldiers and Society in the Seven Years' War* (University of North Carolina Press, Chapel Hill: 1984);

Bernard Bailyn, *The Peopling of British North America: An Introduction* (Knopf, New York: 1986);

Paul Boyer and Stephen Nissenbaum, *Salem Possessed: The Social Origins of Witchcraft* (Harvard University Press, Cambridge, Mass.: 1974);

Alfred W. Crosby, Jr., *The Columbian Exchange: Biological*

and Cultural Consequences of 1492 (Greenwood Publishing Company, Westport, Conn.: 1973);

John Putnam Demos, *Entertaining Satan: Witchcraft and the Culture of Early New England* (Oxford University Press, New York: 1982);

Gregory Evans Dowd, *A Spirited Resistance: The North American Indian Struggle for Unity: 1745-1815* (Johns Hopkins University Press, Baltimore: 1992);

Olaudah Equiano, *The Interesting Narrative of Olaudah Equiano or Gustavus Vassa the African* (London, 1789), from http://www.gliah.uh.edu/black_voiced/voices_display.cfm?id=37

David Hackett Fischer, *Albion's Seed: Four British Folkways in America* (Oxford University Press, New York: 1989);

Rhys Isaac, *The Transformation of Virginia: 1740-1790* (University of North Carolina Press, Chapel Hill: 1982);

Francis Jennings, *The Founders of America: How Indians Discovered the Land, Pioneered in It,* and *Created Great Classical Civilizations* (W.W. Norton, New York: 1993);

Winthrop D. Jordan, *White Over Black: American Attitudes Toward the Negro: 1550-1812* (University of North Carolina Press, Chapel Hill: 1968);

Alvin M. Josephy, ed., America in 1492: *The World of the Indian Peoples Before the Arrival of Columbus* (Vintage Books, New York: 1993);

Kenneth A. Lockridge, *A New England Town: The First Hundred Years, Dedham, Massachusetts: 1636-1736* (W.W. Norton, New York: 1970);

Edmund S. Morgan, *American Slavery, American Freedom: The Ordeal of Colonial Virginia* (W.W. Norton, New York: 1975), and *The Puritan Dilemma: The Story of John Winthrop* (2nd ed., Addison-Wesley, Reading, Mass.: 2000);

Samuel Eliot Morison, *The European Discovery of America: The Northern Voyages, A.D. 500-1600* (Oxford University Press, New York: 1971), and *The European Discovery of America: The Southern Voyages, A.D. 1492-1616* (Oxford University Press, New York: 1974);

Frances Mossiker, *Pocahontas: The Life and the Legend* (Da Capo Press, New York: 1996);

Gary B. Nash, *Quakers and Politics: Pennsylvania: 1681-1726* (Princeton University Press, Princeton, N.J.: 1968);

William D. Phillips, Jr., and Carla Rahn Phillips, *The Worlds of Christopher Columbus* (Cambridge University Press, New York: 1992);

Daniel K. Richter, *Facing East from Indian Country: A Native History of Early America* (Harvard University Press, Cambridge, Mass.: 2002);

Helen C. Rountree, *Pocahontas's People : The Powhatan Indians of Virginia Through Four Centuries* (University of Oklahoma Press, Norman: 1996);

Kirkpatrick Sale, *The Conquest of Paradise: Christopher Columbus and the Columbian Legacy* (Knopf, New York: 1990);

Richard Slotkin, *Regeneration Through Violence: The Mythology of the American Frontier* (Wesleyan University Press, Middletown, Conn.: 1973);

David E. Stannard, *American Holocaust: Columbus and the Conquest of the New World* (Oxford University Press, New Yourk, N.Y.: 1992);

Alan Taylor, *American Colonies* (Viking Press, New York: 2001); John Thornton, *Africa and Africans in the Making of the Atlantic World: 1400-1680* (Cambridge University Press, New York: 1992);

Laurel Thatcher Ulrich, *Good Wives: Image and Reality in the Lives of Women in Northern New England: 1650-1750* (Vintage Books, New York: 1982);

David J. Weber, *The Spanish Frontier in North America* (Yale University Press, New Haven, Conn.: 1992); and

Peter Wood, *Black Majority: Negroes in Colonial South Carolina from 1670 Through the Stono Rebellion* (Random House, New York: 1974).

★ CHAPTER TWO ★
A Revolutionary Age

Charles W. Akers, *Abigail Adams: An American Woman* (2nd ed., Addison-Wesley, Reading, Mass.: 1999);

Bernard Bailyn, *The Ideological Origins of the American Revolution* (Belknap Press, Cambridge, Mass.: 1967);

Ira Berlin, *Many Thousands Gone: The First Two Centuries of Slavery in North America* (Harvard University Press, Cambridge, Mass.: 1998);

Saul Cornell, *The Other Founders: Anti-Federalism and the Dissenting Tradition in America: 1788-1828* (University of North Carolina Press, Chapel Hill: 1999);

Edward Countryman, *The American Revolution* (Hill & Wang, New York: 1985);

David Brion Davis, *The Problem of Slavery in the Age of Revolution: 1770-1823* (Cornell University Press, Ithaca, N.Y.: 1975);

Joseph J. Ellis, *Founding Brothers: The Revolutionary Generation* (Knopf, New York: 2001);

David Hacket Fischer, *Paul Revere's Ride* (Oxford University Press, New York,1994);

Eric Foner, *Tom Paine and Revolutionary America* (Oxford University Press, New York: 1976);

James T. Flexner, *The Traitor and the Spy: Benedict Arnold and John André* (Little, Brown, Boston: 1975);

Edith B. Gelles, Portia: *The World of Abigail Adams* (Indiana University Press, Bloomington: 1992);

Merrill Jensen, *The New Nation: A History of the United States During the Confederation: 1781-1789* (Knopf, New York: 1950);

Linda K. Kerber, *Women of the Republic: Intellect and Ideology in Revolutionary America* (University North Carolina Press, Chapel Hill: 1980);

Jan Ellen Lewis and Peter S. Onuf, eds., *Sally Hemings and Thomas Jefferson: History, Memory, and Civic Culture* (University Press of Virginia, Charlottesville: 1999);

David McCullough, *John Adams* (Simon & Schuster, New York: 2001);

Edmund S. Morgan, *The Birth of the Republic: 1763-89* (3rd ed., University of Chicago Press: 1993);

Edmund S. Morgan and Helen M. Morgan, *The Stamp Act Crisis: Prologue to Revolution* (University of North Carolina Press, Chapel Hill: 1983);

Gary B. Nash, *The Urban Crucible: Social Change, Political Consciousness, and the Origins of the American Revolution* (Harvard University Press, Cambridge, Mass.: 1979);

Mary Beth Norton, *Liberty's Daughters: The Revolutionary Experience of American Women: 1750-1800* (Little Brown, Boston: 1980);

Charles Royster, *A Revolutionary People at War: The Continental Army and American Character: 1775-1783* (University of North Carolina Press, Chapel Hill: 1979);

John Shy, *A People Numerous and Armed: Reflections on the Military Struggle for American Independence* (University of Michigan Press, Ann Arbor: 1990);

Marshall Smelser, *The Winning of Independence* (Quadrangle, Chicago: 1972);

Garry Wills, *Inventing America: Jefferson's Declaration of Independence* (Doubleday, Garden City, N.J.: 1978);

Gordon S. Wood, *The Radicalism of the American Revolution* (Knopf, New York: 1992);

Alfred F. Young, *The Shoemaker and the Tea Party: Memory and the American Revolution* (Beacon Press, Boston: 1999);

Alfred F. Young, et al., *We the People: Voices and Images of the New Nation* (Temple University Press, Philadelphia: 1993).

★ **CHAPTER THREE** ★
The New Republic

Joyce Appleby, *Capitalism and a New Social Order: The Republican Vision of the 1790s* (New York University Press, New York: 1984);

Gregory Evans Dowd, *A Spirited Resistance: The North American Struggle for Unity: 1745-1815* (Johns Hopkins University Press, Baltimore: 1992);

Thomas Dublin, *Women at Work: The Transformation of Work and Community in Lowell, Massachusetts: 1826-1860* (Columbia University Press, New York: 1979);

Stanley Elkins and Eric McKitrick, *The Age of Federalism: The Early American Republic: 1788-1800* (Oxford University Press, New York: 1993);

John Mack Faragher, *Sugar Creek: Life on the Illinois Prairie* (Yale University Press, New Have, Conn.: 1986);

Elizabeth Fox-Genovese, *Within the Plantation Household: Black and White Women of the Old South* (University of North Carolina Press, Chapel Hill: 1988);

Eugene D. Genovese, *From Rebellion to Revolution: Afro-American Slave Revolts in the Making of the Modern World* (Louisiana State University Press, Baton Rouge: 1979), and *Roll, Jordon, Roll: The World the Slaves Made* (Pantheon Books, New York: 1974);

Herbert G. Gutman, *The Black Family in Slavery and Freedom: 1750-1925* (Pantheon Books, New York: 1976);

Peter Kolchin, *American Slavery: 1619-1877* (Hill & Wang, New York: 1993);

Lawrence W. Levine, *Black Culture and Black Consciousness: Afro-American Folk Thought From Slavery to Freedom* (Oxford University Press, New York: 1977);

Forrest McDonald, *Alexander Hamilton: A Biography* (W.W. Norton, New York: 1979);

James Oakes, *The Ruling Race: A History of American Slaveholders* (Knopf, New York: 1982);

Arthur M. Schlesinger, Jr., *The Age of Jackson* (Little, Brown, Boston: 1945);

Charles Sellers, *The Market Revolution: Jacksonian America: 1815-1846* (Oxford University Press, New York: 1991);

Thomas P. Slaughter, *The Whiskey Rebellion: Frontier Epilogue to the American Revolution* (Oxford University Press, New York: 1986);

Christine Stansell, *City of Women: Sex and Class in New York: 1789-1860* (Knopf, New York: 1986);

Anthony F. C. Wallace, *The Death and Rebirth of the Seneca* (Vintage Books, New York: 1969);

Harry L. Watson, *Liberty and Power: The Politics of Jacksonian America* (Farrar, Straus & Giroux, New York: 1990); and

Sean Wilentz, *Chants Democratics: New York City and the Rise of the American Working Class: 1788-1850* (Oxford University Press, New York: 1984).

★ **CHAPTER FOUR** ★
A New Birth of Freedom: Civil War and Reconstruction

Iver Bernstein, *The New York City Draft Riots: Their Significance for American Society and Politics in the Age of the Civil War* (Oxford University Press, New York: 1990);

Stanley W. Campbell, *The Slave Catchers: Enforcement of the Fugitive Slave Law: 1850-1860* (University of North Carolina Press, Chapel Hill: 1970);

William J. Cooper, Jr., *The South and the Politics of Slavery: 1828-1856* (Louisiana State Univ. Press, Baton Rouge: 1980);

Ellen Carol DuBois, *Feminism and Suffrage: The Emergence of an Independent Women's Movement in America: 1848-1869* (Cornell University Press, Ithaca, N.Y.: 1978);

W. E. Burghardt Du Bois, *Black Reconstruction: An Essay Toward a History of the Part Which Black Folk Played to Reconstruct Democracy: 1860-1880* (Harcourt Brace, New York: 1935);

John S. D. Eisenhower, *So Far from God: The U.S. War with Mexico: 1846-1848* (Random House, New York: 1989);

John Mack Faragher, *Women and Men on the Overland Trail* (Yale University Press, New Haven Conn.: 1978);

Don E. Fehrenbacher, *The Dred Scott Case: Its Significance in American Law and Politics* (Oxford University Press, New York: 1978);

Eric Foner, *Free Soil, Free Labor, Free Men: The Ideology of the Republican Party Before the Civil War* (Oxford University Press, New York: 1970), and *Reconstruction: America's Unfinished Revolution: 1863-1877* (Harper & Row, New York: 1988);

Shelby Foote, *The Civil War: A Narrative* (Random House, New York: 1958-1974);

Douglas Southall Freeman, *R. E. Lee: A Biography* (Charles Scribner's Sons, New York: 1935);

Larry Gara, *Liberty Line: The Legend of the Underground Railroad* (University of Kentucky Press, Lexington: 1961);

William E. Gienapp, *The Origins of the Republican Party: 1852-1856* (Oxford University Press, New York: 1987);

Michael F. Holt, *The Political Crisis of the 1850s* (John Wiley & Sons, New York: 1978);

Thomas Holt, *Black Over White: Negro Political Leadership in South Carolina During Reconstruction* (University of Illinois Press, Champaign: 1977);

Julie Roy Jeffrey, *Frontier Women: The Trans-Mississippi West: 1840-1880* (Hill & Wang, New York: 1979);

William S. McFeely, *Grant: A Biography* (W.W. Norton, New York: 1981);

Leon F. Litwack, *Been in the Storm So Long: The Aftermath of Slavery* (Knopf, New York: 1979);

James M. McPherson, *Battle Cry of Freedom: The Civil War Era* (Oxford University Press, New York: 1988);

Stephen B. Oates, *To Purge This Land With Blood: A Biography of John Brown* (Harper & Row, New York: 1970), and *With Malice Toward None: The Life of Abraham Lincoln* (Harper & Row, New York: 1977);

David M. Potter, *The Impending Crisis: 1848-1861* (HarperCollins, New York: 1976);

Benjamin Quarles, *Allies for Freedom: Blacks and John Brown* (Oxford University Press, New York: 1974);

James A. Rawley, *Race and Politics: "Bleeding Kansas" and the Coming of the Civil War* (Lippincott, Philadelphia: 1969);

Kenneth M. Stampp, *America in 1857: A Nation on the Brink* (Oxford University Press, New York: 1990);

George Rogers Taylor, *The Transportation Revolution: 1815-1860* (Economic History of the United States, Vol. 4, 1951, reissued by M. E. Sharp, White Plains, N.Y.1977);

Emory M. Thomas, *The Confederate Nation: 1861-1865* (Harper & Row, New York: 1979);

John D. Unruh, *The Plains Across: The Overland Emigrants and the Trans-Mississippi West: 1840-1860* (University of Illinois Press, Champaign: 1979);

David J. Weber, *The Mexican Frontier: 1821-1846: The American Southwest Under Mexico* (University of New Mexico Press, Albuquerque: 1982);

Bell Irvin Wiley, *The Life of Johnny Reb: The Common Soldier of the Confederacy* (Bobbs-Merrill, Indianapolis: 1943) and *The Life of Billy Yank: The Common Soldier of the Union* (Bobbs-Merrill, Indianapolis: 1952);

C. Vann Woodward, *Reunion and Reaction: The Compromise of 1877 and the End of Reconstruction* (Little, Brown, Boston: 1951); and

Gavin Wright, ed., *The Political Economy of the Cotton South: Households, Markets, and Wealth in the Nineteenth Century* (W.W. Norton, New York: 1978).

★ **CHAPTER FIVE** ★
Industry and Empire

Leonard J. Arrington and Davis Bitton, *The Mormon Experience: A History of the Latter-day Saints* (Vintage Books, New York: 1979);

Edward L. Ayers, *The Promise of the New South: Life after Reconstruction* (Oxford University Press, New York: 1992);

Robert L. Beisner, *Twelve Against Empire: The Anti-Imperialists: 1898-1900* (McGraw-Hill, New York: 1968);

John Bodnar, *The Transplanted: A History of Immigrants in Urban America* (Indiana University Press, Bloomington: 1985);

Alfred D. Chandler, Jr., *The Visible Hand: The Managerial Revolution in American Business* (Harvard University Press, Cambridge, Mass.: 1977);

Melvyn Dubofsky, *Industrialism and the American Worker: 1865-1920* (Thomas Y. Crowell, New York: 1975);

Leon Fink, *Workingmen's Democracy: The Knights of Labor and American Politics* (University of Illinois Press, Champaign: 1983);

Gilbert C. Fite, *The Farmers' Frontier: 1865-1900* (Holt, Rinehart & Winston, New York: 1966);

Joseph Frazier Wall, *Andrew Carnegie* (2nd ed., University of Pittsburgh Press: 1989);

John A. Garraty, *The New Commonwealth: 1877-1890* (Harper & Row, New York: 1968);

Lawrence Goodwyn, *Democratic Promise: The Populist Moment in America* (Oxford University Press, New York: 1976);

Herbert G. Gutman, *Work, Culture, and Society in Industrializing America* (Knopf, New York: 1976);

Samuel P. Hays, *The Response to Industrialism: 1885-1914* (University of Chicago Press: 1957);

John D. Hicks, *The Populist Revolt: A History of the Farmers' Alliance and the People's Party* (University of Minnesota Press, Minneapolis: 1931);

Jacqueline Jones, *Labor of Love, Labor of Sorrow: Black Women, Work and the Family from Slavery to the Present* (Random House, New York: 1985);

Matthew Frye Jacobson, *Barbarian Virtues: The United States Encounters Foreign Peoples at Home and Abroad: 1876-1917* (Hill & Wang, New York: 2000);

Matthew Josephson, *The Robber Barons: The Great American Capitalists: 1861-1901* (Harcourt, Brace, New York: 1934);

Michael Kazin, *The Populist Persuasion: An American History* (Basic Books, New York: 1995);

Alice Kessler-Harris, *Out to Work: A History of Wage-Earning Women in the United States* (Oxford University Press, New York: 1982);

J. Morgan Kousser, *The Shaping of Southern Politics: Suffrage Restriction and the Establishment of the One-Party South: 1880-1910* (Yale University Press, New Haven, Conn.: 1974);

Walter LaFeber, *The Cambridge History of American Foreign Relations: The American Search for Opportunity: 1865-1913* (Cambridge University Press, New York: 1993);

Robert C. McMath, *American Populism: A Social History: 1877-1898* (Hill & Wang, New York: 1993);

Nell Irvin Painter, *Standing at Armageddon: The United States: 1877-1919* (W.W. Norton, New York: 1987);

Glenn Porter, *The Rise of Big Business: 1860-1910* (Thomas Y. Crowell, New York: 1973);

Howard N. Rabinowitz, *Race Relations in the Urban South: 1865-1890* (Oxford University Press, New York: 1978);

Wallace Stegner, *The Gathering of Zion: The Story of The Mormon Trail* (McGraw-Hill, New York: 1964);

Robert M. Utley, *The Last Days of the Sioux Nation* (Yale University Press, New Haven, Conn.: 1963);

Philip Weeks, *Farewell, My Nation: The American Indian and the United States: 1820-1890* (Harlan Davidson, Wheeling, Ill.: 1990);

Robert H. Wiebe, *The Search for Order: 1877-1920* (Hill & Wang, New York: 1967);

C. Vann Woodward, *Origins of the New South: 1877-1913* (Louisiana State University Press, Baton Rouge: 1951), *The Strange Career of Jim Crow* (3rd. ed, Oxford University Press, New York: 1974), and

Tom Watson: *Agrarian Rebel* (Oxford University Press, New York: 1938).

★ CHAPTER SIX ★

Progressivism and the New Deal

Alan Brinkley, *Voices of Protest: Huey Long, Father Coughlin and the Great Depression* (Knopf, New York: 1982);

David M. Chalmers, *Hooded Americanism: The History of the Ku Klux Klan* (Quadrangle Books, Chicago: 1965);

John Whiteclay Chambers, II, *The Tyranny of Change: America in the Progressive Era: 1890-1920* (2nd ed., Rutgers University Press, New Brunswick, N.J.: 2000);

Norman Clark, *Deliver Us from Evil: An Interpretation of American Prohibition* (W.W. Norton, New York: 1976);

Lizabeth Cohen, *Making a New Deal: Industrial Workers in Chicago: 1919-1939* (Cambridge University Press, New York: 1990);

Blanche Wiesen Cook, *Eleanor Roosevelt* (2 vols., Viking Press, New York: 1992: 1999);

Nancy F. Cott, *The Grounding of Modern Feminism* (Yale University Press, New Haven Conn.: 1987);

Allen F. Davis, *Spearheads for Reform: The Social Settlements and the Progressive Movement: 1890-1914* (Oxford University Press, New York: 1967);

Kenneth S. Davis, *FDR* (5 vols., Random House, New York: 1972-1993);

Steven J. Diner, *A Very Different Age: Americans of the Progressive Era* (Hill & Wang, New York: 1998);

Stephen R. Fox, *The American Conservation Movement: John Muir and His Legacy* (Little, Brown, Boston: 1981);

Glenda Elizabeth Gilmore, *Gender and Jim Crow: Women and the Politics of White Supremacy in North Carolina: 1896-1920* (University of North Carolina Press, Chapel Hill: 1996);

Glenda Elizabeth Gilmore, ed., *Who Were the Progressives?* (Palgrave Macmillan, New York: 2002);

James N. Gregory, *American Exodus: The Dust Bowl Migration and Okie Culture in California* (Oxford University Press, New York: 1989);

Grace Elizabeth Hale, *Making Whiteness: The Culture of Segregation in the South: 1890-1940* (Random House, New York: 1998);

Louis R. Harlan, Booker T. Washington: *The Wizard of Tuskegee: 1901-1915* (Oxford University Press, New York: 1983);

John Higham, *Strangers in the Land: Patterns of American*

Nativism: 1860-1925 (Rutgers University Press, New Brunswick, N.J.: 1955);

Richard Hofstadter, *The Age of Reform: From Bryan to FDR* (Knopf, New York, 1955);

David M. Kennedy, *Over Here: The First World War and American Society* (Oxford University Press, New York: 1980), and *Freedom from Fear: The American People in Depression and War: 1929-1945* (Oxford University Press, New York: 1999);

Aileen Kraditor, *The Ideas of the Woman Suffrage Movement: 1890-1920* (Columbia University Press, New York: 1965);

David Levering Lewis, *W.E.B. Du Bois: Biography of a Race: 1868-1919* (Henry Holt, New York: 1993);

William Leuchtenberg, *The Perils of Prosperity: 1914-1932* (University of Chicago Press, Chicago: 1958);

Arthur S. Link and Richard L. McCormick, *Progressivism* (Harlan Davidson, Wheeling, Ill.: 1983);

Leon Litwack, *Trouble in Mind: Black Southerners in the Age of Jim Crow* (Knopf, New York: 1998);

Robert S. McElvaine, *The Great Depression: America: 1929-1941* (Times Books, New York: 1984);

Michael E. McGerr, *The Decline of Popular Politics: The American North: 1865-1928* (Oxford University Press, New York: 2002);

David Montgomery, *The Fall of the House of Labor: The Workplace, the State, and American Labor Activism: 1865-1925* (Cambridge University Press, New York: 1987);

Geoffrey Perrett, *America in the Twenties: A History* (Simon & Schuster, New York: 1982);

William Preston, Jr., *Aliens and Dissenters: Federal Suppression of Radicals: 1903-1933* (Harper & Row, New York: 1966);

Francis Paul Prucha, *The Great Father: The United States Government and the American Indians* (University of Nebraska Press, Lincoln: 1984);

Daniel T. Rodgers, *Atlantic Crossings: Social Politics in a Progressive Age* (Harvard University Press, Cambridge, Mass.: 1998);

Nick Salvatore, *Eugene V. Debs: Citizen and Socialist* (University of Illinois Press, Champaign: 1982);

Elizabeth Sanders, *Roots of Reform: Farmers, Workers, and the American State: 1877-1917* (University of Chicago Press: 1999);

Patricia A. Schechter, *Ida B. Wells-Barnett and American Reform: 1880-1930* (University of North Carolina Press, Chapel Hill: 2001);

Martin J. Sklar, *The Corporate Reconstruction of American Capitalism, 1890-1916: The Market, the Law, and Politics* (Cambridge University Press, New York: 1988);

Rosalyn Terborg-Penn, *African American Women in the Struggle for the Vote: 1850-1920* (Indiana University Press, Bloomington: 1998);

William Tuttle, Jr., *Race Riot: Chicago in the Red Summer of 1919* (Atheneum, New York: 1970);

Robert B. Westbrook, *John Dewey and American Democracy* (Cornell University Press, Ithaca, N.Y.: 1991); and

Donald Worster, *Dust Bowl: The Southern Plains in the 1930s* (Oxford University Press, New York: 1979).

★ CHAPTER SEVEN ★
War, Prosperity, and Social Change

John Morton Blum, *V Was for Victory: Politics and American Culture During World War II* (Harcourt Brace Jovanovich, New York: 1977);

Taylor Branch, *Parting the Waters: America in the King Years: 1954-63* (Simon & Schuster, New York: 1988), and *Pillar of Fire: America in the King Years: 1963-65* (Simon & Schuster, New York: 1998);

David Burner, *John F. Kennedy and a New Generation* (Scott Foresman, New York: 1988);

David Chalmers, *And the Crooked Places Made Straight: The Struggle for Social Change in the 1960s* (Johns Hopkins University Press, Baltimore: 1991);

John Dittmer, *Local People: The Struggle for Civil Rights in Mississippi* (University of Illinois Press, Champaign: 1994);

John D'Emilio, *Sexual Politics, Sexual Communities: The Making of a Homosexual Minority in the United States: 1940-1970* (University of Chicago Press: 1998);

John Dower, *War Without Mercy: Race and Power in the Pacific War* (Pantheon, New York: 1986);

Steve Fraser and Gary Gerstle, eds., *The Rise and Fall of the New Deal Order: 1930-1980* (Princeton University Press, Princeton, N.J.: 1989);

Richard M. Fried, *Nightmare in Red: The McCarthy Era in Perspective* (Oxford University Press, New York: 1990);

John Lewis Gaddis, *We Now Know: Rethinking Cold War History* (Oxford University Press, New York: 1997);

Martin Gilbert, *The Second World War: A Complete History* (Henry Holt, New York: 1989);

Todd Gitlin, *The Sixties: Years of Hope, Days of Rage* (Bantam Books, New York: 1987);

Lewis Gould, *1968: The Election That Changed America* (Ivan R. Dee, Chicago: 1993);

David Halberstam, *The Fifties* (Villard Books, New York: 1993);

Jon Halliday and Bruce Cumings, *Korea: The Unknown War* (Pantheon Books, New York: 1988);

Alonzo Hamby, *Liberalism and Its Challengers: From F.D.R. to Bush* (Oxford University Press, New York: 1992), and *Man of the People: A Life of Harry S. Truman* (Oxford University Press, New York: 1998);

Susan Hartmann, *The Home Front and Beyond: American*

Women in the 1940s (Twayne, Old Tappan, N.J.: 1982);

George Herring, *America's Longest War: The United States and Vietnam: 1950-1975* (Knopf, New York: 1986);

Peter H. Irons, *Justice at War: The Inside Story of the Japanese-American Internment Cases* (University of California Press, Berkeley: 1993);

Kenneth T. Jackson, *Crabgrass Frontier: The Suburbanization of the United States* (Oxford University Press, New York: 1985);

Stanley I. Kutler, *The Wars of Watergate: The Last Crisis of Richard Nixon* (W.W. Norton, New York: 1992);

Nicholas Lemann, *The Promised Land: The Great Black Migration and How It Changed America* (Vintage Books, New York: 1992);

Nelson Lichtenstein, *"The Most Dangerous Man in Detroit": Walter Reuther and the Fate of American Labor* (Basic Books, New York: 1995);

Allen J. Matusow, *The Unraveling of America: A History of Liberalism in the 1960s* (Harper and Row, New York, 1984);

Elaine Tyler May, *Homeward Bound: American Families in the Cold War Era* (Basic Books, New York: 1999);

Thomas J. McCormick, *America's Half-Century: United States Foreign Policy in the Cold War* (Johns Hopkins University Press, Baltimore: 1989);

James Miller, *"Democracy Is in the Streets": From Port Huron to the Siege of Chicago* (Harvard University Press, Cambridge, Mass.: 1994);

Richard Natkiel, *Atlas of World War II* (Bison Books, London, 1985);

Chester Pach, Jr., and Elmo Richardson, *The Presidency of Dwight D. Eisenhower* (University Press of Kansas, Lawrence: 1991);

James T. Patterson, *America's Struggle Against Poverty in the Twentieth Century* (Harvard University Press, Cambridge, Mass.: 2000), and *Grand Expectations: The United States: 1945-1974* (Oxford University Press, New York: 1996);

Richard Rhodes, *The Making of the Atomic Bomb* (Touchstone Books, New York: 1995);

Jonathan Rieder, *Canarsie: The Jews and Italians of Brooklyn Against Liberalism* (Harvard University Press, Cambridge, Mass.: 1987);

Arthur M. Schlesinger, *Robert Kennedy and His Times* (Ballantine Books, New York: 1996);

Ellen Schrecker, *Many Are the Crimes: McCarthyism in America* (Little, Brown, Boston: 1998);

Michael Schudson, *Watergate in American Memory: How We Remember, Forget, and Reconstruct the Past* (Basic Books, New York: 1993);

Martin Sherwin, *A World Destroyed: The Atomic Bomb and the Grand Alliance* (Knopf, New York: 1975);

Harvard Sitkoff and Eric Foner, *The Struggle for Black Equality: 1954-1992* (Hill & Wang, New York: 1993);

Ronald Takaki, *Double Victory: A Multicultural History of America in World War II* (Little, Brow, Boston: 2000),

Studs Terkel, ed., *"The Good War": An Oral History of World War II* (New Press, New York: 1997);

Stephen J. Whitfield, *The Culture of the Cold War* (Johns Hopkins University Press, Baltimore: 1991);

David Wyman, *The Abandonment of the Jews: America and the Holocaust: 1941-1945* (New Press, New York: 1998); and

Marilyn Blatt Young, *The Vietnam Wars: 1945-1990* (Harper Collins, New York: 1991).

★ **CHAPTER EIGHT** ★
The Age of Conservatism

William C. Berman, *America's Right Turn: From Nixon to Clinton* (Johns Hopkins University Press, Baltimore: 1998);

Mary Frances Berry, *Why ERA Failed* (Indiana University Press, Bloomington: 1986);

Dan T. Carter, *The Politics of Rage: George Wallace, the Origins of the New Conservatism, and the Transformation of American Politics* (Louisiana State University Press, Baton Rouge: 1996);

Peter N. Carroll, *It Seemed Like Nothing Happened: America in the 1970s* (Rutgers University Press, New Brunswick, N.J.: 1990);

Clayborne Carson, *In Struggle: SNCC and the Black Awakening of the 1960s* (Harvard University Press, Cambridge, Mass.: 1995);

Alan Dershowitz, *Supreme Injustice: How the High Court Hijacked Election 2000* (Oxford University Press, New York: 2001);

Alice Echols, *Daring to Be Bad: Radical Feminism in America: 1967-1975* (University of Minnesota Press, Minneapolis: 1989);

Thomas Byrne Edsall, with Mary D. Edsall, *Chain Reaction: The Impact of Race, Rights, and Taxes on American Politics* (W.W. Norton, New York: 1991);

Sara Evans, *Personal Politics: The Roots of Women's Liberation in the Civil Rights Movement and the New Left* (Vintage Books, New York: 1979);

John R. Greene, *The Presidency of Gerald R. Ford* (University Press of Kansas, Lawrence: 1995);

Samuel P. Hays, *Beauty, Health, and Permanence: Environmental Politics in the United States: 1955-1985* (Cambridge University Press, New York: 1987);

Jerome Himmelstein, *To the Right: The Transformation of American Conservatism* (University of California Press, Berkeley: 1990);

Godfrey Hodgson, *The World Turned Right Side Up: A*

History of the Conservative Ascendancy in America (Houghton Mifflin, New York: 1996);

Joan Hoff, *Nixon Reconsidered* (Basic Books, New York: 1995);

Maurice Isserman and Michael Kazin, *America Divided: The Civil War of the 1960s* (Oxford University Press, New York: 1999);

Burton I. Kaufman, *The Presidency of James Earl Carter, Jr.* (University Press of Kansas, Lawrence: 1993);

Rebecca E. Klatch, *Women of the New Right* (Temple University Press, Philadelphia: 1988);

Michael Lienesch, *Redeeming America: Piety and Politics in the New Christian Right* (University of North Carolina Press, Chapel Hill: 1993);

Anthony J. Lukas, *Common Ground: A Turbulent Decade in the Lives of Three American Families* (Knopf, New York: 1986);

Jane Mansbridge, *Why We Lost the ERA* (University of Chicago Press: 1986);

David Maraniss, *First in His Class: The Biography of Bill Clinton* (Touchstone Books, New York: 1996);

Kim Moody, *An Injury to All: The Decline of American Unionism* (Routledge, New York: 1997);

Herbert S. Parmet, *George Bush: The Life of a Lone Star Yankee* (Simon & Schuster, New York: 1997);

Kevin Phillips, *Boiling Point: Democrats, Republicans, and the Decline of Middle-Class Prosperity* (Harper Perennial, New York: 1993);

Richard A. Posner, *Breaking the Deadlock: The 2000 Election, the Constitution, and the Courts* (Princeton University Press, Princeton, N.J.: 2001);

Kirkpatrick Sale, *The Green Revolution: The American Environmental Movement: 1962-1992* (Hill & Wang, New York: 1993);

Michael Schaller, *Reckoning with Reagan: America and Its President in the 1980s* (Oxford University Press, New York: 1992);

Philip Shabecoff, *A Fierce Green Fire: The American Environmental Movement* (Hill & Wang, New York: 1993);

Garry Wills, *Reagan's America: Innocents at Home* (Doubleday, Garden City, N.J.: 1987);

David P. Thelen, *Becoming Citizens in the Age of Television: How Americans Challenged the Media and Seized Political Initiative During the Iran-Contra Debate* (University of Chicago Press: 1996); and

Bob Woodward, *The Agenda: Inside the Clinton White House* (Pocket Books, New York: 1995).

Quote Sources

ANB=American National Biography Online

JB=John Bartlett, *Familiar Quotations, 15th ed.* (Little, Brown, Boston: 1980)

Boyd=Julian P. Boyd, ed. *Papers of Thomas Jefferson,* Vol. II, Princeton University Press, 1955.

Cott=Nancy F. Cott, *No Small Courage: A History of Women in America* (Oxford University Press, New York: 2000).

Evans=Sara M. Evans, *Born for Liberty: A History of Women in America* (Free Press, New York: 1989).

Foner=Eric Foner, *Tom Paine and Revolutionary America* (Oxford University Press, New York: 1976).

Hine=Robert V. Hine and John Mack Faragher, *The American West: A New Interpretive History* (Yale University Press, New Haven, Conn.: 2000).

JMF=John Mack Faragher, Mari Jo Buhle, et al., *Out of Many: A History of the American People* (2nd ed., Prentice Hall, Upper Saddle River, N.J.: 1997).

Jordan=Robert Paul Jordan, *The Civil War* (National Geographic, Washington, D.C.: 1969)

Lichtenstein=Nelson Lichtenstein, Susan Strasser, and Roy Rosenzweig, *Who Built America? Working People and the Nation's Economy, Politics, Culture, and Society,* Vol. 2, Since 1877 (Worth Publishers, New York, 2000.)

Nash=Gary Nash, Julie Roy Jeffrey, et al., *The American People: Creating a Nation and a Society* (3rd ed., Vol. 1, HarperCollins, New York: 1994).

OE=Olaudah Equiano, *The Interesting Narrative of Olaudah Equiano or Gustavus Vassa the African* (London, 1789), from http://www.gliah.uh.edu/black_voiced/voices_display.cfm?id=37

Oshinsky=David M. Oshinsky, *A Conspiracy So Immense: The World of Joe McCarthy* (Free Press, New York, 1983.)

Quinn= Paul Hulton and David Beers Quinn, *American Drawings of John White 1577–1590* (Univ. of North Carolina Press, Chapel Hill, 1964.)

★ CHAPTER ONE ★

Vespucci: "A New World...Africa." p. 10 (JB, 152); Columbus: "The best thing...is gold," p. 14 (JMF, 41); "Should your majesties...slaves." p.14 (JMF, 41, 36); "a gourd...liquor," p. 14 (Quinn, 414); Columbus "in the crown...Castile," p. 15; Las Casas: "the entire human is one," p. 15 (JMF, 39)King James: "loathsome...the lungs." p. 19 (Nash, 40); Now...my fate in Virginia. p.19 (JMF, 63); Equiano: "With the loathsomeness...relieve me," p. 20 (OE); Cugoano: "I must own...my own complexion," p. 20 (JMF, 86); "rammed like herring in a barrel," p. 20–21 (JMF, 87); "Ten times...paganism," p. 22 (JMF, 95); "put the power in the people," p.23 (Nash, 63); Penn: "a holy experiment," p. 23 (JMF, 71); "To win and incite...the Christian faith," p.25 (Nash, 51); Winthrop: "We must delight...and suffer together," and "For we must consider...upon us," p. 26 (Nash 48); Reagan: "I have always...city on a hill." p. 26 (1974 address to the Conservative Political Action Conference); "My father came here for religion, but I came for fish," p. 29, (Nash, 58); "The spirit...awfully withdrawn," p. 29 (Nash, 125).

★ CHAPTER TWO ★

Washington: "Liberty, when...rapid growth." p. 30 (Letter to James Madison, March 2, 1788); Henry: "Give me liberty...death." p. 36 (JB, 383); Bernard: "war of plunder" and "distinction between rich and poor," p. 36 (Nash, 152); "The industry...ladies," p. 37 (JMF, 158); "mark the supremacy of Parliament," p. 37 (Nash, 156); Henry: "The distinctions...American," p. 39 (Nash, 160); George III: "Open and avowed Rebellion," p. 40 (Nash, 161); Paine: "O! ye that love mankind. O! receive...an asylum for mankind," p. 41 (Tom Paine, "Common Sense") http://www.gliah.uh.edu/documents/documents_p2.cfm?doc=267); "These are the times that try men's souls.... the more glorious the triumph," p. 41 (Paine, "The Crisis": http://www.ushistory.org/paine/crisis/c-01.htm); "repeated injuries and usurpations," p. 42 (Declaration of Independence); "We hold these truths to be...Happiness." p. 42 (Declaration of Independence); A. Adams: "I desire...ancestors," "All Men would be tyrants if they could," and "We...rebellion," p. 43 (Evans, 56); "her majesty," p. 43 (ANB); J. Adams: "Depend upon it,...Masculine systems." and "despotism of the Peticoat," p. 43 (Letter to Abigail Adams April 14, 1776, *Adams Family Correspondence* 1:382); "Civilization...savages," p. 46 (Nash, 187); Jefferson: "A little rebellion...rebellion." p. 50 (letter to James Madison, January 30, 1787, Boyd p. 93).

★ CHAPTER THREE ★

"We the people...of America." p. 54 (Constitution); Adams: "His Highness...United States," p. 57 (JMF, 214-5); Washington: "a parcel of barbarians," p. 59 (JMF, 207); Washington: "With slight...the spirit of party," p. 59 (JMF, 222); Tecumseh: "These lands are ours...place for us." p. 64 (JB, 419); Sequoyah: "When a writing...the white man." p. 64 (*The Cherokee Advocate*); Tecumseh: "The white race...pale face." p. 65 (JMF, 255–56); Jackson: "the majority...govern," p.70 (JMF, 282); Jackson: "There are no necessary evils...abuses." p. 70 (JB, 419); Turner: "Was...treatment," p. 73 (JMF, 326); Turner: "Ordained...the Almighty," p. 73 (ANB); Turner: "White spirits...battle," p. 73 (JMF, 326); Turner: "arise...weapons," p. 73 (ANB); "the suspicion...explosion," p. 73 (ANB); Jefferson: "This momentous...the Union," p. 74 (JMF, 266).

★ CHAPTER FOUR ★

Lincoln: "A house divided...cannot stand," p. 76 (JB, 520); "I now...isolated household," p. 79 (Cott, 235); "The history of mankind...absolute tyranny over her," p. 80 (Seneca Falls Declaration, http://www.ku.edu/carrie/docs/texts/seneca.htm); Marshall: "Boys...gold mine!" p. 81 (Hine, 234); O'Sullivan: "Our manifest destiny...continent," p. 83 (Hine, 199); Taney: "Beings...bound to respect," p. 85 (Nash, 481); Douglass: "A most scandalous... Constitution," p.85 (Nash, 482); Brown: "It is deemed necessary...let it be done." p. 87 (JB, 486)); Emerson: "The gallows...the cross," p. 87; Thoreau: "An angel of light," p. 87 (JMF, 461); Garrison: "A covenant...hell," p. 88 (ANB); Lincoln: "We must not be enemies." p. 90 (JB, 521); Davis: "The American idea...established," p. 91 (JMF, 467); Lincoln: "The better angels...nature," p. 91 (JMF, 468); Lincoln: "If I could save the Union...I would do it," p. 94 (JMF, 492); Lincoln: "What I do about Slavery...save this Union." p. 94 (JMF, 492); "We are cheered in every town we pass through." p. 96 (JMF, 493); Lincoln: "Four score...can long endure." and "this nation under God...from the earth." p. 97 (JB, 523); Lincoln: "with malice toward none...drawn with the sword," p. 97 (JB, 524); Marshall: "He triumphed...respect to his enemy." p. 99 (Jordan, 200); Stevens: "The whole fabric...changed," p. 99 (JMF, 519); Garfield: "The overwhelming...nothing," p. 103 (JMF, 541).

★ CHAPTER FIVE ★

Rockefeller: "The day of combination...never to return." p. 104

(*Historical Atlas of the United States,* National Geographic p. 174); Rockefeller: "The good Lord...conscience." p. 108 (JMF, 589); "We meet...fortunes," p. 115 (Nash, 596); "We seek...originated," p. 115 (JMF, 627); "From the same...paupers and millionaires." p. 116 (Nash, 596); Sherman: "The more I see...pauper," p.117 (JMF, 551); "kill the Indian...save the man," p. 118 (JMF, 576); Joseph: "Hear me...no more forever," p. 119 (Hine, 374); Joseph: "Treat...Great Spirit Chief," p. 119 (JMF, 552); Black Elk: "I can see... beautiful dream," p. 120 (JMF, 576); Strong: "the rest...Christianized and civilized," p. 121 (JMF, 637); Beveridge: "Has made us...regeneration of the world," p. 121 (JMF, 637); McKinley: "We want no...aggression," p. 122 (JMF, 640); Hay: "a splendid little war," p. 122 (Nash, 682); McKinley: "The American people...wherever they go." p. 123 (Second Inaugural address, 1901, from http://www.cc.ukans.edu/carrie/docs/texts/29mcki2.htm); Gompers: "Perhaps nearer...nation on earth," p.xx (JMF, 644); "The Real 'White Man's Burden,'"p. 125 (Nash, 686).

★ CHAPTER SIX ★

FDR: "The only thing we have to fear is fear itself," p. 128 (JB, 779); B.T. Washington:"The wisest...extremest folly," p. 134 (ANB); B.T. Washington: "In all things...mutual progress," p. 134 (ANB); Du Bois: "The problem...the color line." p. 135 (JB, 724); "One feels...strivings," (JB, 725); "Any discrimination...barbarous," p. 135 (JMF, 675); "Persistent manly...liberty." p. 135 (JMF, 675): Wilson: "The world...democracy," p. 137 (JMF, 696); "The colored soldier...armies return," p. 138 (JMF, 699); Wells-Barnett: "The more...outraged and lynched," p. 140 (ANB); "She has plenty...steel trap," p. 140 (ANB); Wells-Barnett: "Is there no redress..for us," p. 141 (*The American Republic to 1877*, Glencoe-McGraw Hill, p. 543); Harding: "return to normalcy," p. 142 (JMF, 715); "I've given up...no use," p. 146 (JMF, 760); FDR: "I pledge you...the American people," p. 146 (JMF, 763); FDR: "most dangerous men in America," p.148 (ANB) Long: "to break...all the people," and "Every man a king." p. 148 (JMF, 767-8).

★ CHAPTER SEVEN ★

Kennedy: "Let both sides...law." p. 150 (Inaugural Address); Mussolini: "We have buried...liberty," p. 153 (JMF, 794); FDR: "All aid...short of war," p. 154 (JMF, 796); Yoneda: "There were no lights...no toilets or washrooms," p. 156 (JMF, 805); Hughes: "Looky here America...Include me?" p. 157 (JMF, 807); "Strategic monstrosity," p. 163 (JMF, 838); "Are you...a Communist?" p. 164 (JMF, 850); McCarthy: "conspiracy so immense," p. 164 (Oshinsky); "Conduct unbecoming a member," p. 164 (JMF, 850); Kennedy: "Ask not what your country can...country. p. 168 (JB, 890); King: "jobs and freedom," p. 168 (Lichtenstein, 616); King: "I have a dream...created equal." p. 169 (http://www.king-raleigh.org/main.cfm); King: "I just want to do God's will...the promised land," p. 169 (ANB); Friedan: "The feminine mystique...possibilities." p. 172 (*National Geographic Eyewitness to the 20th Century,* 257); "To bring women...American society," p. 172 (JMF, 949).

★ CHAPTER EIGHT ★

Clinton: "The era..over" p. 176 (Lichtenstein, 768); Ford: "Our long national nightmare is over." p. 182 (JMF, 975); "A Democrat...like a Republican," p. 185 (JMF, 977); Reagan: "Those who say..to look" p. 188 (http://www.cc.ukans.edu/carrie/docs/texts/49rega1.htm); Bush: "In crucial things...generosity" p. 192 (Inaugural Address); Franklin: "They that give up..safety" p. 197 (JB, 348).

★ Index ★

Illustrations are indicated by **boldface**. If illustrations are included within a page span, the entire span is **boldface**.

Oliver, Andrew
    effigy 36
Oneida Indians 45–46
Opechancanough (Algonquin Indian)
    17
Oregon 69, 83, 118, 133
Oregon Trail **79**, 82–83
    map 82
O'Sullivan, John L. 83
Oswald, Lee Harvey 168, 171

★ **P** ★

Paine, Thomas 40–42, **41**
Palestine
    leaders **192**
Parks, Rosa **166**, 166–167
PATRIOT Act of 2002 196
Peace Corps **151**, 168
Pearl Harbor, Oahu, Hawaii 151, 155,
    155, 221
Penn, William 22, 23, **23**
Pennsylvania 22, 23, 59, 66
Pentagon, Arlington, Virginia 177,
    195
Perot, Ross 191–192
Persian Gulf War **177**, 190–191, **191**
    map 191
Philadelphia, Pennsylvania 23, **33**, 38
    centennial celebration **104**, 105
    Constitutional Convention 51–52
    iron advertisement **66**
Phonograph **114**
Pilgrims 22
Pinchot, Gifford 133
Pioneers 82–83, **83**
    trail map 82
Plymouth, Massachusetts 22
Plymouth Meeting, Pennsylvania **89**
Pocahontas 10, 18, **18**
Polio vaccine **150**
Political parties 58–59, 115–116
Polk, James K. 75
Ponce de León, Juan **10**
Populists 115–116, 124
Powell, Colin **195**
Powhatan (Algonquin leader) 17, 18
Prescott, Samuel 39
Presley, Elvis **165**
Progressive Party 132–133, 136
Prohibition 143, **143**
Protestant fundamentalism 144
Providence, Rhode Island **66**
Pueblo culture 13
    handprints **10**
Puritans 24–25, **25**, 26, **28**, 28–29

★ **Q** ★

Quakers 23, 25, 89, **89**

★ **R** ★

Racism 124–125, 126, **127**, 133, 143–145,
    180, 188, 189, 197
Radical Republicans 99, 100, 101
Radio
    advertisement **142**
Railroads 66–67, 103
    maps 67, 117
Rankin, Jeannette 155
Rawding, Sylvester **116**
Ray, James Earl 169
Reagan, Ronald 26–27, 186, **186**, 187,
    188
Reconstruction 77, 99–100, **100**,
    100–102
Religions 14, 21–22, 23, 24–25, 73
    see also Christianity
Republicans 59–60, 84, 102, 103, 136,
    192, 193
Revere, Paul 39, **39**
    engraving by **42**
Revolutionary War 37, **37**, 41, 46, **46**,
    220
    map 47
    medals **48**
    money **50**
    recruiting notice **44**
Rhode Island 25, 53
Richmond, Virginia 98, **98**
Riots 96, 156, **170**, **188**, 189–190
Rivera, Diego
    murals by **130**
Roads
    map 67
Rockefeller, John D. 108, 110
Rolfe, John 18, 19
Rolfe, Thomas 18
Roosevelt, Franklin Delano 146–147,
    148, **150**, 160, **160**
    New Deal mural **129**
    World War II 154–155, 156
Roosevelt, Theodore 121, 133, **133**, 136,
    136
Running Bear, Oscar **183**

★ **S** ★

Sacagawea (Shoshone Indian) 54, 62
Sadat, Anwar **185**
Salem, Massachusetts **27**
Salina, Kansas 156–157
Salk, Jonas **150**
Schlafly, Phyllis 173

Schools **11**, **126**, 144, **150**, 166, 180,
    180, 193
Scopes, John T. 144
Scott, Dred **84**, 84–85
Second Great Awakening 70–71, 113
Segregation 105, **127**, 133, 138, 156–157,
    166, 180
Seneca Falls, New York 77, 79, 80
Sequoyah (Cherokee scholar) 64
Seven Years War **30**, 33, 34
    see also French and Indian War
Seward, William 122
Shaw, Robert Gould **95**
Shawnee Indians **55**, 64–65
Shays, Daniel 49
Shays's Rebellion 49–50, **50**
Sherman, William T. 98, 117, 118
Shoshone Indians 62
Sitting Bull (Sioux leader) 107
Slavery 19, 20–22, **22**, 25, 33, 61, **71–77**,
    83–91
    American Revolution 44–45
    emancipation **94**, 94–95
    maps 74, 84, 85
    Middle Passage 20–21, **21**, 25
Smalls, Robert 100
Smith, Buffalo Bob **165**
Smith, John **10**, 18
Smith, Joseph 113
Smith, Samuel A. 87
Smith College, Northampton,
    Massachusetts **173**
Snake
    as symbol **42**
South Carolina 70, 90, 93, 100
Soviet Union 154, 155, 159, 162–163, 168,
    182, 186, 188, 190
Space shuttles **178**
Spain
    colonies 17
Spanish-American War 122–123
St. Augustine, Florida 17
Stalin, Joseph **160**, 162
Stamp Act 30, 35–37
    cartoon **34**
Standard Oil Company
    cartoon **108**
Stanton, Elizabeth Cady 79, 80, **80**
Stanton, Henry 80
"The Star-Spangled Banner" 63, 218
Stars and Stripes (flag) 4
Statue of Liberty, New York 4, **104**
Steamboats **54**, **71**
Stock market 145–146
Stowe, Harriet Beecher 76

★ Illustration Credits ★

Abbreviations:
  NG=National Geographic Image Collection
  t=top, b=bottom, c=center, l=left, r=right

Cover (Statue of Liberty), PhotoLink/Getty Images; (flag), Photographic History Collection, National Museum of American History, Smithsonian Institution, neg. no. 83.7221.

Front Matter
1, Marie-Louise Brimberg; 2, White House Collection, courtesy White House Historical Association (538); 8, White House Collection, courtesy White House Historical Association.

Chapter One: A New World From Many Old Worlds
10 (l), George H. H. Huey; 10 (c-l), Metropolitan Museum of Art; 10 (c-r), The Granger Collection, New York; 10 (r), "The Lookout", by Wm. R. Leigh, Woolaroc Museum, Bartlesville Oklahoma; 11 (l), CORBIS; 11 (c-l), courtesy The Library of Congress; 11 (c-r), The Granger Collection, New York; 11 (r), Metropolitan Museum of Art; 12, Tom Till Photography; 13, courtesy Plimoth Plantation, photograph by Bert Lane; 14 (t), Private Collection / Bridgeman Art Library; 14 (b), British Museum; 15 (t), Warren Morgan; 15 (b), CORBIS; 17, Louis S. Glanzman; 18, The Granger Collection, New York; 19, Farrell Grehan; 21 (t), Margaret Bourke-White/TimePix; 21 (b),woodcut from Thomas Clarkson, reprint London, Frank Cass, 1968; 22, Colonial Williamsburg; 23, Thomas Gilcrease Institute of American History & Art; 24 (t), Wayne McLoughlin; 24 (b), Signing of the Mayflower Compact, Percy Moran, Pilgrim Society; 25, CORBIS; 27, CORBIS; 28, John Berkey; 29, George Whitefield, NPG131, by John Wolloston, National Portrait Gallery Picture Library.

Chapter Two: A Revolutionary Age
30 (l), detail of "The Death of General Wolfe" by Benjamin West, National Gallery of Canada, Transfer from the Canadian War Memorials, 1921 (Gift of the 2nd Duke of Westminster, Eaton Hall, Cheshire, 1918); 30 (l-c), James L. Stanfield, NG; 30 (c-r), The Granger Collection, New York; 30 (r), courtesy Daughters of the American Revolution; 31 (l), Farrell Grehan; 31 (c-l), Collection of The New-York Historical Society; 31 (c-r), John Lewis Stage; 31 (r), courtesy The Library of Congress; 32, courtesy The Library of Congress; 33, I.N. Phelps Stokes Collection, New York Public Library; 34 (t), Prince Consorts Library England; 34 (b), Historical Society of Pennsylvania; 35 (t), John Ward Dunsmore; 35 (b), Anne S. K. Brown Military Collection, Brown University Library; 36, Virginia Historical Society; 37, The Granger Collection, New York; 38 (t), CORBIS; 38 (b), courtesy American Antiquarian Society; 39, courtesy UnumProvident Corporation; 40 (t), Victor R. Boswell, Jr.; 40 (b), painting by W. B. Woollen, with permission of the National Army Museum, Chelsea; 41, George F. Mobley; 42 (t), "Join or Die." Engraving at masthead of the *Massachusetts Spy*, 7 July 1774. MHS 2242, courtesy Massachusetts Historical Society; 42 (b), Historical Society of Pennsylvania; 43, The Granger Collection, New York; 44 (t), courtesy The Library of Congress; 44 (b), Terrill Eiler; 45, Chicago Historical Society; 46, Vladimir Kordic; 48 (t), Ted Spiegel; 48 (b), Victor R. Boswell, Jr.; 49, Lithograph by E.P. & L. Restein, courtesy The Library of Congress; 50 (t), CORBIS; 50 (b), Historical Society of Pennsylvania, photograph by Victor R. Boswell, Jr.; 51, by Junius Brutus Sterns from Virginia Museum of Fine Arts, Gift of Col. & Mrs. Edgar W. Garbisch; 52, Painting by Charles Willson Peale, Independence National Historical Park; 53, courtesy The Library of Congress.

Chapter Three: The New Republic
54 (l), National Museum of American History, Smithsonian Institution; 54 (c-l), George F. Mobley; 54 (c-r), Doris S. Clymer; 54 (r), Museum of the City of New York; 55 (l), The Granger Collection, New York; 55 (c-l), Albany Institute of History & Art; 55 (c-r), Field Museum of Natural History; 55 (r), Texas State Capitol; 56, Emory Kristof, NG; 57, The Granger Collection, New York; 58 (t), Atwater Kent Museum; 58 (b), National Academy Museum; 59, Burning Jay effigy from Edward S. Ellis, Youth's History of the U.S., New York, 1887; 60, Lisa Biganzoli, NG; 61, Eastern National Park & Monument Association; 62, Missouri Historical Society, photograph by Richard S. Durrance; 63 (l), The Granger Collection, New York; 63 (r), The Peale Museum; 65, "The Trail of Tears", by Robert Lindneux, Woolaroc Museum, Bartlesville Oklahoma; 66 (t), Rhode Island School of Design; 66 (b), Historical Society of Pennsylvania; 68 (t), Yale University Art Gallery; 68 (b), IBM Corp; 69 (l), Peabody Essex Museum; 69 (t), Courtesy, Museum of Fine Arts, Boston. Reproduced with permission. c2002 Museum of Fine Arts, Boston. 54.1575. All Rights Reserved; 71, The Granger Collection, New York; 72, Chicago Historical Society; 73, Nat Turner/CORBIS; 75, The Granger Collection, New York.

Chatper Four: A New Birth of Freedom: Civil War and Reconstruction
76 (l), James L. Amos; 76 (c-l), Charles L. Blockson Afro-American Collection; 76 (c-r), Modern Enterprises; 76 (r), Kansas State Historical Society; 77 (l), Anne S. K. Brown Military Collection, Brown University Library; 77 (c-l), U.S. National Park Service ; 77 (c-r), Breton Littlehales; 77 (r), The Granger Collection, New York; 78, The Granger Collection, New York; 79, Scotts Bluff National Monument; 80, courtesy Brigham Young University; 81 (l), courtesy The Library of Congress; 81 (r), Wyoming State Archives, Museums & Histocial Department; 83, Denver Public Library; 84, Missouri Historical Society; 85, Kansas State Historical Society; 87, Courtesy the Friends Historical Library of Swarthmore College; 88, Frederick Douglass daguerreotype, Rubel Collection, courtesy Thackery & Robertson; 89 (t), CORBIS; 89 (b), Patricia A. Topper; 90 (t), Vladimir Kordic; 90 (l), Engraving, 1861 Courtesy Kiplinger Washington Collection; 91, Anne S. K. Brown Military Collection, Brown University; 93, Courtesy Chicago Historical Society; 94, White House Collection, White House Historical Association (212); 95, Tom Lovell; 96, Maryland Historical Society; 97, Lloyd Ostendorf Collection, Dayton, OH; 98, courtesy The Library of Congress; 99, Tom Lovell; 100 (l), from the Penn School Collection, Permission granted by Penn Center, Inc., St. Helena Island, South Carolina; 100 (r), HarpWeek; 101, Breton Littlehales; 102 (t), Virginia Historical Society; 102 (b), HarpWeek; 103, Richard Brooke, "A Pastoral Visit," 1881, Accession No. 81.8, In the Collection of The Corcoran Gallery of Art, Museum Purchase, Gallery Fund.

Chapter Five: Industry and Empire
104 (l), Historical Society of Pennsylvania; 104 (c-l), Edison National Historic Site; 104 (c-r), Campbell Soup Company; 104 (r), Harald Sund/The Image Bank/Getty Images; 105 (l), Western History Collections, University of Oklahoma Libraries; 105 (c-l), Bettmann/CORBIS; 105 (c-r), courtesy The Library of Congress; 106, courtesy The Library of Congress; 107, courtesy The Library of Congress; 108, courtesy The Library of Congress; 109, Lester S. Levy Collection; 110 (t-l), Brown Brothers; 110 (t-r), courtesy George Eastman House; 110 (b), The New York Public Library; 112 (t), courtesy The Library of Congress; 112 (b), William Cahn; 113, National Baseball Hall of Fame Library; 114 (t-l), Chicago Historical Society; 114 (t-r), Courtesy AT&T; 114 (b), Howard Hazelcorn Collection; 115, used by Permission, Utah State Historical Society, all rights reserved; 116, Nebraska State Historical Society; 117, Univeristy of California, Riverside; 118, NG; 119, Cody Patrick Lyons Collection; 120, courtesy, National Museum of the American Indian, Smithsonian Institution; 121, courtesy Oklahoma Historical Society; 123, Chicago Historical Society; 124, The George Meany Memorial Archives ; 125, Culver Pictures; 126 (t), courtesy The Library of Congress; 126 (b), The Granger Collection, New York; 127, The Granger Collection, New York.

Chapter Six: Progressivism and the New Deal
128 (l), CORBIS; 128 (c-l), CORBIS; 128 (c-r), The Granger Collection, New York; 128 (r), Brown Brothers; 129, Walt Disney Productions; 129 (c-l), courtesy The Library of Congress; 129 (c-r), Breton Littlehales; 129, CORBIS; 130, courtesy Detroit Institute of Arts; 131, Brown Brothers; 132 (t), David R. Phillips Collection, Chicago Architectural Photographing Company; 132 (b), Bettmann/CORBIS; 133, Culver Pictures; 134, courtesy The Library of Congress; 135, Mary Evans Picture Library; 136, Bettmann/CORBIS; 137 (l), Brown University; 137 (r), courtesy National Archives; 138, Imperial War Museum; 140, The University of Chicago Library; 141 (t), UPI/CORBIS; 141 (b), Culver Pictures; 142, Collection of Ernest Trova; 143 (l), Bettmann/CORBIS; 143 (r),Joseph H. Bailey, NG; 144, Whitney Museum of American Art; 145 (l), courtesy The Library of Congress; 145 (r), courtesy The Library of Congress; 146 (l), Bettmann/CORBIS; 146 (r), UPI/CORBIS; 147, TimePix; 148, Bettmann/CORBIS; 149 (l), Chris Johns, National Geographic Society; 149 (r), courtesy The Library of Congress.

Chapter Seven: War, Prosperity, and Social Change
150 (l), CORBIS; 150 (c-l), TimePix; 150 (c-r), CORBIS; 150 (r), Bettmann/CORBIS; 151 (l), Molly Blocker; 151 (c-l), Archive Photos/Getty Images; 151 (c-r), Donald J. Crump, NG; 151 (r), Robert Ellison/BLACK STAR; 152, AP/Wide World Photos; 153, Hulton Archives/Getty Images; 154, American Heritage Publishing Co.; 155 (l), Joseph H. Bailey, NG; 155 (r), U.S. Government Army; 156, Culver Pictures; 157 (t), TimePix; 157, courtesy The Library of Congress; 158, Dwight D. Eisenhower Library; 159 (b), Bettmann/CORBIS; 159 (t), courtesy The Library of Congress; 160 (t-l), Bettmann/CORBIS; 160 (t-r), Hulton Archives/Getty Images; 160 (b), U.S. Air Force/Defense Nuclear Agency; 162, UPI/CORBIS; 164, UPI/CORBIS; 165 (t-l), Joseph H. Bailey, NG; 165 (t-r), Edward Clark/TimePix; 165 (b), Culver Pictures; 166, courtesy The Library of Congress; 166 (b), Flip Schulke/BLACK STAR; 167, UPI/CORBIS; 168, Charles Moore/BLACK STAR; 169, Archive Photos/Getty Images; 170 (t), Neal Boenzi/The *New York Times*; 170 (b-l), UPI/CORBIS; 170 (l-r), Louis P. Plummer; 171, Archive Photos/Getty Images; 173, David L. Arnold, NG; 175 (t), Charles Bonnay/BLACK STAR; 175 (b), Bernie Boston.

Chapter Eight: The Age of Conservatism
176 (l), NASA; 176 (c-l), Lisa Quinones/BLACK STAR; 176 (c-r), Joseph H. Bailey, NG; 176 (r), Liaison/Getty Images; 177 (l), CORBIS; 177 (c-l), Abbas/MAGNUM; 177 (c-r), CORBIS; 177 (r), Liaison/Getty Images; 178, Jon Schneeberger, NG; 179, Steve Liss/TimePix; 180 (t), Stanley J. Forman, Pulitzer Prize 1977; 180 (b), Lisa Law; 181 (l), Archive Photos/Getty Images; 181 (r), Vince Mannino/Bettmann/CORBIS; 182 (l), White House Collection, courtesy White House Historical Association; 182 (r), BLACK STAR; 183 (t-l), Todd Gipstein, NG; 183 (t-r), Owen Franken/CORBIS; 183 (b), CORBIS; 184, Arthur Schatz/TimePix; 185 (t), D.B. Owen/BLACK STAR; 185 (b), National Museum of American History, Smithsonian Institution; 186 (l), UPI/CORBIS; 186 (r), Liaison/Getty Images; 187, Robert S. Oakes, NG; 188 (l), Archive Photos/Getty Images; 188 (r), Liaison/Getty Images; 189 (l), CORBIS; 189 (r), Reuters NewMedia Inc./CORBIS; 190, NAMES Project Foundation/Paul Margolies; 191 (t), Steve McCurry; 192 (l), CORBIS; 192 (r), Reuters/Rick Wilking/Archive Photos/Getty Images; 193 (t-l), CORBIS; 193 (t-r), AP/Wide World Photos;193 (b), CORBIS; 195 (l), *The Record* (Bergen, N.J.) Photo by Thomas E. Franklin; 195 (r), GAMMA; 196, CORBIS; 197, CORBIS; 199, Stan Honda/AFP; 200, Yale University Art Gallery; 201, Tim Feresten; 224 (l), NG; 224 (r), NG.